The FLAVOR of FRANCE

The
FLAVOR
of
FRANCE
in Recipes and Pictures

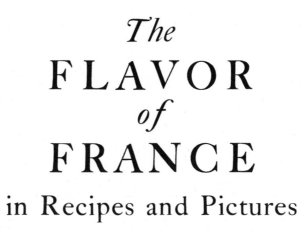

By NARCISSA G. CHAMBERLAIN
and NARCISSE CHAMBERLAIN
Photographs by Samuel Chamberlain

HASTINGS HOUSE, *Publishers*, NEW YORK 10016

Library of Congress Cataloging in Publication Data

Chamberlain, Narcissa G.
The flavor of France, in recipes and pictures.
Includes index.
1. Cookery, French.   2. France—Description and travel—1975-   —Views.
I. Chamberlain, Narcisse, joint author.   II. Title.

TX719.C38 1977   641.5′944   77-14323

ISBN 0-8038-2326-6

Published simultaneously in Canada by
Saunders of Toronto, Ltd., Don Mills, Ontario

Printed in the United States of America

Introduction

❦

THE FLAVOR OF FRANCE was originally published in two volumes, Volume I having been devoted primarily to the simpler classics of French family cooking and Volume II generally to regional specialties. This master edition of both volumes is made possible by the loyal readership of the original books and by our publisher's long-lived faith in them and in their readers, past and future.

We did not entirely perceive what we had wrought over the years until the lengthy task of collating the indexes of recipes and illustrations for the two volumes began. Then we saw that what had started as a modest essay on our family predilection—the home and provincial food of France—had become a fat compendium of 432 recipes, 432 photographs, plus assorted menus and commentary. The following extracts from the introductions to the earlier books describe our enthusiasm for our subject . . .

The association of the landscapes of France with her cooking is irresistible, as any traveler in that remarkable country remembers. The returned tourist is as likely to refer to a French cathedral town as "the one where we had that marvelous *pâté en croûte*" as to quote its proper name. One cannot possibly set out to see this lovely country without at the same time daily pleasing one's palate. It can even reasonably be maintained that sightsee-ers are exposed to a good many French cultural meccas largely because they know of a top-notch restaurant on the way.

A day's motoring through the countryside is inevitably punctuated by a meal with the overtones of a feast, even if it is only a picnic gathered together from the pushcarts of a village market or lunch in an anonymous bistro. In the provinces, the occasion may produce regional specialties as characteristic of their native areas as the roof lines of the local architec-

v

ture. And occasionally one must indulge in a feast in earnest at a gastronomic shrine. In each case, like wine in a sauce, the setting is a tangible ingredient of such memorable meals.

So a profile of France in pictures seemed the most logical embellishment a collection of her recipes could have. They appear in this book to add a little of the flavor of France herself to the reconstruction of some of those memorable meals and they are as varied and as French as the recipes that accompany them. They cost the photographer many a French lunch when the sun was shining photogenically at high noon on a scene as delectable as a *poulet en cocotte,* as majestic as an Escoffier recipe, or as simple as a French hors-d'oeuvre. But in France, if lunch is skipped that may sometimes be wise, dinner is never far away, and châteaux and villages, fields of wheat or lettuce or spring carrots will adorn the scenery on the way. Gothic spires and magnificent cheeses tempt one equally across the land and the word "art" is applied to the fabrication of them both. The French—to echo the feelings of generations of francophiles—know how to live.

To describe in words what it is that makes a French dish French, a poet, a chef, and an historian would have to combine their talents to do. Yet one needs only to sit down at table to *know* what it is. From Flanders to the Pyrenees, from Brittany to the Italian border, the produce and recipes, the style and traditions change, creative cooks and chefs borrow freely across every border. They tamper with the classics and invent dishes of their own in restaurants, cookbooks, and family kitchens. All this variety remains French not through any special effort to stay that way, but through a common understanding of what is good to eat that is stronger than all the prejudices of Basque or Burgundian, Alsatian or Breton, Provençal or Parisian.

Yet there is a difficulty in bringing to life in one's own kitchen the memories of gastronomic travels. Most of us do not wish to eat at home as we do in restaurants, nor would we want to cook like expert chefs every day even if we knew how. There is something missing in the traveling epicure's experience of French food which indeed can be brought to life in our own kitchens. Ironically, this missing link is the most common cuisine of the country, *la cuisine bourgeoise,* made up of the day-to-day offerings of the good *cuisinière,* or family cook. We do not apologize for presenting here many recipes that are commonplace old favorites. These are the dishes that win new friends and influence new cooks and keep firm hold on those who no longer need to be persuaded that there is nothing in the world quite like a good French meal.

On page 442 is a list of some of these stand-bys, a number of them main dishes around which a down-to-earth family meal is constructed, often with nothing more elaborate to complete it than the well-known triumvirate of salad, cheese, and fruit. A sampling of regional specialties begins on page 443. A good number of these are as familiar all over France as they are in their native provinces and they are household recipes.

We have also included a selection of menus (page 433) that in part might puzzle a French housewife because certain of the lunches and suppers would seem to her too simple to need to be printed in a book. But we think Americans will welcome these plain little meals as a guide to French eating in an everyday way. And then, to take care of every eventuality, we did go on to more lavish recipes and menus for dinner parties and holidays. Various categories of dishes, from hors-d'oeuvre and soups through desserts and pastries, can also be located through the Menu Planner on page 441. From these we hope you will create French menus of your own, for ours are meant primarily as help in planning others.

And now, *bon appétit* whenever you cook with THE FLAVOR OF FRANCE.

NARCISSE CHAMBERLAIN
NARCISSA G. CHAMBERLAIN

The FRENCH PROVINCES

Contents

❦

This edition of *The Flavor of France*
is dedicated with love and gratitude
to Sam Chamberlain

THE EIFFEL TOWER AND THE STATUE OF MARSHAL JOFFRE   *Paris*

French Vanilla Ice Cream

Glace Vanille

(Milk, vanilla bean, egg yolks, sugar, cream)

Scald 2 cups of milk in a saucepan. Turn off the flame and steep a vanilla bean in the milk for 20 minutes. Beat 6 egg yolks in the top of a double boiler until they are thick and lemon colored. Stir in ½ cup of granulated sugar, then slowly add the warm milk. Cook the mixture over barely simmering, never boiling, water, stirring constantly for about 7 minutes, or until it just coats the spoon. Remove the top of the double boiler immediately, set it in cold water to cool the custard, and stir in 2 cups of heavy cream.

This ice cream should, of course, be made in a hand freezer. However, if it *must* be done in the refrigerator, turn the controls to "very cold" and put the custard in a deep ice tray in the freezing compartment until it reaches the mushy stage. Then spoon it into a chilled bowl and beat it hard with an egg beater. Return it to the tray, freeze it some more, beat it again, then leave it to freeze solid for at least 3 hours, covered with wax paper to keep crystals from forming on top. Makes 3 pints.

FOUNTAIN OF NEPTUNE, PLACE STANISLAS—NANCY   *Lorraine*

Hot Lorraine Tart

Quiche Lorraine

(Pastry, ham, onion, eggs, milk, spices)

Line a 10-inch pie pan with a thin layer of your favorite pastry dough. Over this scatter ⅓ cup of finely diced ham. Slice 2 onions, sauté them gently in butter until they are soft but not brown, and spread them over the ham. Beat 4 eggs with a pinch of salt, a little grated nutmeg and a few grains of cayenne pepper. Very gradually stir 2 cups of hot milk into the eggs. Heat the mixture slowly over a low fire and stir it until it just begins to thicken. Pour this custard carefully into the pie shell. Bake the *quiche* in a 375° oven for about ½ hour or until it is set and golden on top. Serve hot, directly from the pan.

VILLAGE IN THE MIDI *Provence*

Noëlie's Eggplant Toulouse

Aubergine Toulousaine à la Noëlie

(Eggplant, oil, garlic, parsley, croutons, tomato sauce)

Peel and slice an eggplant, salt the slices and let them stand under pressure for ½ hour. Drain and dry the slices. Dip them in flour and brown them on both sides in hot oil almost ½ inch deep in the pan. The eggplant will absorb the oil very fast. Put the eggplant on a hot platter and keep it warm. Chop finely 1 clove of garlic and 2 or 3 sprigs of parsley and heat them in the remaining oil; be careful not to burn them and add more oil if necessary. Add ¾ cup of bread cut in small dice and brown it lightly. The bread will absorb the oil and turn into crisp, garlic-flavored croutons. Sprinkle them over the slices of eggplant and serve with tomato sauce.

THE YACHT BASIN—MONTE CARLO   *Riviera*

Stewed White Beans from Southern France
Haricots Blancs à la Moustierenco
(Dried white beans, herbs, onion, olive oil, tomato, meat juice, garlic)

Soak 2 cups of dried white beans overnight in water to cover. Drain them, cover them with boiling salted water, and add a *bouquet garni,* 1 stalk of celery with its leaves, and 1 small onion stuck with a clove. Cook the beans slowly until they are tender but still firm; drain them and remove the onion, celery and herbs. In a skillet sauté 1 medium onion, chopped, in 1 tablespoon of olive oil until it is golden. Add 1 large tomato, peeled, seeded and chopped, and simmer together for 4 or 5 minutes. Add a little brown juice from a roast, or 1 teaspoon of meat glaze dissolved in ¼ cup of the water in which the beans were cooked. Then add the beans, cover, and simmer them for 20 minutes. A few minutes before serving, taste for seasoning and add a very finely minced half clove of garlic. The beans should be very tender but not mushy. Serves six.

THE LAC D'ANNECY AT TALLOIRES *Savoy*

Creamed Water Cress Soup

Velouté Cressonière

(Potatoes, water cress, cream, egg yolks, butter)

Peel and slice 1 pound of potatoes. Cut off about 3 dozen perfect leaves from a large bunch of water cress and put them aside. Chop the rest of the water cress coarsely and sauté it in a soup kettle in 1 tablespoon of butter until it is somewhat softened. Add 5 to 6 cups of salted boiling water and the sliced potatoes, and simmer all together for 20 minutes, or until the potatoes are soft. Pour the soup through a sieve into a saucepan and force through as much as possible of the vegetables. Bring the soup back to the boil, add the reserved water cress leaves, and simmer it another 2 or 3 minutes only.

In a small bowl mix together ¼ cup of heavy cream and 2 egg yolks and stir in a few spoonfuls of the hot soup. Take the soup off the fire and slowly stir in the egg and cream mixture. Add a lump of butter, taste the *velouté* for seasoning, and reheat it briefly without letting it boil. Serve immediately. Serves six.

5

REMNANTS OF A MEDIEVAL TOWN—TRÈVES   *Anjou*

Curried Chicken in Cream

Fondue de Poulet à l'Indienne

(Chicken, onion, curry powder, brandy, cream)

French cooks use curry only to flavor a sauce, not to make it exotically hot or spicy. A curried dish is nevertheless poetically named *à l'indienne*.

Cut a roasting chicken into pieces as for a fricassee. In a heavy skillet brown the pieces on all sides in 4 tablespoons of butter. Add 1 minced onion, 1 cup of chicken stock, cover the skillet and simmer the chicken gently until it is tender. Then pour in a liqueur glass of warmed brandy and set it aflame, shaking the pan back and forth until the flame dies. Remove the chicken to a serving dish and keep it warm. Add 1½ cups of heavy cream and 1 teaspoon of curry powder to the pan juices and simmer the sauce until it is slightly reduced. Work 1 teaspoon of butter to a smooth paste with 1 teaspoon flour and blend this into the sauce. Strain the sauce through a fine sieve and pour it over the chicken.

6

HAMLET IN THE FOOTHILLS—ASPERS-SUR-BUECH *Dauphiny*

Strawberry Tart

Tarte aux Fraises

(Pastry, strawberries, raspberry jelly)

Use your favorite pastry recipe for this *tarte aux fraises*. Line a pie plate (or a straight-sided tart ring) with a thin layer of the pastry dough and press a circle of waxed paper over it to keep it flat as it bakes. Bake the pastry shell for ¼ hour in a 450° oven. Cool the shell and fill it with neat rows of raw, hulled strawberries, stem ends down. Stir 1 cup of raspberry jelly thoroughly with 2 tablespoons of water and spoon it over the strawberries. Heat the tart for 5 minutes in a hot oven just before serving.

7

SUNDAY MORNING IN CLAMECY *Nivernais*

Ham in Cream Nivernaise

Jambon à la Crème Nivernaise

(Ham, unsalted butter, white wine, chicken consommé, cream)

In a heavy skillet heat 8 slices of cooked ham in 2 tablespoons of unsalted butter. Cook the ham on both sides but do not let it brown. Add 1 cup of dry white wine and let the liquid in the pan reduce to a very small quantity. Put the slices of ham on a warm platter and keep it hot. Blend a teaspoon of flour into the pan juices, stir in 1 cup of chicken consommé and simmer the sauce for about 5 minutes. Then add ½ cup of heavy cream and pour the sauce over the ham. Serves four.

PLACE DE LA CONCORDE   *Paris*

Filets of Beef Béarnaise

Tournedos Béarnaise

(Beef tenderloin, croutons, and a sauce of egg yolks, cream, butter, vinegar, herbs)

Brown 4 1-inch-thick slices of beef tenderloin on each side in a little butter, leaving the meat rare in the center. Meanwhile trim 4 slices of bread to fit the size and shape of the tenderloins. Sauté these croutons in butter until they are golden brown and crisp, and put one under each tenderloin.

Serve with the following luxurious *sauce béarnaise:* In a small earthenware bowl mix 2 egg yolks with 2 tablespoons of heavy cream, ¼ teaspoon of salt, a pinch of cayenne pepper and 1 tablespoon of tarragon vinegar. Fit the bowl into the top of a small pan of barely simmering water and stir the sauce with a wire whisk until it begins to thicken. Bit by bit add 4 tablespoons of butter, still stirring constantly. When the butter is melted and the sauce has become fairly thick, add 1 teaspoon of chopped tarragon and ½ teaspoon each of chopped parsley and chives. Serves four.

9

THE STEEP VALLEY   *Auvergne*

Braised Carrots

Carottes Vichy

(Carrots, butter, sugar)

Scrape a bunch of young carrots and slice them paper-thin. Cook them over a very low flame in a heavy pan, tightly covered, with ¼ cup of water, a pinch of salt, 1 teaspoon of sugar and a good lump of butter. In about 20 minutes the water should be completely evaporated and the carrots should be cooked and just beginning to glaze. Sprinkle them with chopped parsley before serving.

CASTLE ON A CLIFF—BEYNAC-ET-CAZENAC *Périgord*

Creamed Ham Omelette

Omelette au Jambon à la Crème

(Eggs, ham, nutmeg, cream)

Heat 3 tablespoons of chopped ham in 1 tablespoon of butter and season it with a little nutmeg and freshly ground pepper. Blend in a scant teaspoon of flour, add 4 tablespoons of cream and stir the mixture until it is hot and slightly thickened. Spread the *jambon à la crème* across the center of a 4- or 6-egg omelette just before it is folded.

11

VINEYARDS AT BERÈZE-LA-VILLE *Burgundy*

Veal Stew with Red Wine

Etuvée de Veau au Vin Rouge

(Veal, red wine, garlic, herbs)

Cut 1½ pounds of young veal into 1-inch cubes. Brown the veal in a heavy casserole in 2 tablespoons of butter. Add 1½ cups of red wine, ½ cup of water, salt and pepper, 2 whole cloves of garlic, parsley, and 1 bay leaf. Cover the casserole and simmer the veal for about 2 hours, adding more liquid if the sauce reduces too fast. Dissolve 1 tablespoon of flour in a little water or red wine, add it to the sauce, and cook the *étuvée* about ½ hour longer. Serves four.

QUAI DES ÉTATS-UNIS—NICE *Riviera*

Lamb Chops Niçoise

Côtelettes d'Agneau à la Niçoise

(Lamb chops, green beans, potatoes, tomatoes, white wine, garlic, tomato paste)

The mark of a dish from the Riviera is its gentle Mediterranean aroma of garlic, olive oil and ripe tomatoes. This particular recipe requires a modest effort in presentation.

Pan-broil 8 small rib lamb chops in 2 tablespoons of olive oil. Arrange them in the center of a hot platter. Around the chops arrange neat, alternating piles of buttered young green beans and small new potatoes browned in butter, and 8 tiny whole tomatoes sautéed in oil until partly softened.

To the juices in the pan in which the chops were cooked add 1 small chopped and mashed clove of garlic, 2 or 3 tablespoons of white wine, the same amount of veal or chicken stock, 1 teaspoon of tomato paste and ½ teaspoon of chopped tarragon. Heat the sauce, stirring briskly, and pour it over the chops. Serves four.

13

CHÂTEAU À LA FRANÇAISE—VAUX-LE-VICOMTE   *Ile-de-France*

Broiled Calf's Liver à la Française
Foie de Veau Grillé
(Calf's liver, garlic, tarragon vinegar, herbs)

The secret of good calf's liver is, above all, to use only young, tender liver that is very light in color. Secondly, liver must never be overcooked. Have your butcher slice it not too thin. Cook it only briefly, in hot butter, over a brisk fire; 2 minutes on each side should be plenty. The slices should be pale pink in the center and very tender. When the liver is almost cooked, add for each slice ½ finely chopped and mashed clove of garlic. Arrange the liver on a hot platter. For each slice stir 1 teaspoon of tarragon wine vinegar into the pan juices and add a little butter if the pan is dry. Pour this sauce over the liver. A dusting of finely chopped parsley is the indispensable last touch. If you have fresh tarragon to sprinkle on too, so much the better.

14

Breton Roast Lamb with White Beans

Gigot à la Bretonne

(Leg of lamb, garlic, white beans, tomato, onion)

A roast of lamb is unthinkable in provincial France without stewed white beans (*haricots*) to go with it. The Bretons perfect the combination by serving the *gigot* on a large, deep platter with the beans, which can then soak up every drop of the juice as the roast is carved. When planning this dish, first put 2 cups of dried white beans to soak in cold water overnight.

Cut 2 cloves of garlic in half lengthwise and insert the pieces near the bone at each end of a leg of young lamb. Remove as much skin and fat as possible from the roast, spread it with butter, give it a light dusting of freshly ground pepper, and roast it until it is done but still somewhat pink and juicy in the center.

Meanwhile drain the water from the beans and cover them with boiling salted water, add 2 whole peeled onions and a *bouquet garni*. Cook the beans slowly and drain them when they are tender but still firm. In another saucepan melt a generous lump of butter, add the 2 onions from the bean pot and 2 peeled, ripe tomatoes. Cook this mixture down to a purée, stir in the beans carefully so as not to break them, add a little juice from the roasting pan and simmer the *haricots* just long enough to heat them. Serves six.

15

CHÂTEAU DE TOUFFOU NEAR POITIERS   *Poitou*

Veal Chops Poitou

Côtes de Veau Poitou

(Veal chops, shallots, bacon, stock, white wine, egg yolk)

In a heavy skillet brown lightly 3 chopped shallots and 2 tablespoons of diced lean bacon, or ham, in 2 tablespoons of butter. Add 2 veal chops and brown them slowly, turning them from time to time. When the chops are done, remove them to a heated platter, discard part of the fat in the pan and add ¼ cup of veal stock, ¼ cup white wine, and salt and pepper. Simmer the sauce briefly and thicken it at the last minute by pouring it very gradually into 1 beaten egg yolk, stirring constantly. Add a few drops of wine vinegar and 1 teaspoon of chopped parsley. Reheat the sauce carefully without letting it boil and pour it over the chops. Serves two.

OLD MONTMARTRE   *Paris*

Onion Soup

Soupe à l'Oignon

(Onions, stock, bread, cheese)

When you are left with the carcass of a roast chicken, boil it down with seasonings to make a stock. Then try, instead of the usual chicken soup, a Parisian *soupe à l'oignon:* In a heavy kettle sauté 4 or 5 finely sliced onions in a generous tablespoon of butter. Cook the onions until they are soft and lightly browned and stir them often as they may tend to burn. Season the onions with a little salt and pepper (remember your stock is seasoned), and pour in 5 cups of the hot stock. Simmer the soup for 5 to 8 minutes, pour it into an ovenproof casserole and float slices of French bread on top. Sprinkle the bread with plenty of grated Swiss or Parmesan cheese and brown the bread and cheese lightly under a hot broiler. Serve from the casserole. Serves four.

17

MARKET DAY—KAYSERSBERG *Alsace*

Pears Amandine

Poires Amandines

(Pears, almonds, sugar syrup, strawberries, whipped cream)

Boil together 1 cup of water and ½ cup of sugar for 3 or 4 minutes and add 2 drops of vanilla. Peel 3 firm fresh pears, cut them in half and scoop out the cores. Cook the pears slowly in the syrup for 5 to 8 minutes. Arrange the pear halves in a circle on a platter, round side up, and stick several slivers of toasted almond into each one. Reduce the remaining syrup to about one-half. Add 1 cup of sliced strawberries with their juice and boil the mixture down again to a good syrupy consistency. Force the strawberry sauce through a fine sieve, spoon it carefully over the pears and chill them in the refrigerator. Serve with whipped cream.

HOSTELLERIE DU VIEUX PÉROUGES *Bresse*

Sautéed Veal Kidneys with Red Wine

Rognons de Veau au Vin Rouge

(Veal kidneys, onion, mushrooms, red wine, rice)

Veal kidneys must not be cooked too long or they will be tough. This recipe gives succulent results, and it will work equally well with cubes of calf's liver.

Wash 2 veal kidneys, remove all the fat, skin, and the hard center membrane, and cut the kidneys into small pieces. Brown the pieces quickly in plenty of hot butter, with salt and pepper, 1 small finely chopped onion and ¾ cup of sliced mushrooms. Sprinkle a scant tablespoon of flour over the kidneys, blend the mixture thoroughly and add ½ cup of dry red wine and ½ cup of water. Let the liquid simmer down briefly and pour the kidneys and sauce into a ring of fluffy rice. Serves four.

19

PROVINCIAL CAFÉ—VERSAILLES   *Ile-de-France*

Braised Sweetbreads

Ris de Veau Braisés au Madère

(Sweetbreads, onion, carrot, herbs, chicken stock, Madeira)

Wash 2 pairs of sweetbreads and soak them in ice water for 1 hour. Put them in a saucepan with fresh water to cover, the juice of ½ a lemon, and a little salt. Bring the water to a boil, then simmer the sweetbreads gently for 15 minutes. Drain them, chill them in ice water, and remove the tough sinews and outside membranes. Flatten the sweetbreads between two plates, weighing them down with some handy object, and keep them cold.

Use an ovenproof casserole just large enough to hold the sweetbreads without overlapping them. Melt 2 tablespoons of butter in the casserole and add 1 onion and 1 carrot, both sliced, 1 bay leaf, 2 sprigs of parsley and a pinch of thyme. When the vegetables begin to brown, blend in 1 teaspoon of flour. Season the sweetbreads with salt and pepper, arrange them on top of the vegetables, and add 1 cup of chicken stock or consommé. Bake them, uncovered, and basting occasionally, in a 400° oven for 45 minutes, or until they are brown on top and the liquid is half cooked away. Remove the sweetbreads to a hot platter. Add 2 tablespoons of Madeira to the juices in the casserole, strain this sauce over the sweetbreads and serve immediately. Serves four.

20

PLACE ST. LAZARE—AVALLON *Burgundy*

Chicken in Red Wine

Coq au Vin

(Chicken, onion, garlic, red wine)

In a heavy saucepan sauté 1 sliced onion and 1 minced clove of garlic in 1½ tablespoons of butter until the onion is soft. Add the neck, wing tips and giblets of a roasting chicken. When these have browned a little, add 4 cups of dry red wine and a bay leaf, cover the saucepan and simmer the mixture over the lowest possible flame for about 2 hours. Shortly before servingtime, in an iron skillet sauté the rest of the chicken, cut in serving pieces, in 2 tablespoons of butter. When the chicken is brown and almost cooked, strain the red-wine stock and blend into it 1 tablespoon of butter creamed with 2 teaspoons of flour. Pour the wine sauce over the chicken and simmer the *coq au vin,* covered, for 30 minutes. Serve with rice or boiled potatoes. Serves four to six.

21

HOSPICE DE BEAUNE   *Burgundy*

Liver Pâté

Pâté de Foie

(Pork, chicken livers, shallot, spices, brandy, Madeira, bacon)

An aromatic slice of *pâté maison*, served with French bread, butter and little sour pickles, is a classic hors-d'oeuvre all over France.

Put 1 pound of fresh lean pork and 1 pound of chicken livers (or ½ pound chicken livers and ½ pound calf's liver) several times through the finest blade of the meat grinder. Add 1 chopped shallot, 2 tablespoons of chopped parsley, 2 teaspoons of freshly ground pepper, ⅔ teaspoon of powdered ginger, ¼ teaspoon of cinnamon, 2¼ teaspoons of salt, 1 tablespoon of brandy and 1 tablespoon of Madeira. Mix all the ingredients together thoroughly.

Line a loaf pan with strips of bacon, pack in the pork-and-liver mixture, and bake the pâté in a 350° oven for about 1½ hours. Cool the pâté under pressure, preferably under another loaf pan containing any handy object heavy enough to pack the meat down to a firm consistency. Chill before serving.

THE RIVER LOIRE AT BEAUGENCY   *Orléanais*

Baked Stuffed Shad

Alose au Four Gourmandine

(Shad, shallots, parsley, garlic, ham, mustard)

American fishermen will get as much pleasure from this recipe as do French anglers on the river Loire.

Chop finely together 2 shallots, a sprig of parsley and ½ clove of garlic. Add 2 tablespoons of chopped ham, gently simmer this stuffing for 3 minutes in 1 tablespoon of oil and add 1 teaspoon of prepared French mustard. Stuff a whole, dressed shad with this mixture and sew up the slit side of the fish. Slash a few shallow diagonal cuts along the top of the shad, put it in a buttered baking dish and over it pour ¼ cup of melted butter. Sprinkle the shad with salt and pepper and fine bread crumbs, and bake it in a moderately hot oven for about 25 minutes. Serve shad *gourmandine* in the baking dish, with quarters of lemon.

23

VACATION AT ST. CAST   *Brittany*

Baked Oysters with Almonds

Huîtres aux Amandes

(Oysters, almonds, butter, brandy, cayenne)

Allow about ½ cup of dressing for each dozen oysters. Cream together equal parts of finely ground blanched almonds and sweet butter. For each ½ cup of this dressing blend in thoroughly ½ a minced and crushed clove of garlic, 1½ teaspoons of brandy and a cautious sprinkling of cayenne pepper. Pour off most of the liquor from oysters on their half-shells, and cover each one with about 2 teaspoons of dressing. Bake them in a 450° oven for 5 minutes and serve immediately.

24

THATCHED FARMHOUSES—ILE-DE-FEDRUN   *Brittany*

Anchovy Baked Mashed Potatoes
Purée de Pommes de Terre aux Anchois
(Potatoes, anchovies, butter, eggs, cream, Swiss cheese, bread crumbs)

Mince 4 anchovy fillets and work them to a paste with 2 tablespoons of butter. Cut 4 more fillets into ¼-inch pieces. In a bowl mix together 2 cups of hot mashed potatoes, 2 lightly beaten egg yolks, ½ cup of warm cream, the anchovy butter and diced fillets, ¼ cup of grated Swiss cheese and a little pepper. Fold in 2 beaten egg whites and turn the mixture into a well-buttered soufflé dish. Sprinkle the top with fine bread crumbs and bake the potatoes in a preheated 375° oven for 25 minutes, or until the top is golden brown and a little puffed. Pour melted butter over the top just before serving. Serves six.

25

THE MARKET CHURCH OF ST. PIERRE—SENLIS *Ile-de-France*

Lamb Chops Argenteuil

Côtelettes d'Agneau Argenteuil

(Lamb chops, bread crumbs, asparagus tips, new potatoes)

The word Argenteuil traditionally indicates a dish served with asparagus.

Dip 6 well-trimmed lamb chops in melted butter and fine bread crumbs. In a skillet brown the chops quickly on each side in 3 tablespoons of butter; then cook them slowly until done but still juicy and a little pink in the center. Boil 4-inch asparagus tips in salted water, drain them, put them on a hot platter and pour melted butter over them. Arrange the chops in a ring around them, and around the chops place tiny new potatoes sautéed in butter. Serves six.

26

ROLLING FIELDS NEAR METZ   *Lorraine*

Pork Tenderloin Lorraine

Filet de Porc Lorraine

(Pork tenderloin, bread crumbs, onion, shallot, garlic, parsley, stock, vinegar)

In a small roasting pan on top of the stove brown a lean pork tenderloin on all sides in 2 tablespoons of butter. Cover the tenderloin with a generous layer of fine bread crumbs mixed with salt and pepper. Mince 1 onion, 1 shallot, 1 clove of garlic, and 2 or 3 sprigs of parsley, and sprinkle them on the meat. Put the roast in a hot oven to brown the layer of bread crumbs, basting it several times with melted butter. Once the crumbs are brown, lower the oven temperature to medium, add 1 cup of stock to the pan, cover it, and bake the meat until it is done, or for about 50 minutes. Then uncover the pan, raise the oven temperature and brown the crumbs again for another 10 minutes. Put the roast on a hot platter, and stir 1 tablespoon of wine vinegar into the sauce before serving it. Serves four.

27

PALAIS DU GOUVERNEMENT—NANCY   *Lorraine*

Brussels Sprouts and Chestnuts

Choux de Bruxelles Sautés aux Marrons

(Brussels sprouts, chestnuts, butter, consommé)

Prepare ½ pound of boiled chestnuts, or use well-drained canned chestnuts. Trim 1 pound of firm Brussels sprouts and soak them in salted water. Boil them in fresh salted water for 15 minutes, or until they are just tender, and drain them. In a skillet sauté the chestnuts in 2 tablespoons of hot butter until they are nicely browned. Add the Brussels sprouts and more butter if necessary. When the sprouts take on a little color, moisten with ¼ cup strong beef consommé and simmer all together until the liquid is reduced. Serves four to six.

THE RIVER DOUBS   *Franche-Comté*

Cheese and Ham Stuffed Rolls

Petits Pains au Fromage

(Soft rolls, milk, cheese, ham, butter)

Serve these *petits pains* at a buffet supper or with cocktails.

Use the smallest available soft rolls, or cut larger ones in halves or quarters just before serving them. Split the rolls in half horizontally and scrape out as much of the soft centers as you can without damaging the crusts. Prepare a mixture of equal parts of freshly grated cheese and minced ham. Moisten the soft bread crumbs with a very little boiling milk and mix them with an equal amount of the cheese and ham mixture. Stuff and reassemble the split rolls and arrange them on a buttered cooky sheet. Brush the tops with melted butter, and heat the rolls in a slow oven until the cheese has melted and they just begin to toast. Serve the pieces of halved or quartered rolls on toothpicks.

GATEWAY TO DIANE DE POITIERS' CHÂTEAU—ANET *Orléanais*

Hot Cheese and Ham Sandwiches

Croque Monsieur

(Bread, Swiss cheese, ham, cream, butter, cream sauce)

Trim the crusts from thin slices of white bread. Mix grated Swiss cheese with just enough heavy cream to make a paste and spread a generous layer of it on each piece of bread. Put the slices together into sandwiches, with a thin slice of ham in between. Dip the sandwiches in beaten egg and sauté them in hot butter until they are crisp and golden on each side. Make a cream sauce with 1 table-spoon of butter, melted and blended with 1 teaspoon of flour, 1 cup of cream, stirred in gradually, 2 tablespoons of grated Swiss cheese, and salt and pepper. Blend the cream sauce well, let it thicken slightly and serve it over the *croque monsieur*.

VILLAGE SCHOOLHOUSE, ONCE A SMALL CHÂTEAU   *Champagne*
—RUMILLY

Cream of Cucumber Soup

Potage Crème de Concombre

(Cucumbers, milk, potato starch, egg yolks, cream, chives or dill)

Peel 2 fresh cucumbers, cut them lengthwise, scoop out the seeds and cut the cucumbers into 1-inch pieces. Sprinkle the pieces with salt, let them stand for several hours, drain them, drop them into 2 cups of boiling water, and let them cook for 5 minutes. Drain the cucumbers again, reserve the cooking water, and sauté them gently for 5 minutes in 1 tablespoon of butter. Do not let the butter brown. Force the cucumbers through a fine sieve and add 1½ cups of the cooking water and 1½ cups of milk. Add 1 tablespoon of potato starch dissolved in a little milk, and salt and pepper to taste. Beat 2 egg yolks with 3 tablespoons of heavy cream and pour a little of the cucumber soup into this mixture to blend it without cooking the eggs. Pour the eggs and cream into the soup and heat it, stirring, until it is slightly thickened. Do not let it boil. Serve the *crème de concombre* with a sprinkling of chopped chives or dill. Serves four.

31

TOUR GABRIEL—RAMPARTS OF MONT ST. MICHEL   *Normandy*

Lobster in Cream

Homard à la Crème

(Lobster, brandy, seasoning, egg yolks, cream, sherry)

Slice the meat of a 2-pound boiled lobster and heat the pieces in 2 tablespoons of hot butter for 1 or 2 minutes. Add salt, pepper and a little paprika. Pour on 1 tablespoon of warmed brandy, set it aflame and shake the pan back and forth until the flame dies. Beat 2 egg yolks with ¾ cup of cream, add 2 tablespoons of sherry and pour this sauce over the lobster. Keep the lobster over a low fire, stirring constantly, until the sauce thickens, but do not let it boil. Serves two.

VILLAGE FOUNTAIN—RIQUEWIHR   *Alsace*

Beef à la Mode

Boeuf à la Mode

(Beef, white wine, herbs, veal knuckle, brandy, carrots, onions)

Boeuf à la mode is one of the most delicious commonplaces of French cooking. Serve it hot one day and cold the next, when the sauce will have jelled rather like an aspic.

Remove the fat from a 4-pound piece of beef suitable for a pot roast. Run a few narrow strips of salt pork through it with a larding needle. In a deep iron casserole brown the meat on all sides in 1 tablespoon of butter. Add 1 cup of hot water, 2 cups of white wine, salt and pepper, a bay leaf, a sprig of parsley, a good pinch of thyme, a pinch of nutmeg, and a piece of cracked veal knuckle. Simmer the beef, covered, over a low flame for about 2 hours, then add 2 tablespoons of brandy, 4 carrots, cut in pieces, and 6 small whole onions. Stick 2 or 3 cloves into one of the onions. Simmer the *boeuf à la mode* for another 1½ hours, or until it is tender. Remove the veal knuckle and the cloves before serving. The sauce should be fairly brown and rich; if there is too much, pour it into another pan and reduce it over a brisk flame.

33

BASQUE COUNTRY TOWN—USTARITZ   *Pyrenees*

Basque Omelette

Pipérade

(Eggs, green pepper, onion, tomato, ham)

A *pipérade* is neither quite an omelette nor quite scrambled eggs, but something in between. And it is neither quite French nor quite Spanish — it is Basque.

In 2 tablespoons of oil sauté 1 small green pepper and 1 small onion, both thinly sliced, 1 small clove of garlic, chopped and mashed, and 1 large ripe tomato, peeled, seeded and chopped. Add 2 tablespoons of chopped ham and let the mixture simmer over a low fire for 20 to 30 minutes. When the vegetables are soft, stir in 1 tablespoon of butter, let it melt and pour in 4 lightly beaten eggs. Add more salt and pepper if necessary, stir just once or twice, let the eggs set and serve the *pipérade* from the pan. Serves two.

BARLES, A MOUNTAIN VILLAGE   *Dauphiny*

Scalloped Potatoes

Gratin Dauphinois

(Potatoes, milk or cream, seasoning)

The secret of this dish is to slice the potatoes paper-thin and to cook them just long enough to brown them on top without drying them out underneath. The recipe is very simple, and yet it may require practice.

Slice raw potatoes very thinly and spread the slices in layers in a shallow baking dish. Sprinkle a little salt and pepper on each layer and add a dash of nutmeg if you like it. Fill the dish with milk, or even better, with thin cream, just to the level of the top layer of potatoes. Dot the *gratin* with bits of butter and bake it in a very slow oven for 1¼ to 1½ hours, or just to the point where the milk is all absorbed, the potatoes are soft and the top layer is delicately browned. Serve from the baking dish.

PONT ST. BÉNÉZET—AVIGNON   *Provence*

Braised Beef Avignon

Boeuf à la Façon d'Avignon

(Beef, herbs, white wine, bacon, shallots, onions, tomato, mushrooms)

Marinate a 4-pound piece of beef (top of the round, rump, or a similar piece) with ½ lemon, sliced, 2 cloves of garlic, cut in pieces, a good pinch of thyme, 1 bay leaf, ½ teaspoon each of chopped tarragon and chives, a little pepper, 2 cups of white wine and 4 tablespoons of olive oil. Let the meat stand for 12 hours and turn it from time to time in the marinade.

Put the beef in an earthen casserole with a piece of bacon rind under it. Add 4 shallots, cut in pieces, 3 or 4 peeled and seeded tomatoes, cut in quarters, 2 cloves of garlic, chopped, 6 or 8 small onions, 2 tablespoons of diced bacon, ¼ pound of mushrooms, and a sprig of parsley. Pour 1 cup of beef stock and the marinade over the beef. This dish should be cooked in the slowest possible oven for 5 to 6 hours. For best results the casserole should be hermetically sealed. The French way of doing this is to make a paste of flour and water, shape it into a long, narrow roll, fit the roll around the edge of the casserole and press the lid firmly down upon it.

AMBOISE   *Touraine*

Salmon in White Wine

Saumon au Vin Blanc

(Salmon steaks, white wine, butter, steamed potatoes, green peas)

In the Touraine this dish is made with Vouvray, but any good dry, white table wine will do. For a Gallic version of the American 4th of July salmon-and-green peas, why not serve *saumon au vin blanc* with *petits pois à la française?*

In a heavy skillet brown 4 salmon steaks on each side in plenty of butter. Add salt and a little pepper and when the salmon is half cooked, pour in 1½ cups of white wine. Simmer the steaks over a brisk fire until the butter and wine are reduced to a rich but still juicy sauce. Serve the salmon with steamed potatoes and green peas.

Here is the incomparable French method for preparing peas: In a covered pan, over a low flame, simmer 2 cups of green peas in ¼ cup of water with 4 green lettuce leaves, 1 small sliced onion, 2 tablespoons of butter, a sprig of parsley, ¼ teaspoon of sugar, a pinch of thyme, and salt and pepper to taste. The peas should be tender and the liquid almost absorbed in about ½ hour. Serves four.

37

ALPHONSE DAUDET'S WINDMILL—FONTVIEILLE *Provence*

Eggplant and Tomato Hors-d'Oeuvre

Aubergine à la Turque

(Eggplant, tomatoes, onions, peppercorns, olive oil)

A la turque here means a general Mediterranean style. Eggplant is often served this way in the south of France.

Peel an eggplant and slice it rather thinly. Salt the slices, pile them together, let them stand under pressure for ½ hour, and drain off the liquid. Peel and slice 6 large ripe tomatoes and 3 or 4 onions. In the bottom of a shallow baking dish arrange a layer of onion slices, put a layer of eggplant over the onions, then a layer of tomato over the eggplant. Sprinkle in a few whole peppercorns and a little salt. Keep this up until you have used all of the vegetables, finishing off with a layer of tomato slices each neatly decorated with a round of onion. Fill all the corners and empty spaces with bits of tomato. Fill the dish just to the top layer of tomato with olive oil, and bake it in a 250° oven for 3 hours or more. Baste the juices over the top several times. Serve chilled.

VILLAGE DRY-DOCK—YPORT *Normandy*

Scallops Saint-Jacques

Coquilles Saint-Jacques

(Scallops, shallot, white wine, parsley, bread crumbs, cheese)

Slice ¾ pint of sea scallops. Sauté the pieces gently for 3 minutes in 2 tablespoons of butter with a little pepper and 1 chopped shallot. Add 2 tablespoons of fine bread crumbs and ¾ cup of white wine, and simmer the scallops for 8 to 10 minutes, or until the sauce is slightly reduced and thickened. Add 1 teaspoon of finely chopped parsley, and salt if necessary, and fill 4 scallop shells with the mixture. Sprinkle the *coquilles* with bread crumbs and grated Parmesan, dot them with butter and brown them lightly under a hot broiler. Serves four.

THE NORTH PORCH OF THE CATHEDRAL
OF NOTRE-DAME—CHARTRES

Orléanais

Blanquette of Veal

Blanquette de Veau

(Veal, onion, carrots, mushrooms, egg yolks)

A *blanquette de veau* is a veal stew almost too delicate to be called a stew. Every cook in France knows the recipe well.

Cut 1½ pounds of young, white stewing veal into cubes and put the meat in a bowl with boiling water to cover. Put a lid on the bowl and let the meat stand for 20 minutes. Drain off the water and put the veal in a heavy saucepan with 2 onions and 2 carrots, all cut in pieces, salt and pepper and a sprig of parsley, and cover the veal again with boiling water. Simmer the *blanquette,* covered, over a low fire for about 1½ hours. Then add ½ pound of sliced mushrooms and simmer for another ½ hour. In a separate saucepan melt 1 tablespoon of butter, blend in 1 tablespoon of flour and stir in gradually 2 cups of the veal stock. Simmer this sauce until it is slightly reduced. Beat 2 egg yolks in a bowl with 1 teaspoon of lemon juice and add the hot sauce gradually. Return the mixture to the saucepan and stir it over a very low flame until it just begins to thicken. The sauce should be almost white. Pour it over the meat and vegetables, which have been drained and kept hot, and serve the *blanquette* with rice. Serves four.

TAKING ON SUPPLIES—CAMARET-SUR-MER *Brittany*

Cod Brittany

Cabillaud à la Bretonne

(Codfish, cider, parsley, shallots, mushrooms)

Put a 2-pound piece of fresh cod, boned and skinned, in a baking dish first greased with 3 tablespoons of salad oil. Sprinkle the fish with salt and pepper and with 2 shallots, 1 teaspoon of parsley, and 4 or 5 mushrooms, all chopped. Add 2 cups of hard cider. Work 1 teaspoon of flour to a smooth paste with 1 tablespoon of butter and add it to the cider. Bake the codfish in a moderately hot oven and baste it several times. It should be done in 20 to 30 minutes. Serves four.

SCREEN OF POPLARS—OZENAY   *Burgundy*

Duck with Olives

Canard aux Olives

(Duck, Italian vermouth, olives)

Spread a duck with softened butter, salt and pepper it, and roast it in a hot oven. Add ½ cup of water and ½ cup of sweet Italian vermouth to the fat in the pan and baste the duck often. Fifteen minutes before the duck is done, add 1 cup of small pitted green Italian olives. Serve the duck and the olives together. Skim most of the fat from the pan juices and serve them in a sauceboat.

PASTORALE   *Normandy*

Creamed Camembert Cheese

Crème de Camembert

(Camembert, white wine, butter)

Crème de camembert will be at its best if it is served with French bread and a bottle of red wine.

Take a ripe Camembert cheese (whole or in sections), scrape off the skin carefully and thoroughly and let the cheese stand in a bowl, covered with dry white wine, for 12 hours. Drain it, wipe it dry and cream it thoroughly with ⅓ cup of sweet butter. Shape the Camembert cream into the form of the original cheese, coat it on all sides with very fine toast crumbs and chill it well before serving.

RAMPARTS OF THE CHÂTEAU—FARCHEVILLE   *Ile-de-France*

Baked Eggs with Mushrooms

Oeufs Bonne Femme

(Croutons, mushrooms, butter, eggs)

Cut slices of good white bread into circles about 3 inches across. Sauté the circles in butter until they are crisp and brown on both sides. In another skillet, over a low flame, sauté finely minced mushrooms in butter until they are soft and the liquid they give off is reduced. Arrange the sautéed croutons close together in a shallow, buttered baking dish, spread them with the cooked mushrooms and carefully break an egg over each one. Season with salt and pepper and bake the *oeufs bonne femme* in a 350° oven for 10 minutes, or until the whites are set but the yolks are still soft.

44

THE OLD AUBERGE—BEAULIEU-SUR-DORDOGNE   *Limousin*

Puréed Vegetable Soup

Potage aux Légumes

(Onion, carrots, turnips, potatoes, celery, butter, cream)

In a large saucepan sauté 1 large sliced onion in 1 tablespoon of butter until it is soft and lightly browned. Add 2 carrots, 2 small white turnips, 3 medium potatoes and 2 stalks of celery, all cut in small pieces, a sprig of parsley, and salt and pepper. Cook the vegetables for a few minutes in the butter, stirring often. Then add 5 cups of hot water, cover the saucepan and simmer the soup over a low flame for 1 hour. Pass the soup through a sieve into another saucepan, and force through all the vegetables. To serve this traditional French *potage*, reheat it with a big lump of butter and add 2 tablespoons of extra-heavy sweet or sour cream. Serves six.

45

THE CHÂTEAU AND THE HORSESHOE STAIRCASE —FONTAINEBLEAU   *Ile-de-France*

Artichokes with Mousseline Sauce

Artichauts, Sauce Mousseline

(Artichokes, and a sauce of eggs, butter, lemon juice, cream)

Cover 6 handsome artichokes with boiling salted water and cook them for about 45 minutes, or until the bases are tender when pricked with a sharp knife. Drain them and serve them hot. Eat the ends of the artichoke leaves and the bases with a frothy *sauce mousseline:*

In an earthenware bowl lightly beat 4 egg yolks with 4 tablespoons of cream. Fit the bowl into the top of a pan of barely simmering water. Let the yolks thicken slightly, stirring them constantly with a wire whisk. Divide ¼ pound of butter into 4 pieces and stir in the pieces one at a time, letting each one melt before adding the next. When the eggs and butter have thickened somewhat, take the bowl off the pan of hot water, stir in 2 teaspoons of lemon juice and a pinch each of salt and pepper. Add about ¾ cup of stiffly whipped cream. Put the bowl back over the hot water and stir the sauce, very gently this time, until it is hot. If the flame under the pan of water is low enough and the earthenware bowl is thick enough, there should be no danger of this *sauce mousseline* curdling. Serves six.

HARVEST—NEAR LUSSAC-LE-CHÂTEAU   *Poitou*

Fowl with Rice

Poule au Riz

(Fowl, herbs, vegetables, rice, egg yolks)

Put a whole, dressed fowl in a deep kettle with salt, pepper, parsley, 1 bay leaf, a pinch of thyme, 2 cloves of garlic, 1 stalk of celery and 1 quartered onion. Add water to cover, put the lid on the kettle and simmer the fowl gently for about 2 hours, or until it is tender.

Wash 1½ cups of rice and cook it in 3 cups of stock from the chicken pot. Add a little more stock if the liquid is absorbed before the rice is tender. Beat 2 egg yolks in the top of a double boiler, add gradually 2 cups of the chicken stock, strained, and heat the sauce over simmering water. Stir the sauce with a whisk until it just begins to thicken and add 1 tablespoon of butter. Put the rice on a hot platter, carve the chicken and put the pieces on the bed of rice. Serve the sauce separately. Serves six.

ROMAN ARCH (49 B.C.)—ORANGE   *Provence*

Grilled Pepper Hors-d'Oeuvre

Poivrons Grillés

(Green peppers, olive oil, French dressing, onion)

Split large green peppers in half lengthwise and remove the stems, seeds and all the white membranes. Soak the peppers in a little olive oil for 30 minutes; then drain them and broil them under a low flame, turning them occasionally, until they are slightly browned and blistered. (Ideally this should be done over a charcoal fire.) Cut the peppers into thin strips and sprinkle them with a little finely minced onion. Marinate them for an hour or more in a French dressing made of 1 part vinegar, 3 parts olive oil, and mustard, salt and pepper to taste, and serve them cold but not chilled.

REFLECTED LANDSCAPE NEAR LANNE   *Pyrenees*

Cucumber Hors-d'Oeuvre

Concombres à la Grecque

(Cucumbers, salad oil, lemon juice, herbs, spices)

Peel 2 large or 3 small cucumbers, quarter them lengthwise, scoop out the seeds and cut the quarters into 1-inch pieces. Heat to the boiling point 1 cup of water, 6 tablespoons of salad oil and the juice of 2 lemons with a *bouquet garni* composed of parsley, celery leaves, thyme, a bay leaf, and a stalk of fennel or some fennel seeds, adding also salt, pepper and a dozen coriander seeds. Add the cucumbers and cook them over a medium flame for 10 minutes. Remove the *bouquet garni* and cool the cucumbers in the cooking liquid. Serve them chilled, with just enough liquid to serve as a dressing. Serves four.

THE CHÂTEAU AT CHANTILLY *Ile-de-France*

Strawberries with Whipped Cream

Fraises Chantilly

(Strawberries, cream, powdered sugar, vanilla)

Hull a basket of ripe strawberries and cut them in half. Stir them into a bowl of fluffy whipped cream flavored with a little powdered sugar and vanilla. The cream should not be too stiff and there should be enough of it to smother the strawberries completely. Let the *fraises Chantilly* stand in the refrigerator for 2 hours before serving them. They will be nicely chilled and the cream will be streaked with pink strawberry juice.

THE ROOFTOPS OF CHINON   *Touraine*

Caramel Custard

Crème Renversée

(Eggs, sugar, milk, vanilla)

Heat ½ cup of sugar in a heavy pan over moderate heat until it melts and browns, stirring it constantly. Add very slowly ½ cup of boiling water, stirring to keep it from boiling over. Simmer the caramel for 2 or 3 minutes and pour it into a china or glass baking dish, turning and tilting the dish to coat all the inside. Beat 2 whole eggs and 3 egg yolks in a bowl with a pinch of salt, 4 tablespoons granulated sugar and 1 teaspoon of vanilla. Stir in gradually 1½ cups of hot milk. Pour this custard into the baking dish. Set the dish in a shallow pan of water and bake the custard for 1 hour in a 250° oven. It will be done when a knife inserted in the center comes out clean. Serve the *crème renversée* chilled and turned out on a platter. The caramel will cover it like a sauce.

51

PALACE OF THE POPES—AVIGNON   *Provence*

Avignon Flambéed Filets Mignons

Filets Mignons Flambés à l'Avignonnaise

(Beef tenderloin, garlic, butter, croutons, brandy)

Rub slices of beef tenderloin, cut 1½ inches thick, on both sides with a cut clove of garlic. Season them generously with salt and coarsely ground pepper. Sauté circles of bread, cut to fit the filets, in plenty of butter until the croutons are crisp and brown on both sides. In a separate skillet, cook the filets in hot butter over a high flame. They should be very brown, but also very rare inside. Then slip a crouton under each filet and add a little melted butter to the pan. Pour in about 1 teaspoon of warmed brandy for each filet, put a match to it, and shake the pan until the flame dies out. Transfer croutons and filets to a large hot platter, pour on the pan juices, and garnish the platter with water cress, broiled tomatoes, and French-fried shoe-string potatoes.

HARNESS SHOP—NOGENT-LE-ROI

Orléanais

Cauliflower Purée

Purée de Chou-fleur

(Cauliflower, mashed potatoes, cream, butter, parsley)

Trim off the leaves and the tough end of the stem of a firm, white cauliflower. Soak it head down in salted water for ½ hour, and boil it in fresh salted water for about 20 minutes, or until the core is just tender. Drain it, mash it through a colander, and reheat it to reduce any excess liquid. Combine the purée with approximately the same amount of mashed potatoes, and add a little heavy cream and plenty of butter. Beat well with a wooden spoon and serve very hot with another lump of butter and sprinkled with parsley. Serves six.

53

THE SEINE AND THE PONT MARIE *Paris*

Leek and Potato Soup

Potage Parisien

(Leeks, potatoes, cream, herbs)

Clean 2 large leeks, remove most of the green tops and slice the rest very thinly. Peel 3 potatoes and cut them into small dice. Melt 1 tablespoon butter in a saucepan, add the leeks and cook them over a low flame for 5 minutes without letting them brown. Add the potatoes and cook another minute. Then add 1½ quarts of boiling water and a little salt and simmer the soup gently for 30 minutes, skimming off the surface once or twice. The soup should reduce to about 1 quart. Stir in 1 teaspoon of butter and 3 tablespoons of heavy cream and taste for seasoning. Serve with a sprinkling of chopped chives or parsley. Serves four.

54

THE YACHT BASIN AT CANNES   *Riviera*

Niçoise Salad

Salade Niçoise

(Lettuce, vegetables, eggs, anchovies, black olives, tuna fish)

A *salade niçoise* should be pretty as a picture when it comes to the table, but you must then courageously spoil the picture by tossing the salad thoroughly before serving it. Rub a wooden salad bowl with a cut clove of garlic. On a bed of lettuce in the bowl arrange the following traditional ingredients: 4 quartered small red tomatoes, 1 cup of cooked green beans, 2 sliced boiled potatoes, 2 quartered hard-boiled eggs, thin slices of mild Spanish onion and of green pepper, 8 anchovy fillets cut in small pieces, 10 black Italian olives, and pieces of white canned tuna fish. Over all of this pour the standard French dressing made of salt and freshly ground black pepper to taste, ½ teaspoon of prepared mustard, 2 tablespoons of red wine vinegar, and 6 tablespoons of olive oil. Serves four.

THE PORT OF AURAY *Brittany*

Lobster Alexander

Homard Alexandre

(Cold lobster, and a sauce of herbs, seasoning, eggs, oil, vinegar)

Slice the meat of a boiled lobster and arrange it on a platter. Mix ½ teaspoon each of chopped chervil, parsley, tarragon and chives with the mashed yolks of 2 hard-boiled eggs. Add salt and pepper, a little English mustard, 1 tablespoon of wine vinegar and a few drops of Worcestershire sauce. When the mixture is smoothly blended, add gradually about ½ cup of cold olive oil, stirring constantly until the sauce thickens into a sort of mayonnaise. Add a few drops of Madeira or sherry and drop a neat spoonful of sauce on each piece of lobster just before serving.

THE CHÂTEAU AT DUINGT—LAC D'ANNECY *Savoy*

Trout with Almonds and Cream

Truite aux Amandes

(Trout, almonds, cream)

Clean, wash and dry 4 small fresh trout (or 2 large ones), dip them lightly in flour and sauté them on both sides in plenty of hot butter. Remove the trout to a hot platter when they are brown. In the butter left in the pan (add more if the pan is dry) lightly brown ½ cup of blanched and slivered almonds. Add ½ cup of heavy cream, stir it briskly so it will take up the brown color of the butter, let the liquid reduce a little, and pour this sauce over the trout. Serves four.

57

NOTRE-DAME DE PARIS   *Paris*

Mushroom Salad

Salade de Champignons

(Mushrooms, French dressing, herbs)

This is an exceptionally delicious salad. In France it is usually found on the tray of assorted hors-d'oeuvre served as a first course.

Wash and dry, but do not peel, firm white mushroom caps. Slice them thinly, pour French dressing over them, toss them carefully and let them stand a while to absorb the dressing. Sprinkle them with chopped chives and parsley before serving. The usual French dressing of salt, pepper, 1 part red wine vinegar and 3 parts olive oil may be varied for *salade de champignons* by using a little less vinegar and adding a little lemon juice.

GOTHIC CHURCH AT ST. RIQUIER   *Picardy*

Roast Goose with Fruit Stuffing

Oie Rôtie aux Pruneaux

(Goose, onion, orange, apple, prunes, bread crumbs, seasoning)

Sauté 2 chopped onions in 3 tablespoons of butter until they are soft, add salt and pepper and 1 peeled, coarsely chopped orange. Simmer this mixture for 3 minutes and add 3 large apples and 14 large soaked and pitted prunes, all coarsely chopped. Add 2 tablespoons of sugar, ½ teaspoon each of thyme and marjoram, ¼ teaspoon each of cinnamon and nutmeg, and 1 tablespoon each of brandy and Madeira. Mix in thoroughly the chopped liver of the goose, 2 cups of coarse dry bread crumbs soaked with ¼ cup of milk, and add a little more salt and pepper. Rub the inside of the goose with salt and a little sage and thyme and pack it loosely with the stuffing. Roast the goose in a 325° oven, allowing 20 to 25 minutes per pound. Prick the skin well all over to allow the fat to run out. When the goose is ready, put it on a hot platter, skim most of the fat from the pan juices and stir in a cup of stock made from the giblets and neck, simmered in water with 1 onion, salt and pepper and a bay leaf. Reduce the sauce and serve it separately.

59

THE FARM GATE—MANOIR DE QUERVILLE *Normandy*

Fried Cheese Puffs

Délicieuses au Fromage

(Swiss cheese, egg whites, bread crumbs)

This is a delectable hot hors-d'oeuvre. Make a paste of 2 lightly beaten egg whites mixed with ¼ pound of grated Swiss cheese. Form the paste into little balls no bigger than marbles, roll them in fine bread crumbs and fry them in very hot, deep oil. The *délicieuses* will puff up and become light and delicious, just as their name implies. Serve them immediately, with French-fried parsley.

THE NOBLE DOVECOTE, MANOIR D'ANGO—NEAR DIEPPE   *Normandy*

Omelette with Herbs

Omelette Fines Herbes

(Eggs, parsley, chives, tarragon, chervil)

Add 1 tablespoon of water and a little salt and pepper to 6 eggs and beat them briefly with a fork. Stir in 1 teaspoon each of finely chopped parsley, chives, tarragon and chervil. Put 1 tablespoon of butter in an omelette pan just hot enough to make the butter sizzle but not brown. Pour in the eggs and stir them twice quickly with the flat of the fork. Shake the pan to keep the omelette free. As soon as it is set but still soft, fold over one edge of the omelette with a spatula. Slide the unfolded edge right out of the pan onto a platter, then turn the pan completely over the platter. The omelette should land with two edges neatly tucked under and the top golden and unbroken. It should be cooked through but quite soft.

REFLECTIONS IN THE RIVER TARN—ALBI   *Languedoc*

Beef Tongue with Sauce Piquante
Langue de Boeuf, Sauce Piquante
(Beef tongue, shallots, wine vinegar, white wine, herbs, capers, pickles)

Wash and scrape a fresh beef tongue and cook it slowly in a large kettle with 3 or more quarts of water, salt, several peppercorns, 1 onion, cut in half, 1 carrot, cut in pieces, parsley, 1 bay leaf, and a good pinch of thyme. Simmer the tongue for about 3 hours. Then skin it and serve it sliced and garnished with water cress.

With *langue de boeuf* serve this spicy *sauce piquante:* Simmer 4 finely chopped shallots in ¼ cup of wine vinegar and ¼ cup of white wine. Add salt and pepper to taste. When the liquid is reduced to about one-half, add 1 cup of the stock in which the tongue was cooked and simmer the sauce 10 minutes longer. In a small bowl dissolve 1 teaspoon of potato flour in a little of the tongue stock and stir this mixture into the sauce to thicken it slightly. Add 2 teaspoons of fresh herbs (parsley, tarragon and chervil) and 1 small sour pickle, all finely chopped, 1 teaspoon of capers and a little freshly ground pepper.

SIXTEENTH-CENTURY STREET CORNER—BOURGES   *Berry*

Germaine's Creamed Spinach with Madeira

Epinards au Madère à la Germaine

(Spinach, mushrooms, cream, Madeira, croutons)

Epinards au madère is no ordinary vegetable; it deserves to be eaten as a separate course.

Cook 2 pounds of spinach, covered, with ¼ cup of water for about 10 minutes, or until it is just soft. Drain it thoroughly and put it through the finest blade of the meat grinder. Drain the spinach again, add 1 tablespoon of butter, a dash of nutmeg, salt and pepper, and ¼ cup of heavy cream. Sauté ¼ pound of sliced mushrooms in 1 tablespoon of butter for 4 or 5 minutes, add them to the spinach and stir in 2 tablespoons of Madeira. Sauté 1 cup of diced white bread in 2 tablespoons of butter until the croutons are crisp and golden brown. Reheat the spinach and sprinkle it with the croutons. Serves four.

THE INNER PORT—HONFLEUR *Normandy*

Fillets of Flounder in White Wine

Filets de Sole au Vin Blanc

(Flounder fillets, white wine, shallot, mushrooms, cream, egg yolks)

Spread 1½ pounds of fillets of flounder in a shallow baking dish. Add 1 cup of dry white wine, sprinkle the fillets with salt and pepper and add 1 finely chopped shallot and ¼ pound of sliced mushrooms. Dot the fish with butter and bake it in a moderate oven for 20 minutes, or until it is cooked but still firm. Drain off the liquid in the baking dish and simmer it down to about 1 cup. Mix 2 egg yolks with ½ cup of heavy cream and stir them carefully into the reduced fish stock. Add 1 teaspoon of chopped parsley, pour the sauce over the flounder and glaze it briefly under a hot broiler. Serves four.

THE FORTIFIED BRIDGE—CAHORS

Gascony

Chestnut Pudding

Mont-Blanc

(Chestnuts, milk, sugar, vanilla, egg yolks, butter, whipped cream)

Slash the shells of 2 pounds of chestnuts on the flat side. Put the chestnuts in a frying pan with a little hot oil and heat them until the shells begin to loosen. Let them cool, peel them and boil them in salted water for 10 minutes; drain them and remove the remaining bits of the inner skin. Cover the chestnuts with 2¼ cups of milk, add ½ teaspoon of vanilla and 6 tablespoons of sugar, and boil them gently until they are soft. Force the mixture through a colander and add 2 tablespoons of butter and enough hot milk to give the purée a moderately thick consistency. Mix it thoroughly and let it cool. Then add 2 egg yolks and chill it in the refrigerator. Shape the chestnut purée into a low pyramid on a serving platter and cover it with sweetened whipped cream.

THE PALACE OF VERSAILLES   *Ile-de-France*

Francine's Chocolate Cream

Marquise au Chocolat à la Francine

(Milk, sugar, eggs, butter, chocolate)

Over a low flame dissolve ½ cup of granulated sugar in a scant ½ cup of milk. Put in a vanilla bean for a little while for flavor, or use a few drops of vanilla extract. When the milk has boiled, let it cool and stir it into 3 beaten egg yolks. Thicken the custard over barely simmering water and stir it constantly. Put it aside to cool.

Put ¾ of a pound of unsalted butter in a bowl and cream it until it is very soft. (This may take about ½ hour.) Melt ¼ pound of bittersweet chocolate with 2 tablespoons of water in the top of a double boiler. Let the chocolate cool and stir it a little at a time into the creamed butter. Add the cooled custard, and then settle down to some 20 minutes of constant stirring. This may seem like a lot of work, but the *marquise* will acquire a beautiful consistency. Pour the *marquise* into a mold and chill it. Unmold it onto a platter and serve a small slice to each guest (this is a very, very rich dessert) with the following custard sauce: Boil 2 cups of milk with 6 lumps of sugar and a vanilla bean. When the sugar is dissolved, remove the vanilla bean, cool the milk a little and stir it slowly into 6 beaten egg yolks. Thicken the sauce over simmering water, stirring constantly, and serve it cold.

INFORMAL FARM ARCHITECTURE *Guyenne*

Steak with Bordelaise Sauce

Steak Bordelaise

(Steak, shallot, red wine, stock, herbs, lemon)

The French seldom bother about outdoor barbecue cooking, but it just so happens that this great French provincial recipe is perfection for a charcoal-broiled steak. The sauce can be made ahead of time in the kitchen.

Broil a good thick steak over a charcoal fire until it is brown on both sides but rare in the center. Carve it and serve it with this *sauce bordelaise:* Combine 1 chopped shallot, freshly ground pepper, ¼ teaspoon salt, a pinch each of marjoram and thyme, and a small bay leaf with ½ cup of red wine. Simmer this mixture until the wine is reduced to about half its original quantity. Now add ½ cup of good strong beef stock and reduce the sauce again to about one-half. Add ½ teaspoon lemon juice, strain the sauce through a fine sieve, add a good lump of butter and 1 teaspoon of chopped parsley. A true *sauce bordelaise* also contains sliced marrow from the center of a boiled marrowbone, but this is not absolutely necessary.

ARC DE TRIOMPHE   *Paris*

Chicken Salad Boulestin

Salade de Poulet Boulestin

(Rice, cold chicken, French dressing, peppers, mayonnaise, mustard, eggs, herbs)

For leftover chicken deluxe: Season freshly boiled rice while it is still hot with a French dressing made of 1 part wine vinegar, 3 parts olive oil, salt, pepper and a little prepared mustard. Mix in a little green pepper and sweet pimento, both minced, and cool the rice thoroughly. Just before serving, put the rice in a glass bowl, cover it with diced cooked chicken, and cover the chicken with homemade mayonnaise spiced with a little mustard. Decorate the salad with a circle of hard-boiled egg slices and sprinkle it with chopped fresh tarragon, chives and parsley. Mix the *salade de poulet* thoroughly at the table. There should be plenty of French dressing and not too much mayonnaise.

CATHEDRAL OF ST. MAURICE—ANGERS   *Anjou*

Artichoke Hearts and Peas

Artichauts à la Clamart

(Frozen artichoke hearts, green peas, butter, herbs)

Thaw a package of frozen artichoke hearts, cut them in half lengthwise, and pat them dry in a cloth. Sauté them slowly in 2 tablespoons of butter until they are lightly browned, turning them several times. Add 2 cups of green peas, ½ cup of water, 1 tablespoon of butter, a *bouquet garni,* a pinch of sugar, and salt and pepper. Cover and simmer together over a very low flame for 25 minutes, or until the peas are tender and the liquid has almost evaporated. Serves four.

THE MARKET—PARTHENAY   *Poitou*

Cream of Cauliflower Soup

Potage Crème de Choufleur

(Cauliflower, milk, egg yolks)

Wash a cauliflower and break it into pieces. Cook the pieces in boiling salted water until they are soft but still whole, drain off the water and reserve it. Force the cauliflower through a fine sieve and add to it enough liquid (half cauliflower water and half chicken stock) to make a moderately thick soup. Simmer the soup for about 15 minutes, take it off the fire and add gradually 1 cup of milk beaten with 2 egg yolks. Add a lump of butter and reheat the soup very slowly, stirring constantly. Do not let it boil or the egg will turn. Serves four.

MEDIEVAL BUTCHER SHOP—BESSE-EN-CHANDESSE *Auvergne*

Pork Chops with Piquante Sauce

Côtelettes de Porc, Sauce Piquante

(Pork chops, onions, vinegar, pickles, Madeira)

In a heavy skillet brown 4 trimmed pork chops in butter on each side. Add 3 coarsely chopped onions and salt and pepper, and cook the onions and chops together until the onions are browned. Remove the chops. Add 1 tablespoon of flour to the pan, blend it into the juices and let this *roux* brown a little more. Stir in gradually 1 cup of water and add 1 teaspoon of vinegar and 2 or 3 small sliced sour pickles. Simmer the sauce for a minute, return the chops to the pan and simmer them 10 minutes longer over the lowest possible flame. Add 1 tablespoon of Madeira 2 or 3 minutes before serving. Serves four.

THE IDYLLIC CHÂTEAU—AZAY-LE-RIDEAU   *Touraine*

Flambéed Bananas

Bananes Flambées

(Bananas, lemon juice, butter, sugar, brandy or orange Curaçao)

Peel 8 ripe bananas and remove the strings. Arrange the bananas close together in a shallow baking dish, add 4 tablespoons of water and sprinkle the bananas with 4 teaspoons of lemon juice. Put several dots of butter and 1 tablespoon of sugar on each banana. Bake them in a 400° oven, basting once or twice and adding a little water if necessary. In 20 minutes the bananas should be soft and beginning to glaze. Bring a pony of warmed brandy or orange Curaçao and the bananas, piping hot, to the table. Put a match to the liqueur, pour it flaming over the bananas and shake the dish gently until the flame dies. Serves six.

LATE AFTERNOON IN OLD MENTON

Riviera

Riviera Pizza

Pissaladière

(Hot roll or French bread dough, onions, garlic, olive oil, anchovies, black olives)

A *pissaladière* should be made with French bread dough (see *Index*), but a standard American hot roll mix will do very nicely. Line an oiled cookie sheet with a layer of dough ⅛ inch thick and roll the edges to make a border. In an iron skillet over a low flame cook 3 pounds of sliced onions and 2 minced cloves of garlic in 1 cup of olive oil until they are quite soft. Drain the onions well, cool them and spread them evenly over the dough. Make a lattice work of anchovy fillets, not too close together, over the onions and in each square place a pitted black Italian olive. Bake the *pissaladière* in a 350° oven for 20 minutes, or until the edges of the crust are brown, and serve it hot.

SHEPHERD WITH HIS FLOCK — PACY-SUR-EURE   *Normandy*

Lamb Stew

Navarin de Mouton

(Stewing lamb, onions, garlic, herbs, white wine, stock, carrots, potatoes, turnips)

In a deep casserole brown together 1½ pounds of good lean stewing lamb, cut in cubes, 1 chopped onion and 6 small whole onions in 2 or 3 tablespoons of oil or lard. Pour off any excess fat and sprinkle the lamb with 1 tablespoon of flour. Blend in the flour and add salt and pepper, 1 minced clove of garlic, a *bouquet garni,* ½ cup of white wine, 1 cup of veal stock or chicken consommé, and just enough hot water to cover. Cover the casserole and simmer the stew over the lowest possible flame for 1½ hours. Add 2 carrots, 2 small white turnips and 2 potatoes, all cut in pieces. Simmer the *navarin* for another ½ hour, or until the meat and vegetables are all tender. Serves four.

74

ROQUEFORT HILLSIDE *Guyenne*

Epicures' Canapés

Diablotins d'Epicures

(Roquefort cheese, butter, walnut meats, red pepper, French bread)

These are hot hors-d'oeuvre of generous proportions, intended for hungry and appreciative guests and not for mere nibblers.

Cream together to a smooth paste 1 cup of crumbled Roquefort cheese and ¼ pound of butter. Mix in thoroughly ½ cup of finely chopped walnut meats and a pinch of red pepper. Toast slices of French bread on one side, spread the cheese mixture on the untoasted side and brown the *diablotins* briefly in a hot oven.

HILLSIDE VILLAGE — ST. ROME-DE-CERNAN   *Gascony*

Vermicelli and Onion Soup
Tourin des Landes

(Onions, butter, bacon fat, vermicelli, tomato paste, stock or consommé, Parmesan)

In a heavy casserole or saucepan sauté 4 chopped onions in 1 tablespoon each of butter and bacon fat until they are soft and just beginning to brown. Stir in ¾ cup of fine vermicelli, broken in pieces, and let them take on a little color. Blend in 3 tablespoons of tomato paste and add 6 cups of good beef or chicken stock or consommé. Simmer the soup for 10 minutes and serve it with grated Parmesan. Serves six.

THE CHÂTEAU — LUNÉVILLE *Lorraine*

Baked Whole Liver

Foie de Veau Bourgeoise

(Calf's liver, salt pork, brandy, herbs, spices, onions, carrots, white wine, egg yolk)

This splendid dish does require time and trouble, but it is a masterpiece. If any is left over it will be delectable cold, served as a pâté.

Moisten 4 ounces of salt pork, cut in long thin strips, with a little brandy. Roll the strips in a mixture of minced parsley, pepper and a pinch each of powdered cinnamon and clove. With a larding needle run the seasoned salt pork through a small whole calf's liver (about 3 pounds). Marinate the liver for 4 hours, in a covered bowl just big enough to hold it, with 3 tablespoons of olive oil, the juice of ½ a lemon, salt, pepper and a little more cinnamon and clove.

Melt 2 tablespoons of butter in a heavy casserole, add the liver, the marinade, 1 onion and 1 carrot, both cut in small pieces, and a *bouquet garni*. Bake the liver, covered, in a 350° oven for 45 minutes, basting it often. Then add a *garniture bourgeoise* (see *Index*) and bake it for another 15 minutes. Remove the liver to a hot platter and surround it with the *garniture*. Add ½ cup of dry white wine to the juice in the casserole, simmer the sauce for 5 minutes and strain it into a small saucepan. Mix a spoonful of the sauce with 1 beaten egg yolk, slowly stir the egg mixture into the sauce, reheat it, stirring constantly, until it just begins to thicken and pour it over the liver. Serves six to eight.

THE PONT DU GARD, NEAR NÎMES *Languedoc*

Spiced Onion Hors-d'Oeuvre

Oignons à la Grecque

(Onions, consommé, vinegar, raisins, tomato paste, herbs, spices)

In a skillet brown 1½ pounds of very small white onions on all sides in 2 tablespoons of butter. In a saucepan combine ¾ cup of strong consommé, ¼ cup wine vinegar, ¾ cup of seedless raisins, 3 tablespoons of tomato paste, 1 tablespoon of salad oil, 2 tablespoons of sugar, ½ teaspoon salt, ⅛ teaspoon of crushed red pepper, ¼ teaspoon of dried thyme, 1 bay leaf and a generous grinding of black pepper. Simmer this sauce for 2 or 3 minutes. Arrange the browned onions close together in a shallow baking dish and cover them with the sauce. Bake them in a 325° oven for 1 hour, or until they are tender when pricked with a fork. Serve *oignons à la grecque* chilled, as an hors-d'oeuvre or with cold meats.

78

THE WALLS OF THE CITE — CARCASSONNE *Languedoc*

Veal Scallops with Tarragon

Escalopes de Veau à l'Estragon

(Veal scallops, consommé, tomato paste, tarragon)

Use 4 large veal scallops cut very thin and pounded even thinner with a wooden mallet or potato masher. Salt and pepper the scallops and dip them lightly in flour. Sauté them in an iron skillet over a medium flame with 2 tablespoons of hot butter until they are brown on each side. Put the scallops on a platter and keep them hot. Stir ½ cup of consommé or juices from a roast, 1 tablespoon of tomato paste and 1 teaspoon of chopped fresh tarragon into the pan juices. Simmer the sauce for 2 or 3 minutes and pour it over the scallops. If you use dried tarragon, it will have more flavor if it is soaked in a few drops of hot water before it is added to the sauce. Serves four.

CATHEDRAL OF ST. PIERRE—ANGOULÊME   *Angoumois*

Pork Chops and Baby Turnips

Côtelettes de Porc aux Navets

(Pork chops, butter, small blue-nose turnips, white wine, parsley)

In a large heavy skillet brown well-trimmed pork chops on both sides in butter. For each chop add 1 young blue-nose turnip, peeled and quartered, and 2 or 3 tablespoons of white wine or chicken consommé, and season with salt and pepper. Cover the skillet, lower the flame, and cook the chops and turnips together, shaking the pan occasionally, for 40 minutes, or until the turnips are tender and browned on all sides. Serve sprinkled with chopped parsley.

DETAIL OF THE CATHEDRAL PORCH—BOURGES *Berry*

Sausages in White Wine Sauce

Saucisses au Vin Blanc

(Country sausage, butter, shallot, herbs, white wine)

Use fresh pork sausages of the kind generally known as country sausage. Brown the sausages slowly in a skillet, pricking the skins first so they will not burst. Remove the sausages when they are done and drain them on brown paper. Pour off all the fat in the skillet. For 1 pound of sausages (enough to serve 3 or 4), melt 1 tablespoon of butter in the skillet and add 1 minced shallot. Sauté the shallot for about 30 seconds, then blend in ½ tablespoon of flour and cook the mixture for 2 or 3 minutes. Then add a *bouquet garni* and 1½ cups of dry white wine, and simmer the sauce for 20 minutes. Remove the *bouquet*, return the sausages to the skillet and reheat them in the sauce. Serve with mashed potatoes.

HEMING, A FARM VILLAGE IN THE ARDENNES *Champagne*

Ardennes Stuffed Baked Potatoes

Pommes de Terre à l'Ardennaise

(Potatoes, cream, egg yolks, butter, grated cheese, nutmeg, parsley, mushrooms)

Slit the tops of 6 baked Idaho potatoes lengthwise and scoop out the pulp. Mash the potato and beat in 2 tablespoons of butter, ¾ cup cream mixed with 3 egg yolks, and 2 tablespoons of grated Parmesan. Add salt and pepper to taste, a pinch of nutmeg and 1 tablespoon of minced parsley. Parboil 6 mushrooms in salted water for 4 or 5 minutes, drain them, chop them finely and add them to the potatoes. Stuff the potato skins with this delicious purée, sprinkle them with more grated Parmesan, dot them with butter, and return them to a 350° oven for 15 minutes, or until the cheese is lightly browned. Serves six.

THE CHURCH OF NOTRE-DAME-DE-L'ÉPINE *Champagne*

Fresh-water Fisherman's Stew

Matelote Champenoise

(Fresh-water fish, shallots, garlic, spices, herbs, white wine, brandy)

This dish from the Champagne country is a stand-by of the vacationing angler. The more fish you catch for it yourself, the better it will taste.

Melt 4 tablespoons of butter in a large saucepan and add 3 shallots and 2 cloves of garlic, all minced, salt, freshly ground black pepper, a pinch of cinnamon, 2 cloves and a *bouquet garni*. When the butter is hot, add 4 pounds of cleaned fresh-water fish cut in 1½-inch slices. Eel is essential and the others may be pickerel, pike, carp, trout or whitefish. Whatever the selection you have available, use roughly equal quantities of each kind of fish. Heat the fish in the butter for several minutes, then add 3 cups of dry white wine, cover the saucepan and cook the *matelote* over a fairly brisk flame for 20 minutes.

Warm a tablespoon of brandy, put a match to it and pour it flaming over the fish stew. When the flame dies, ladle the fish into a deep serving dish and remove the *bouquet garni*. Add a tablespoon of butter creamed with a teaspoon of flour to the sauce, and let it simmer and thicken slightly for a few minutes. Pour the sauce over the fish and garnish the *matelote* with chopped parsley and slices of French bread sautéed in butter until they are crisp and golden. Serves six.

FLANDERS FIELDS NEAR CALAIS   *Flanders*

Flemish Red Cabbage and Apples

Choux Rouges à la Flamande

(Red cabbage, onion, bacon fat, apples, red wine, sugar, spices)

Soak 4 cups of finely shredded red cabbage in cold water for 1 hour and drain it. Chop 2 medium onions and sauté them in a heavy saucepan in 2 tablespoons of bacon fat until they are golden. Add 2 tart apples, peeled, cored and sliced, and simmer together for 5 minutes. Then add the cabbage, 2 tablespoons of brown sugar, salt, pepper and a pinch of either powdered clove or nutmeg. Add ½ cup each of water and red wine, cover the pan, and simmer the cabbage gently until it is very tender, or for at least 1 hour. Add a little red wine if the liquid cooks away too fast. Serves four to six.

VINEYARDS AT VERZENAY *Champagne*

Spinach Purée with Stuffed Eggs

Epinards à la Chimay

(Spinach, eggs, onion, shallot, mushrooms, butter, cream, nutmeg)

Simmer 1 small onion, 1 small shallot and 4 large mushrooms, all finely minced, in 1 tablespoon of butter until they are soft and reduced. Season with salt, pepper and grated nutmeg. Cut 6 hard-boiled eggs in half lengthwise; remove the yolks and mash them with the mushroom mixture, 2 teaspoons of butter, a little cream and a touch of cayenne. Stuff the egg whites with the yolk mixture, sprinkle them lightly with fine bread crumbs, and dot them with butter.

Meanwhile, in a covered kettle cook 3 pounds of spinach with ½ cup of water for 10 minutes, or until it is just soft, and purée it in an electric blender. Reheat the spinach over a good flame to cook away all excess liquid, then add a lump of butter, ⅓ cup of extra-heavy cream or sour cream, and salt and pepper. Brown the stuffed eggs lightly under the broiler; put the spinach purée in a deep serving dish, arrange the eggs in a circle on top and serve immediately. Serves six.

THE PRÉFECTURE OF THE OISE — BEAUVAIS *Ile-de-France*

Roast Tenderloin of Beef Jardinière

Filet de Boeuf Jardinière

(Tenderloin of beef, beef stock or consommé, garden vegetables)

This is a perfectionist's dish. Not complicated, just perfect. The *jardinière* is a panorama of tiny vegetables with which only your own *jardin* or a green-grocer with an exceptional conscience can supply you.

Salt and pepper a tenderloin of beef (about 3½ pounds), tie a thin layer of salt pork over it and roast it in a 350° oven for 50 minutes, basting it frequently. Remove the salt pork and put the roast on a large, hot platter. Skim the excess fat from the pan juices, stir in briskly a little hot beef stock or consommé and serve the juice in a sauceboat.

Around the roast arrange alternating piles of the smallest possible garden vegetables: carrots and blue-nose turnips cooked separately in beef stock or consommé; green peas cooked in a minimum of water with a few lettuce leaves and a small onion; green beans cooked in a minimum of water and sprinkled with minced parsley; and instead of potatoes, white shell beans boiled until tender but not broken and also sprinkled with parsley. Pour a little melted butter on all the vegetables. The final touch of perfection, if you still have the patience, would be flowerettes of steamed cauliflower for which a sauceboat of hollandaise sauce should come separately to the table.

MONDAY ON THE OLD CANAL — STRASBOURG *Alsace*

Alsatian Sauerkraut

Choucroute Garnie Alsacienne

(Sauerkraut, white wine, spices, bacon, frankfurters, ham, potatoes)

Canned sauerkraut is excellent for this, but it will need a little doctoring. Use a standard can, or about 1¾ pounds. Wash the sauerkraut thoroughly in cold water, drain it and press out the excess liquid. Put it in a heavy saucepan, tightly covered, with 1 cup of dry white wine, 2 tablespoons of vinegar, 20 juniper berries, 10 whole peppercorns and ½ pound of lean bacon, cut in chunks. Cook the sauerkraut over the lowest possible flame for 1¼ hours, or until most of the liquid is absorbed. Ten minutes before servingtime, prick the skins of 6 frankfurters or *knackwurst* with a fork and add them and 6 generous slices of baked ham to the sauerkraut. Heat the *choucroute* thoroughly, still covered; then pile the sauerkraut in the center of a large platter, cover it neatly with the ham and surround it with the sausages, the pieces of bacon and 6 boiled potatoes. Serve with a pot of strong mustard. Serves six.

CHÂTEAU DE VALENÇAY   *Touraine*

French Butter Cookies

Sablés

(Flour, sugar, salt, egg yolk, ice water, vanilla, butter)

From their short and granular texture, the name *sablé*, or "sandy," was coined for these traditional cookies:

Sift together into a bowl 1¼ cups of flour, 4 tablespoons of sugar, and a pinch of salt, and make a well in the center. Into the well put 1 egg yolk, 1 tablespoon of ice water, ½ teaspoon of vanilla extract, and 6½ tablespoons of butter, cold and cut into small bits. With the fingers quickly work the butter into the liquids and gradually draw in the flour, mixing the pastry as fast as possible so as not to warm the butter. Sprinkle on a little more flour if necessary, until the dough just holds together and is not sticky. Gather it together into a ball, put it in a floured bowl, and let it stand for ½ hour in the refrigerator. Then roll it out quickly on a floured board to a thickness of a little less than ¼ inch. Cut it into circles with a 2½-inch scalloped cooky cutter and bake the *sablés* on a buttered cooky sheet in a preheated 350° oven for 18 minutes, or until they are cooked through but pale gold, not brown. Cool on a cake rack.

MARTIGUES, "THE VENICE OF PROVENCE"   *Provence*

Eggplant and Tomato Ragout

Ratatouille

(Eggplant, tomatoes, onions, peppers, zucchini, oil, garlic, herbs)

Peel a medium eggplant and cut it in slices ½ inch thick. Salt the slices lightly, pile them together and let them stand under a weight for ½ hour. In a large skillet, over a low flame, sauté 2 large sliced onions and 2 diced green peppers, or sweet red ones, in ½ cup of olive oil. When the vegetables begin to soften, add 4 ripe tomatoes, peeled, seeded and coarsely chopped, the slices of eggplant, drained and cut into dice, and 2 zucchini, cut in ½-inch slices. Add salt and pepper, 1 tablespoon of chopped parsley, and a pinch each of marjoram and basil. Simmer the *ratatouille* for about 45 minutes, or until the vegetables are all soft and the liquid is quite reduced, but be careful not to let them cook to a purée. About 15 minutes before the *ratatouille* is ready, add 1 small minced and crushed clove of garlic. Serves four as a hot vegetable, eight or more as a cold hors-d'oeuvre.

89

THE VILLAGE AT NOONTIME — EVRY-LES-CHÂTEAUX *Ile-de-France*

Calves' Brains with Black Butter

Cervelles au Beurre Noir

(Calves' brains, butter, vinegar, capers)

Soak 4 calves' brains in cold water for 1 hour. Drain them, remove the outer membranes, rinse the brains and drop them into boiling water with a little lemon juice and salt. Simmer them for 15 minutes, drain them again and let them stand covered with ice water until they are thoroughly cooled. Dry the brains with a towel and dip them in a little flour seasoned with salt and pepper. In a skillet sauté them gently in butter until they are lightly browned on all sides and remove them to a heated platter. Add 6 tablespoons of butter to the skillet and when it takes on a nut-brown color take the skillet off the fire and stir in 1 tablespoon of vinegar. Heat the mixture until it foams and add 4 teaspoons of drained capers. Pour this *beurre noir* over the brains and serve immediately. Serves four.

THE RIVER TARN — MONTAUBAN   *Guyenne*

Sautéed Lobster Cettoise

Homard à la Cettoise

(Lobster, onion, olive oil, garlic, ham, parsley, tomato paste, stock, egg yolk)

Split a 2-pound live lobster down the center and cut it in thick pieces, shell and all, discarding the head. This is not as hard as it sounds, but have someone at the fish market do it for you if you'd rather. In a heavy skillet sauté 1 medium onion, chopped, in 3 tablespoons of olive oil until it is soft. Add the cut up lobster and turn the pieces to color the shells on all sides. Add 1 clove of garlic, chopped and mashed, 2 tablespoons of chopped ham and 1 tablespoon of minced parsley and sauté everything together over a low flame for 10 minutes. Sprinkle 1 scant tablespoon of flour over the lobster, add 1 heaping tablespoon of tomato paste and blend these thoroughly into the pan juices. Add ¾ cup of chicken stock or consommé and salt and pepper to taste, and simmer the *homard*, covered, for another 10 minutes. Remove it to a deep serving dish and keep it hot. Add a spoonful of the sauce to 1 beaten egg yolk and stir the egg mixture gradually into the sauce. Heat it, stirring constantly, without allowing it to boil and pour it over the lobster. Serves two.

CLOISTER OF THE BENEDICTINE ABBEY — CHARLIEU   *Lyonnais*

Green Beans and Onions

Haricots Verts à la Lyonnaise

(Green beans, onion, wine vinegar, parsley)

Lyons is famous for its wonderful food. Most *lyonnais* recipes have a characteristic savor of sautéed onion.

Snap off the stems and tips of 1 pound of young green beans. Leave the beans whole, boil them in a minimum of salted water until they are tender but still firm, and drain them thoroughly. In a heavy pan sauté 1 chopped onion in 2 tablespoons of butter until it is soft and golden. Add the green beans, mix them well with the onion and butter and reheat them over a low flame for a few minutes. Add salt and pepper to taste and ½ teaspoon of wine vinegar. Sprinkle the beans with finely chopped parsley before serving. Serves four.

THE CHÂTEAU DE CHAMBORD   *Orléanais*

Upside-down Apple Tart
Tarte Tatin

(Apples, butter, sugar, pie pastry, whipped cream)

Use a round, glass baking dish about 2 inches deep. Butter it very generously and cover the bottom with a ¼-inch layer of sugar. On the sugar arrange a layer of neatly overlapping slices of tart apples, peeled and cored. Then fill the dish to the top with more sliced apples, sprinkle them with sugar and dot them lavishly with butter. Cover the dish with a circle of flaky pie dough and bake the tart in a 375° oven for about 30 minutes. The tart is ready when the apples are golden and the sugar is beginning to caramelize. Then loosen the crust all the way around, put a serving platter upside down over the baking dish, turn the whole thing over and remove the baking dish. Serve the *tarte Tatin* hot, with chilled whipped cream.

THE LOWER TOWN — SEMUR-EN-AUXOIS   *Burgundy*

Burgundian Beef Stew
Boeuf Bourguignon

(Beef, red wine, onions, carrots, garlic, shallots, veal knuckle, brandy, mushrooms)

Boeuf bourguignon comes from the province of the most fabulous vineyards of France and is a great classic of regional cookery.

In an iron *cocotte* or a heavy casserole brown 2 pounds of good lean stewing beef, cut in 1½-inch cubes, in 2 tablespoons of hot butter. Sprinkle the meat with 1 tablespoon of flour, blend it in thoroughly and add salt and pepper and 1½ cups of red wine. In a small frying pan brown 2 coarsely chopped onions in 1 tablespoon of butter. Add the onions to the meat, together with 1 carrot, cut in pieces, 1 clove of garlic and 2 shallots, all finely chopped, a *bouquet garni,* and a piece of cracked veal knuckle if one is available. Add just enough water to cover the meat, cover the *cocotte* and simmer the stew over a low flame for 3 hours, or until the meat is very tender and the sauce is a rich, dark brown.

Half an hour before servingtime, add 1 tablespoon of brandy, 4 tablespoons of Madeira if you have some, and ½ pound of raw mushroom caps. Remove the *bouquet garni* and serve the *boeuf bourguignon* with buttered rice. Serves four.

VILLAGE ARCADE — LOUHANS   *Bresse*

Madame Blanc's Chicken in Cream
Poulet à la Crème Madame Blanc
(Chicken, onion, heavy cream)

Cut a small chicken into serving pieces. In a heavy skillet over a low flame heat the pieces in 2 tablespoons of hot butter, covered, for 5 minutes, being sure not to let them brown. Sprinkle the pieces with 1 tablespoon of flour, blend it thoroughly into the pan juices and add 1 whole onion, salt and pepper and enough hot water almost to cover the chicken. Cover the skillet and simmer the chicken for 20 to 30 minutes, or until it is tender and the stock is reduced to about 1 cup. Discard the onion, put the chicken in a deep serving platter and keep it hot. Add 1 cup of very heavy cream to the stock, simmer the sauce briefly, taste it for seasoning and pour it over the chicken. This *sauce à la crème* should be plentiful and almost white. Serves four.

95

MONT BLANC IN SUMMER *Savoy*

Marinated Roast Leg of Lamb

Gigot à la Génoise

(Leg of lamb, oil, white wine, vegetables, anchovies, bacon, herbs, spices)

Remove as much fat and skin as possible from a small leg of lamb. Insert a cut clove of garlic near the bone at each end of the roast and marinate it for 24 hours with ½ cup of oil, ½ cup of white wine, 1 onion and 1 carrot, both sliced, and 4 whole cloves. The next day put the leg of lamb in a roasting pan and over it slice 2 stalks of celery and 2 small sour pickles. Sprinkle it with a little chopped terragon and across the top arrange 4 anchovy filets and 2 strips of bacon. Roast the *gigot* in a 400° oven for 18 minutes per pound, basting it often, until it is done but still pink in the center. Carve it at the table and serve the pan juices, diluted with a little hot water or stock, in a sauceboat. Be sure to skim the excess fat from them first.

BACK GARDENS OF SAINTES   *Saintonge*

Marinated Beef Hors-d'Oeuvre

Salade de Boeuf

(Cooked beef, onions, carrot, French dressing, parsley)

This is a thrifty classic of the French hors-d'oeuvre tray: Cut leftover cooked beef into thin julienne strips and put it in a shallow serving dish. Over the meat scatter very thin slices of small white onions and a few thin circles of raw carrot. Marinate the salad for 2 or 3 hours in a generous amount of French dressing made of 1 part of wine vinegar, 3 parts of olive oil, and salt, pepper and prepared mustard to taste. Sprinkle the *salade de boeuf* with chopped parsley just before serving.

97

THE INLET — ST. VALERY-SUR-SOMME *Picardy*

Baked Eggs in Tomatoes

Oeufs aux Pommes d'Amour

(Tomatoes, parsley, garlic, eggs, cheese, bread crumbs)

Cut a slice from the stem ends of ripe tomatoes, shake out the seeds and scoop out some of the pulp. Sauté the tomatoes, cut side up, in a little olive oil for 3 or 4 minutes. Transfer them carefully to a shallow baking dish and sprinkle them with chopped parsley and a little chopped and mashed garlic. Break an egg into each tomato and sprinkle them with salt, pepper, grated Swiss cheese, bread crumbs and a little melted butter. Bake the *pommes d'amour* in a 400° oven for 10 minutes, or until the eggs are set and the crumbs are lightly browned.

98

ROMANESQUE REMNANTS — CHAUVIGNY   *Poitou*

Poached Eggs Saint-Germain

Oeufs Pochés Saint-Germain

(Purée of split green peas, eggs, cream sauce, Swiss cheese, butter)

The traditional ingredient in any dish called *Saint-Germain* is a purée of green peas, either dried or fresh ones.

Spread a ½-inch layer of hot purée of green peas in a shallow baking dish. Poach 4 eggs and arrange them on the purée. Over the eggs pour a cream sauce made with 1 tablespoon of butter melted and blended with 1 teaspoon of flour, 1 cup of cream, stirred in gradually, salt and pepper and 2 tablespoons of grated Swiss cheese. Pour a little melted butter over the sauce and glaze the *oeufs pochés* briefly under a hot broiler. Serves four.

THE BUSY HARBOR — MARSEILLES   *Provence*

Mackerel with Olives

Maquereaux aux Olives

(Mackerel, green olives, black olives, lemon)

Grease the bottom of a shallow glass or earthenware baking dish with a little salad oil. Choose small fresh mackerel, allowing one per person, and stuff each one with 5 or 6 small pitted green olives. Arrange the fish in the baking dish, sprinkle them with a little more oil and with salt and freshly ground black pepper. Scatter a handful of small black Italian or Greek olives around the fish and bake the *maquereaux aux olives* in a 350° oven for about 25 minutes. Garnish the mackerel with circles of lemon and serve them from the baking dish.

PROVENÇAL FARMHOUSES — LES BAUX   *Provence*

Provençal Tomatoes

Tomates Provençale

(Tomatoes, olive oil, garlic, parsley, bread crumbs)

Cut 4 large, red tomatoes in half, shake out the seeds, and season with salt and pepper. In an iron skillet cook the tomatoes lightly on both sides in 4 table-spoons of hot olive oil. Add 2 minced cloves of garlic and cook the tomatoes another 2 or 3 minutes. Remove them to a heated platter and sprinkle them plentifully with chopped parsley. Add 2 heaping tablespoons of coarse bread crumbs to the oil remaining in the skillet, sauté them for a minute or two until they are brown and have absorbed the oil, and sprinkle them over the tomatoes. Serves four.

101

THE ARCADED FARM — ST. CYR-SUR-MENTHON   *Bresse*

Pumpkin Soup

Soupe au Potiron

(Pumpkin, onion, milk, cream, eggs, butter)

Cut 1 pound of pumpkin into pieces, peel them and put them in a soup kettle with 1 sliced onion and 6 cups of salted water. Cover the kettle and boil the pumpkin for 15 minutes, or until it is soft. Drain off the water and reserve it, and force the pumpkin through a sieve. Put this purée in the top of a double boiler and add 1¾ cups of milk and ¼ cup of cream. *Soupe au potiron* should be quite rich and thick, but you will probably still need to dilute the pumpkin and milk mixture with some of the reserved cooking water. Add salt and pepper to taste and cook the soup over simmering water for 20 minutes.

Mix a few spoonfuls of soup with 2 beaten eggs. Add the egg mixture gradually to the soup, stirring constantly, and keep stirring until it begins to thicken. Then stir in a lump of butter and serve immediately. Serves four.

HILLSIDE HABITATIONS — ROC-AMADOUR   *Guyenne*

Veal Chops en Cocotte

Côtes de Veau en Cocotte

(Veal chops, onions, new potatoes, mushrooms)

In an iron skillet sauté a dozen very small whole onions in hot butter. When they are brown, add a little water, salt and pepper, and 1 teaspoon of sugar. Simmer the onions, covered, until they are almost cooked through and the water is absorbed. Scrape and wipe dry 16 small new potatoes. Sauté them very slowly in another skillet, uncovered, in plenty of butter, tossing them often. They should brown gradually and cook through at the same time.

Meanwhile, in an iron *cocotte* or a heavy casserole brown 4 veal chops quickly on both sides in 3 tablespoons of butter. Lower the flame, cover the *cocotte* and simmer the chops gently for about 20 minutes. When they are almost done, add the onions, ¼ pound of quartered raw mushrooms, salt and pepper if necessary, and 3 or 4 tablespoons of consommé. Simmer the chops and vegetables together, uncovered, for 5 to 10 minutes. Add the potatoes and sprinkle the dish with chopped parsley before serving. Serves four.

VIEUX PALAIS—ESPALION *Guyenne*

Baked Fillet of Sole Gironde

Sole Gratinée comme en Gironde

(Fillets of sole, mushrooms, shallots, herbs, bread crumbs, white wine, stock)

Butter a shallow baking dish with 1 tablespoon of butter creamed with 1 teaspoon of flour. Mix together ¼ pound of mushrooms and 2 shallots, all finely chopped, 1 teaspoon of minced chives, and 1 tablespoon of minced parsley. Spread half this mixture in the baking dish, sprinkle it lightly with fine bread crumbs, and arrange 8 fillets of sole or flounder on top. Cover the fish with the rest of the chopped vegetables, sprinkle lightly again with bread crumbs and with a little grated Swiss cheese, and dot with butter. Add ½ cup each of white wine and chicken stock or consommé, and bake the fish in a moderate oven for 20 to 25 minutes. Serves four.

THE CHÂTEAU OF MADAME DE MAINTENON *Orléanais*

Lamb Kidneys de Latour

Rognons de Mouton de Latour

(Kidneys, onion, butter, flour, beef stock, vinegar, mustard, shallot or garlic)

Soak 12 lamb kidneys in cold water for 20 minutes. Remove the skins, split the kidneys lengthwise with a sharp knife, removing the central gristle, and arrange them in a shallow pan for broiling. Prepare the following sauce first, then broil the kidneys under a brisk flame for about 10 minutes, turning them often.

In a small heavy saucepan sauté 1 tablespoon of minced onion in 2 tablespoons of butter until the onion is soft. Blend in 1½ teaspoons of flour and let the mixture thicken slightly and take on a little color. Add 1¼ cups of beef stock or consommé, 2 teaspoons of wine vinegar, 1 teaspoon of mild prepared mustard, and 1 small minced shallot or clove of garlic. Season with salt and pepper and let the sauce simmer very slowly for 20 minutes. When the kidneys are done, transfer them to a hot platter and strain the sauce over them. Serves four to six.

THE FORTIFIED HARBOR — LA ROCHELLE   *Aunis*

Artichoke and Shrimp Hors-d'Oeuvre
Fonds d'Artichauts aux Crevettes

(Artichokes, oil, vinegar, shrimp, green pepper, mayonnaise, lemon juice, paprika)

Boil 6 artichokes in salted water for 45 minutes or until the bases are tender when pricked with a sharp knife. Drain them and remove the leaves and chokes. Marinate the bases for 1 hour in 3 tablespoons of salad oil, 1½ tablespoons of wine vinegar and salt and pepper. Mix 1 cup of cooked shrimp, cut in small pieces, with ½ a finely diced green pepper and ⅓ cup of mayonnaise seasoned with lemon, freshly ground pepper and paprika. Fill the artichoke bases with the shrimp mixture, mask them with a very thin layer of mayonnaise and decorate each one with half a whole shrimp, split lengthwise, and a tiny sprig of parsley. Chill thoroughly. Serves six.

PLACE DU PALAIS — RENNES   *Brittany*

Chocolate Mousse

Mousse au Chocolat

(Bittersweet chocolate, vanilla, eggs)

Over simmering water in the top of a double boiler melt ½ pound of bitter-sweet chocolate, broken in pieces, with ¼ cup of water. Stir the chocolate until it is smooth and set it aside to cool. Then add 5 egg yolks beaten with 1 teaspoon of vanilla extract. Transfer the mixture to a bowl and carefully but thoroughly fold in 5 stiffly beaten egg whites. Fill small individual ramekins or *pots de crème* with the mousse and chill for at least 2 hours before serving. Serves six.

COUNTRY ROAD IN THE FINISTÈRE
Brittany

Split-Pea Soup

Purée Saint-Germain

(Split peas, bacon, beef consommé, herbs, croutons)

Soak 1 pound of green split peas for 4 hours. Drain them and cook them, covered, in 4 cups of salted water, skimming once or twice, until they are soft. Drain the peas again, reserving the cooking water, and force them through a sieve. In a heavy saucepan sauté 3 tablespoons of finely minced fat bacon. Add the cooking water, 1½ cups of beef consommé or stock, the puréed peas and a *bouquet garni*. Simmer the soup for 15 minutes, remove the *bouquet garni*, stir in 1 tablespoon of butter creamed with 1 teaspoon of flour, and serve the *purée Saint-Germain* with a sprinkling of crisp brown croutons sautéed in butter. Serves six to eight.

PORCH OF THE CATHEDRAL—AMIENS *Picardy*

Poached Salmon with Green Mayonnaise
Saumon Poché, Sauce Verte
(Salmon, herbs, sour cream, homemade mayonnaise, tomatoes, cucumbers)

In 2 quarts of water simmer for 15 minutes 1 carrot and 1 onion, both cut in pieces, 2 sprigs of parsley, 1 bay leaf, ½ teaspoon of thyme, ½ dozen pepper corns, 1 tablespoon of salt and ½ cup of white wine. Then put in a 3-pound piece of salmon wrapped in a square of cheese cloth. When the liquid returns to the boil, turn the flame very low and poach the salmon, covered, for 25 minutes. Remove the cover and cool the fish in the cooking liquid; then drain and unwrap it, chill it and skin the top side before masking it with the following *sauce verte:*

Trim the stems from fresh spinach, water cress, parsley and tarragon. Measure, quite firmly packed, 1 cup of spinach, ½ cup of water cress, ½ cup of parsley and ¼ cup of tarragon. Drop all these greens into boiling water and let them boil for 3 minutes, uncovered. Turn them into a sieve, cool them under running water, and squeeze them dry in a cloth. Chop them as finely as possible, add about ¼ cup of sour cream and reduce them to a fine purée in an electric blender. Mix the green purée thoroughly with 1½ cups of homemade mayonnaise; use part of this sauce to mask the salmon and serve the rest in a sauceboat. Garnish the platter with water cress and with peeled, hollowed and well-drained tomatoes stuffed with diced cucumbers seasoned with French dressing and minced parsley.

MEDITERRANEAN AFTERNOON — ANTIBES

Riviera

Baked Zucchini

Zucchini au Four

(Zucchini, shallots, bread crumbs, bacon)

Split 6 small zucchini lengthwise and parboil them in salted water for 5 minutes. Drain them, arrange them, skin side down, in a shallow baking dish and sprinkle them lightly with 6 minced shallots, bread crumbs and salt and pepper. Dot them with butter and put a strip of bacon on each one. Bake the zucchini in a 350° oven for about 30 minutes, or until they are tender and the bacon is brown. Serves four to six.

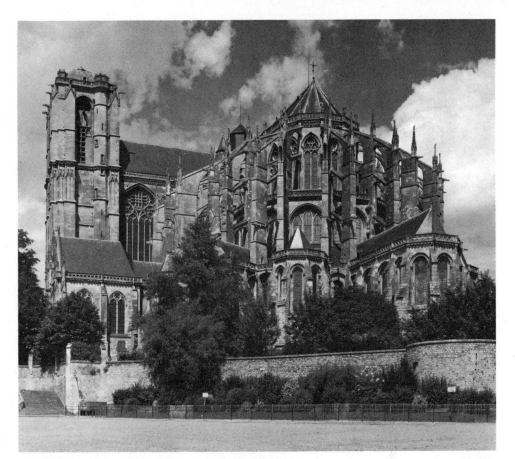

CATHÉDRALE ST. JULIEN — LE MANS *Maine*

Mushrooms in Cream

Champignons à la Crème

(Mushrooms, onion, butter, heavy cream)

This is an epicure's dish for the season when the finest fresh mushrooms are in the markets.

In an iron skillet sauté 1 small minced onion in 2 tablespoons of butter until it is soft but not brown. Add 1 pound of fresh mushrooms, sliced, and cook them over a medium flame until most of the liquid has evaporated. Season them with salt and pepper and blend in 1 teaspoon of flour. Add ¾ cup of warm, heavy cream and simmer the *champignons à la crème* for 2 or 3 minutes, or until the sauce thickens slightly. Serve them on buttered toast or with rice. Serves four.

111

CHAPEL OF STE. CROIX—ABBAYE DE MONTMAJOUR *Provence*

Steamed Salt Cod with Garlic Mayonnaise

Aïoli Provençal

(Salt cod, vegetables, garlic mayonnaise)

The *aïoli* is a pungent Mediterranean mayonnaise which is served in large quantities, thoroughly chilled, with hot, steamed salt cod fillets, hard-boiled eggs and boiled vegetables; whole new potatoes in their jackets, small whole artichokes, leeks with the green tops trimmed off, and carrots and blue-nose turnips, cut in pieces, are the usual assortment.

Use as many cloves of garlic in the *aïoli* as you dare. The correct recipe calls for 8 cloves per cup of homemade mayonnaise; 3 cloves is about the minimum if the dish is to keep its character. Start with the garlic, minced and mashed to a pulp, in a bowl. With a sauce whisk beat in 2 egg yolks. Add ¼ teaspoon of salt and a little freshly ground pepper; then add, drop by drop, 4 tablespoons of chilled olive oil, stirring furiously. Pour this mixture into an electric blender, turn the blender on and slowly add the juice of ½ a lemon and 1 tablespoon of lukewarm water. Then add gradually 1 cup of chilled olive oil. Do not make more than one cup of *aïoli* at a time in an electric blender.

112

MANOIR AT OUILLY-LE-TESSON *Normandy*

Eggs Poached in Cream

Oeufs Cocotte à la Crème

(Eggs, butter, heavy cream)

For each egg use a small ovenproof custard cup. Put a small piece of butter in the bottom of each cup, break an egg over the butter and add 2 teaspoons of very heavy cream. Sprinkle lightly with salt and freshly ground black pepper or paprika. Put the custard cups in a large shallow pan and carefully fill the pan with boiling water just to the level of the cream in the cups. Cover the pan, keep the water barely simmering on the top of the stove and cook the eggs for about 6 minutes, or until the whites are set. Test the edges of the *oeufs cocotte* with a spoon before serving as the cooking time depends somewhat on the thickness of the custard cups.

113

STILL WATERS — ST. JEAN-PIED-DE-PORT *Béarn*

Duck with Orange Sauce

Caneton à l'Orange

(Duck, oranges, lemon, vinegar, sugar, liqueur, chicken stock or consommé)

Roast a duck in a 325° oven for 20 to 25 minutes per pound. Prick the skin several times to release the fat and baste the duck often.

Meanwhile grate coarsely the rind of 2 oranges and 1 lemon. Blanch the rind in boiling water for 20 seconds and drain it. In a small saucepan simmer 3 tablespoons of vinegar with 1 tablespoon of sugar until the mixture begins to caramelize. Add the juice of the 2 oranges and the lemon, simmer together briefly and add the blanched rinds. When the duck is done, remove it to a hot platter and decorate it with thin slices of orange, peeled and halved. Skim all the excess fat from the pan juices. Pour in 2 tablespoons of Cointreau or brandy and ¼ cup of hot chicken stock or consommé and scrape in all the brown glaze around the pan. Add this juice to the orange sauce, reheat it, and serve it in a sauceboat.

LOW TIDE AT DOUARNENEZ *Brittany*

Stuffed Crab Armoricaine

Crabe Armoricaine

(Crab meat, onion, mushrooms, brandy, tomato paste, curry powder, bread crumbs)

Crabe armoricaine may be served in individual ramekins, but the Bretons serve it more picturesquely in real crab shells.

Chop 1 small onion and ¼ pound of mushrooms and sauté them gently in 1 tablespoon of butter until the onions are soft. Add 1 tablespoon of brandy, 3 tablespoons of tomato paste, ½ teaspoon of curry powder and a pinch each of salt and pepper. Simmer the vegetables for 3 more minutes. If the mixture is very thick, dilute it with a little water or white wine. Add ¾ pound of cooked crab meat, stir the mixture well and stuff 6 crab shells with it. Sprinkle the stuffed shells with fine bread crumbs, dot them with butter and brown them lightly under a hot broiler. Serves six.

THE TOWN GATE — AMMERSCHWIHR
Alsace

Alsatian Garlic Potatoes
Pommes de Terre Alsacienne

(Potatoes, eggs, garlic, parsley, nutmeg)

Mash 2 pounds of boiled potatoes and beat in 2 tablespoons of butter and 2 beaten eggs. Mix in thoroughly 2 tablespoons of flour, 2 or 3 minced and crushed cloves of garlic, 2 tablespoons of very finely chopped parsley, a pinch of nutmeg and salt and pepper to taste. Transfer the potatoes to a buttered baking dish and bake them in a 350° oven for 15 minutes, or until the top is lightly browned. Pour a little melted butter over the crust before serving. Serves four.

116

ARC DE TRIOMPHE DU CARROUSEL *Paris*

Roast of Veal Bourgeoise
Rôti de Veau Bourgeoise

(Veal, onions, carrots, white wine, bacon, herbs, stock or consommé)

In an iron casserole or *cocotte* brown a 3½-pound piece of young veal in 2 tablespoons of butter. Add 1 carrot and 1 onion, both cut in pieces, ½ cup of white wine, ¼ cup of water, a *bouquet garni,* salt and pepper, a piece of bacon rind, and ½ teaspoon of meat glaze. Bake the roast, covered, in a 300° oven for 1½ hours, then uncover it and bake it another 30 minutes to brown the meat and reduce the sauce. Serve the *rôti de veau* sliced on a hot platter with the sauce and surrounded by the following *garniture bourgeoise:*

In a skillet sauté 3 strips of lean bacon, diced, in 1 tablespoon of butter. Add a dozen very small onions and, when these are lightly browned on all sides, add 6 young carrots cut in small pieces, salt, pepper, and 1 teaspoon of sugar. When the carrots begin to brown, add 1 cup of beef stock or consommé and simmer the vegetables, covered, until they are tender and very little liquid remains. Serves six to eight.

117

CHÂTEAU DE MENTHON, NEAR ANNECY *Savoy*

Chicken Livers Marianne

Foies de Volailles Marianne

(Chicken livers, shallot, red wine, consommé, mushrooms, bacon)

Cut a dozen fresh chicken livers in half. In an iron skillet sauté the pieces briefly in 2 tablespoons of hot butter and remove them while they are still quite pink in the center. To the butter left in the skillet add 1 shallot, minced, and ½ cup of dry red wine. Simmer the liquid down to about one half its original quantity, add ½ cup of consommé and simmer the sauce again for 5 or 6 minutes.

Meanwhile, sauté a dozen small mushroom caps in 1 tablespoon of butter for 3 minutes and blanch ½ cup of very finely diced bacon in boiling water. Drain the bacon and add the mushrooms, bacon and a little freshly ground black pepper to the red wine sauce. Add a little salt if necessary, add the chicken livers, and reheat all together thoroughly. Sprinkle the *foies de volailles Marianne* with chopped parsley and serve them with buttered rice. Serves four.

THE CHÂTEAU DE TANLAY *Burgundy*

Sliced Steak with White Wine Sauce

Steak Morvandiau

(Steak, shallots, mustard, white wine, parsley)

For a thick, rare and juicy steak (about 2 pounds for 4 people) here is a simple sauce in the best tradition of French cooking.

In an iron skillet over a low flame sauté 2 minced shallots in 1 tablespoon of butter for 2 or 3 minutes, or until they are soft. Add 1 tablespoon of mild prepared mustard (*moutarde de Dijon* if you can get it) dissolved in ½ cup of dry white wine, 1 teaspoon of minced parsley, and salt and pepper. Simmer the sauce 2 more minutes, slice the steak on a hot platter, London-broil fashion, pour the sauce over it and serve immediately.

119

WHEAT FIELDS NEAR CHÂTEAU-THIERRY   *Champagne*

French Bread

Pain de Ménage

(Flour, water, yeast, salt, sugar, butter or egg white)

Making your own French bread is not really as enormous an effort as you may think. To get a crust on the loaves that is as wonderfully tender as it is crisp, be sure to put a large shallow pan of boiling water on the lowest rack of the oven during the baking.

In a large bowl dissolve 1 envelope of dried yeast, 2 teaspoons of salt and 1 tablespoon of sugar in 2 cups of lukewarm water. Mix in gradually 4 or more cups of sifted flour, until the mixture absorbs no more flour. Knead the dough on a floured board until it is slightly elastic, or for about 3 or 4 minutes. Let it rise for 1 hour in a greased bowl, covered with a damp cloth, in a warm corner of the kitchen.

Butter a cookie sheet, sprinkle it with corn meal and shake off the excess. Without working the dough too much, divide it into 2 parts and shape them into long narrow loaves on the cookie sheet. Mark a row of diagonal slits across the tops with a sharp knife and let the loaves rise another 45 minutes. Brush them lightly with melted butter or egg white and bake them in a pre-heated 450° oven for 5 minutes, then lower the temperature to 375° and bake them another 35 minutes.

120

THE ANCIENT COVERED MARKET — DOMME *Périgord*

Chicken Marengo

Poulet Marengo

(Chicken, garlic, tomatoes, white wine, tomato paste, mushrooms)

Cut a small roasting chicken into serving pieces and salt and pepper them. In a large skillet sauté the pieces in 2 tablespoons of oil and 1 tablespoon of butter until they are brown on all sides and almost cooked through. Remove the chicken and keep it warm. In a small saucepan simmer a dozen mushroom caps in ¾ cup of salted water for 5 minutes, drain them and reserve the water.

To the juices left in the skillet add 1 finely minced clove of garlic and a heaping teaspoon of flour. Blend the mixture well, add 2 large ripe tomatoes, peeled, seeded and chopped, simmer them a few minutes and add ½ cup of dry white wine and ½ cup of the mushroom liquor. Simmer the sauce, uncovered, for 15 minutes and add 1 tablespoon of tomato paste and salt and pepper to taste. Return the chicken to the skillet, add the mushrooms and simmer all together for 5 minutes. Serves four.

FARMHOUSE IN PASSY   *Nivernais*

Jellied Ham with Parsley

Jambon Persillé

(Ham, chicken stock, herbs, shallots, white wine, gelatin, parsley)

This is a family version of a Burgundian specialty which is usually presented, by expert chefs, elaborately molded and made of pieces of a whole ham.

Cut enough leftover ham into small chunks to make 4 cups of lean meat. Simmer 3 cups of chicken stock or consommé with 1 teaspoon of minced fresh tarragon, a *bouquet garni*, 2 chopped shallots, and 1 cup of dry white wine for 20 minutes. Strain the stock through a cheesecloth and stir in 2 envelopes of gelatin, dissolved in ½ cup of cold stock, and 1 tablespoon of tarragon vinegar. Put the ham in a glass serving bowl and pour over it just enough of the stock to half cover it. Put the remaining stock in the refrigerator and when it just begins to thicken stir in 4 tablespoons of finely minced parsley. Pour the stock over the ham and chill the *jambon persillé* thoroughly before serving.

THE ANCIENT CHÂTEAU — FOIX   *Comté de Foix*

Cheese Soufflé

Soufflé au Fromage

(Butter, flour, milk, Swiss cheese, Parmesan cheese, eggs)

Make a thick cream sauce with 4 tablespoons of butter, 4 tablespoons of flour, 2 cups of milk, and salt, pepper and a pinch of nutmeg. Simmer the sauce, stirring constantly, for 5 minutes; then stir ¾ cup each of grated Swiss cheese and grated Parmesan into the hot sauce. When the mixture is smooth, take the pan off the fire, let it cool and add slowly 5 beaten egg yolks, stirring constantly.

Beat 6 egg whites stiff but not dry and fold one third of them carefully but thoroughly into the mixture; then fold in the rest very lightly. Pour the batter into 1 large or 2 small buttered soufflé molds. The mold should not be more than ¾ full. Bake the soufflé in a 375° oven for 20 minutes, or until it is puffed high and delicately browned. Serve immediately, of course. Serves six.

THE GOTHIC BRIDGE — ST. AFFRIQUE   *Gascony*

Francine's Apple Fritters

Beignets de Pommes à la Francine

(Apples, rum, sugar, and a batter of flour, water, oil, egg)

In a small bowl blend 3 tablespoons of flour smoothly into 4 tablespoons of lukewarm water. Stir in 1 lightly beaten egg yolk mixed with 1½ tablespoons of oil and a pinch of salt. Add a few drops of water if the mixture is too thick and set it aside to rest at room temperature for 2 hours. The batter should just coat the spoon like heavy cream. (It can be used, incidentally, for almost any fruit or vegetable of your choice.)

Shortly before servingtime, peel and core 2 medium apples, slice them into rings ¼ inch thick and sprinkle the slices lightly with rum and sugar. Beat one egg white stiff but not dry, and with a spoon fold it very gently but thorougly into the batter. Heat vegetable oil ½ inch deep in a large frying pan. It will be the right temperature (about 360°) when a 1-inch cube of bread browns in it in 60 seconds. Dip the slices of apple in the batter, coating both sides, drop them in the hot oil and fry them, turning them once, until they are golden brown on both sides. Drain the fritters on brown paper, sprinkle them with sugar and serve them immediately. Serves four.

PALAIS DU LUXEMBOURG   *Paris*

Chestnut Turkey Stuffing
Farce de Dinde aux Marrons
(Chestnuts, shallots, sausage, bread crumbs, celery, mushrooms, brandy, Madeira)

For a 15-pound Thanksgiving turkey prepare the following stuffing: Peel 2 pounds of chestnuts and boil them in salted water until they are tender (or use canned chestnuts packed in brine). In a large skillet sauté 2 shallots and 1 onion, all chopped, in 1 tablespoon of butter. Add ½ pound of sausage meat, heat it briefly, pour off the excess fat and mix in 1½ cups of bread crumbs moistened with ½ cup of hot chicken stock or consommé. Add the chestnuts, crumbled, 2 stalks of celery and 6 mushrooms, all chopped, 1 tablespoon of minced parsley, 1 teaspoon of dried thyme, salt and pepper, ¼ cup of brandy and, if possible, 2 tablespoons of Madeira. (A French chef would use a 2-ounce can of truffles, chopped with their juice, instead of the mushrooms.) Mix the stuffing thoroughly, cool it, and pack it loosely inside the turkey.

TIMBERED SIDE STREET — MOULINS   *Bourbonnais*

Braised Endive

Endives Braisées

(Endive, butter, onion, parsley)

For each serving use 2 plump heads of endive, 1 teaspoon of butter and
3 tablespoons of water. Cook the endive over a very low flame in a tightly covered, heavy saucepan with the butter, water, a few slices of onion, a sprig of
parsley and a sprinkling of salt and freshly ground pepper. The liquid should
be absorbed and the endive should be cooked through and just beginning to
glaze in about 30 minutes. Serve them with a dusting of finely chopped parsley.

THE SHELTERED WALK TO CHENONCEAUX *Touraine*

Fresh Stewed Fruit with Mousseline Sauce

Compote, Sauce Mousseline

(Pears, peaches, cherries, with a sauce of sugar, cream, eggs, sweet wine)

Boil 1 cup of sugar with 1 cup of water for 5 minutes. Add a few drops of vanilla and in this syrup poach 2 firm pears and 2 peaches, all peeled and halved, and a dozen or so ripe black cherries. Remove each piece of fruit when it is tender but still firm and serve the compote hot, with a frothy *sauce mousseline:*

In the top of a double boiler over barely simmering water beat together with a sauce whisk ½ cup of cream, 2 tablespoons of sugar and 3 egg yolks beaten with 2 egg whites. Stir the sauce constantly and when it has thickened, beat in 3 tablespoons of Marsala (or Madeira or sherry). Serves four.

127

THE CATHEDRAL SQUARE—STRASBOURG

Alsace

Mirasol Pork and Veal Pâté

Terrine de Viande Mirasol

(Pork, veal, sausage meat, bacon, olive oil, white wine, herbs, spices)

Cut 1 pound each of lean fresh pork and veal into ¼-inch slices and cut the slices into 2-inch squares. Marinate the meat for 24 hours in ½ cup of olive oil and 1 cup of dry white wine, with 1 onion, 2 cloves of garlic and 2 shallots, all chopped, 1 sliced carrot, 2 sprigs of parsley, 2 bay leaves, ½ teaspoon of thyme, salt, pepper and grated nutmeg. Line the bottom and sides of an earthenware *terrine* (an ovenproof dish with a lid) with bacon. Fill the *terrine* with alternating layers of the marinated meat, drained and free of herbs, and fresh sausage meat (about 1 pound). Fill the *terrine* with the strained marinade barely to the level of the top layer of meat, and cover the pâté with more bacon.

Make a stiff paste of flour and water, shape it into a narrow roll and fit the roll around the edge of the *terrine*. Press the lid on firmly and bake the sealed pâté in a 300° oven for 3 hours. Take off the lid and the flour paste, cover the pâté with aluminum foil and cool it under pressure, using any handy object heavy enough to pack the meat down firmly. Chill the pâté for 2 days before serving it sliced, as an hors-d'oeuvre or with salad.

THE CLASSIC FOUNTAIN—ARBOIS   *Franche-Comté*

Eggs in Aspic with Madeira

Oeufs en Gelée au Madère

(Eggs, consommé, gelatin, Madeira, tarragon, ham)

Boil 6 eggs for 6 minutes, cool them under running water and shell them carefully when they are cold. Soak 1 tablespoon of gelatin in ¼ cup of cold water. Heat 1½ cups of clear chicken consommé, add the gelatin and stir until it dissolves completely. Add 2 tablespoons of Madeira (or port or sherry) and set this aspic aside to cool.

Use small molds or ramekins just wide and deep enough to hold 1 egg each with a little space to spare. Trim 6 thin slices of ham just to fit the tops of the molds. Spoon a little aspic into the bottom of each mold to make a layer about ¼ inch thick. When this is almost firm, decorate it with 2 crossed leaves of fresh tarragon or a tiny sprig of parsley. Gently place an egg in each ramekin, spoon aspic over them until the molds are almost full, and cover each egg with a circle of ham. Glaze the ham with a final spoonful of aspic, chill the eggs and serve them unmolded.

129

VILLAGE ON THE LOIRE — ST. MATHURIN   *Anjou*

Black Pepper Steak

Steak au Poivre

(Steak, peppercorns, butter, white wine)

Use a good cut of beef, trimmed and cut at least 1½ inches thick, about 2 pounds for 4 people. Cover both sides of the steak very generously with peppercorns first coarsely crushed in a mortar or on a board with a potato masher. Pound the pepper firmly into the meat with the potato masher. In an iron skillet, over a high flame, brown both sides of the steak in 1 tablespoon of butter and a few drops of oil. A French cook would, of course, leave the steak rare. When it is done, remove it to a hot platter. Stir ½ cup dry white wine (and 1 tablespoon of brandy, if you wish) into the pan juices, simmer the sauce for 2 minutes, add a lump of butter and pour it, loose pepper and all, over the steak. Serve with French-fried potatoes.

CHÂTEAU D'O, NEAR MORTRÉE   *Normandy*

Flambéed Apricot Omelette

Omelette Flambée aux Abricots

(Eggs, apricot preserves, almonds, rum, whipped cream)

Make a 6-egg omelette and when it is cooked through but still soft spread across the center ⅓ cup of apricot preserves and a few slivers of blanched almonds. Fold the omelette and turn it out on a platter. Sprinkle the top with sugar and a few more almonds and pour on 3 tablespoons of warmed rum. Light the rum, bring the omelette flaming to the table and serve it with a bowl of chilled whipped cream flavored with sugar and almond extract. Serves four.

131

THE CITY HALL—BORDEAUX

Roast Beef Bordeaux

Rôti de Boeuf à la Bordelaise

(Rump roast of beef, white wine, olive oil, onion, shallots, herbs, vinegar)

Remove the fat from a 3-pound rump roast of beef and reserve it. Marinate the meat overnight in 1 cup of white wine and ½ cup of olive oil, with 1 sliced onion, 2 chopped shallots, 1 bay leaf, several sprigs of parsley, ¼ teaspoon of thyme, and salt and pepper.

Spread part of the beef fat in the bottom of the roasting pan, add the chopped vegetables from the marinade, and put in the roast, lightly salted and with a strip of beef fat tied over the top with kitchen string. Pour in ¼ cup of the marinade and roast the meat, uncovered, in a 350° oven for 1¼ hours, basting it often. Remove the roast to a hot platter and cut off the string. Strain the pan juices into a saucepan, add the rest of the marinade, and simmer the sauce over a good flame to reduce it a little. Let it stand for a few minutes until the excess fat rises to the top, skim off the fat, and add a dash of wine vinegar. Reheat and serve in a sauceboat.

CHÂTEAU DE LOCHES   *Touraine*

Cheese Tart

Tarte au Fromage Touraine

(Pastry, Swiss cheese, eggs, cream, spices)

Line a 9-inch pie pan with a thin layer of rich pastry dough and chill it. Beat 4 eggs thoroughly and combine them with 1½ cups of cream and ½ pound of grated Swiss cheese. Season with grated nutmeg, a touch of cayenne pepper, and salt to taste. Pour this filling into the pie shell, bake the *tarte* in a preheated 400° oven for 15 minutes, then lower the heat to 325°. The cheese custard should be set and golden brown in about 30 minutes. Serve directly from the pan.

MARKET DAY IN PONT L'ABBÉ

Brittany

Fish Salad with Ravigote Sauce

Salade de Poisson Ravigote

(Fish fillets, eggs, anchovies and a sauce of mayonnaise, herbs, seasonings)

Simmer together for 20 minutes 2 cups each of white wine and water with 1 teaspoon of salt, 1 small carrot and 1 small onion, both sliced, a few peppercorns and a *bouquet garni*. In this *court-bouillon* poach 1½ pounds of white fish (bass, pike or Lake Michigan whitefish would be good choices) until it is cooked but still whole and firm. Drain the fish and chill it.

Fillet the fish, cut it into serving pieces and arrange each one on a green lettuce leaf on a serving platter. Split 4 hard-boiled eggs lengthwise, place an anchovy fillet on each one and arrange these between the pieces of fish. Mask each fish fillet with a generous spoonful of *sauce ravigote:*

To ¾ cup of mayonnaise add 1 teaspoon of lemon juice, 2 tablespoons of cream, 1 shallot and 2 small sour gherkins, all finely chopped, 2 teaspoons each of capers and minced parsley, 1 teaspoon of chopped chives and a little freshly ground pepper. Let the sauce steep for an hour or two before using it. Serves four.

THE RIVERBANK — BAYONNE *Béarn*

Ham Mousse

Mousse au Jambon

(Ham, chicken stock, gelatin, eggs, cream, Port)

Put enough cooked ham through the finest blade of a meat grinder to make 3½ cups. Grind the ham several times if necessary, to give it a very fine, smooth consistency. Dissolve 1 envelope of gelatin in ¼ cup of chicken stock. Heat another 1¼ cup of stock in a saucepan and stir the gelatin mixture into it. Beat 2 egg yolks lightly in a bowl and gradually stir in the warm chicken stock. Return this mixture to the saucepan, reheat it, stirring constantly, until it just begins to thicken, then set it aside to cool.

Whip ½ cup of cream and beat 2 egg whites stiff. Mix together the ground ham, the thickened chicken stock and the whipped cream. Stir in 4 tablespoons of Port and then fold in the beaten egg whites. Pour the mousse into a mold and chill it for at least 3 hours. Turn it out onto a platter and garnish it with water cress and unpeeled, thinly sliced cucumber just before serving.

135

TOWN HALL—MOLSHEIM *Alsace*

Roast Leg of Veal with Mustard

Rôti de Veau à la Moutarde

(Veal roast, butter, mustard, stock)

Salt and pepper a roast of veal and place it in an open roasting pan. Cream together equal amounts of butter and mild prepared mustard, preferably *moutarde de Dijon,* and spread half of this generously on the meat. Roast the veal in a 300° oven for 30 minutes per pound for a leg, breast or shoulder, 40 minutes per pound for a loin or rolled roast, basting often with the pan juices, and adding a little chicken stock if the pan gets dry. When the roast is half done, spread it with the rest of the mustard and butter mixture. When the meat is done, remove it to a hot platter. Dilute the pan juices with a little hot chicken stock and serve them in a sauceboat. Serve with buttered noodles.

136

PATHWAY BY THE SEINE—PETIT ANDELY   *Normandy*

Normandy Roast Duck Champsaur

Caneton Champsaur

(Duck, russet apples, bread, cinnamon, white wine, stock, Calvados, cream)

Sauté 1 cup of diced soft white bread in 2 tablespoons of hot butter until it is lightly browned. Peel, core and chop coarsely enough tart or russet apples to make 2 cups and add them to the bread. Cook until the apples begin to soften. Season this stuffing with ⅛ teaspoon of cinnamon, and salt and freshly ground pepper. Moisten it with a very little white wine.

Stuff the duck, truss it, and rub it with salt and pepper. Roast it, uncovered, in a 325° oven for 20 to 25 minutes per pound; prick the skin several times to release the fat. Add ½ cup each of white wine and chicken stock (or consommé) to the roasting pan and baste the duck often. When the duck is done, remove it to a hot platter and skim most of the fat from the pan juices. Pour in 2 tablespoons of Calvados or apple brandy and ¼ cup of heavy cream. Reheat the sauce, stirring briskly, and pour it through a strainer into a sauceboat.

THE WOODED HILLS, NEAR ST. NECTAIRE *Auvergne*

Pork Chop Casserole
Côtes de Porc à l'Auvergnate

(Pork chops, cabbage, cream, white wine, sage, grated cheese)

Remove the outside leaves of a small young cabbage, slice it finely and boil it for 7 minutes in salted water. Drain the cabbage thoroughly, add salt and pepper and 1 cup of cream, and simmer it, covered, for 30 minutes. Meanwhile, in an iron skillet sauté 4 lean, well-trimmed pork chops in a little butter until they are brown and cooked through. Remove the chops and season them with salt and freshly ground pepper. Stir ½ cup of white wine briskly into the pan juices, add a good pinch of sage and simmer the mixture for a couple of minutes. Stir this juice into the creamed cabbage.

Spread half of the cabbage in the bottom of an ovenproof casserole. Add the pork chops, cover them with the rest of the cabbage, sprinkle generously with grated Parmesan and a little melted butter, and bake the casserole, uncovered, in a 350° oven for 20 minutes, or until the top is golden brown. Serves four.

THE ARCHED CLIFF — ÉTRETAT   *Normandy*

Fresh Shrimp Pâté

Pâté de Crevettes

(Shrimp, lemon, seasoning, olive oil)

Shell and devein ½ pound of cooked shrimp and put them twice through the finest blade of a meat grinder. Add 3 tablespoons of lemon juice, freshly ground pepper, a generous dash of paprika and a pinch of salt, and mix well. Then add gradually about ½ cup of olive oil, blending the shrimp to a creamy paste. Store the pâté in a covered jar in the refrigerator and serve it on circles of toast or crackers.

RESTAURANT LAPÉROUSE   *Paris*

Cold Madrilène Consommé

Consommé Madrilène

(Chicken stock or consommé, tomatoes, celery salt, herbs)

This is one of the simpler ways to make one of the great soups of classic cuisine. You can use canned chicken consommé, or make your own chicken stock by boiling the carcass and bones of a roast chicken with the neck and giblets, 1 carrot and 1 onion, both cut in pieces, 1 stalk of celery, several peppercorns, salt, a *bouquet garni* and enough water to cover well. Simmer the stock until it is reduced and flavorful. For each cup of strained stock add 1 small ripe tomato, peeled, seeded and chopped, and celery salt and freshly ground pepper to taste. Simmer the madrilène for 30 minutes, strain it through a fine sieve or cheesecloth and serve it chilled with a little minced parsley and chives.

140

THE GOTHIC PORTAL — CHÂTEAU DE BLOIS *Orléanais*

Honey Cakes

Gâteaux au Miel

(Eggs, sugar, honey, flour)

Blend thoroughly ½ cup of sugar and a scant ¼ cup of honey into 2 well-beaten eggs. Sift 1 cup of flour and mix it gradually into the batter which should remain quite thin. Set it aside to rest for 45 minutes, then spread it about ⅜ inch thick on a buttered cookie sheet and bake the *gâteau* in a 375° oven for 20 minutes. Cut it in squares while it is still hot and transfer the squares to a cake rack to cool and harden.

ANGRY SEAS AT PARAMÉ   *Brittany*

Baked Turbot (or Halibut) in Cream

Turbot au Four à la Crème

(Turbot, mushrooms, onions, bay leaf, garlic, white wine, cream, new potatoes)

Wipe a 3-pound piece of turbot or halibut with a cloth and rub it with a little flour seasoned with salt and pepper. Put the fish in a generously buttered baking dish and dot it with 4 tablespoons of butter. Bake the fish in a 350° oven for 20 minutes and baste it often. Then add ½ pound of whole button mushrooms, ¾ cup of thinly sliced white onions, 1 bay leaf, 1 cut clove of garlic and 1 cup of dry white wine. Cover the baking dish with a piece of buttered brown paper to keep the fish from drying and bake it for another 20 minutes, still basting it frequently. Transfer the fish, mushrooms and onions to a heated platter and discard the bay leaf and garlic. To the liquid left in the baking dish add 1 cup of warm heavy cream. Heat the sauce to the boiling point, taste it for seasoning and pour it over the fish. Finish the platter with boiled new potatoes and several decorative sprigs of parsley. Serves six.

142

THE STATELY METROPOLIS — BORDEAUX *Bordelais*

Broiled Lamb Kidneys

Rognons de Mouton en Brochette

(Lamb kidneys, water cress, butter, parsley, broiled tomatoes)

For each serving soak 2 lamb kidneys in cold water for 20 minutes. Remove the skin and split the kidneys from the rounded sides, leaving the two halves attached on the indented side. Run a skewer into the cut surface of one half and then back through the other half from the outside, so as to hold the kidney flat on the skewer. Season the kidneys with salt and pepper, brush them with oil and grill them under a hot broiler for 3 minutes on each side. Serve the *brochettes* on a bed of water cress and on each kidney put a small lump of butter creamed with minced parsley. Garnish the platter with broiled tomatoes.

143

THE RHÔNE VALLEY AT BEAUCAIRE *Provence*

Chicken Casserole from Southern France

Poule en Cocotte du Midi

(Fowl, onions, bacon, herbs, tomatoes, carrots, red wine, brandy)

Cut a fowl into serving pieces and salt and pepper them. Heat 3 tablespoons of salad oil in an iron *cocotte* or a heavy casserole and add 4 small whole onions (or a large one, quartered), 3 slices of bacon, diced, and a *bouquet garni*. Add the pieces of chicken and brown them on all sides. Add 4 peeled and seeded tomatoes, 2 carrots, cut in pieces, 2 cups of red wine and a liqueur glass of brandy. Cover the casserole and let the chicken simmer over a low fire for about 2½ hours, or until it is very tender. Add more wine or a little chicken consommé during the cooking if the sauce reduces too quickly. Serves four to six.

RESTAURANT "MAISON DES TÊTES"—COLMAR *Alsace*

Ham with Madeira Sauce

Jambon, Sauce Madère

(Baked ham, onion, flour, tomato paste, chicken consommé, Madeira, spinach)

In a heavy saucepan sauté 1 small minced onion in 1 teaspoon of butter until it is soft. Blend in 1 teaspoon of flour and brown it lightly, stirring briskly. Stir in 1 teaspoon of tomato paste, add 1½ cups of chicken consommé, and simmer the sauce over a low flame until it is reduced to about 1 cup. Just before servingtime, heat but do not brown 8 thin slices of baked ham in a skillet with a little butter. Spread a bed of well-drained purée of spinach on a hot platter and arrange the ham on top. Add 2 tablespoons of Madeira to the hot sauce, strain it over the ham, and serve immediately. Serves four.

CHÂTEAU DE SAUMUR

Anjou

Eggplant Purée

Purée d'Aubergines

(Eggplant, shallots, chicken consommé, milk, nutmeg, butter)

Peel 2 medium eggplants and cut them into ¾-inch dice. Put them in a heavy saucepan with 3 minced shallots, ⅓ cup of chicken stock or consommé, 2 tablespoons of milk, and salt, freshly ground pepper and a pinch of nutmeg. Cook the eggplant, covered, over low heat for about 25 minutes, or until it is quite soft. Force it through a strainer; if the purée is too thin, reduce it quickly over high heat. Add a good lump of butter and sprinkle with chopped parsley before serving. Serves four.

REFLECTION IN THE YONNE—JOIGNY   *Burgundy*

Burgundian Snails

Escargots de Bourgogne

(Canned snails, butter, parsley, garlic, nutmeg)

Providing one is equipped with a taste for garlic and a set of metal snail dishes, shell-shaped clamps and little two-pronged forks, this famous specialty should present no serious problems even to the amateur cook. The classic Burgundian butter sauce is simplicity itself. The snails are imported in quantity nowadays, with the snails in a can and their shells usually in a separate package; the shells are reuseable.

Allow 6 snails per person for a first course, or a full dozen for a main course. They can be prepared well in advance, chilled, and heated at the last moment. For four dozen snails, cream together 1¾ sticks of butter, ½ cup of minced parsley, 8 to 10 minced and crushed cloves of garlic, 4 or 5 minced shallots, a pinch of nutmeg, and pepper and just a little salt to taste. Wash and drain the shells. Drain the brine from the canned snails, place one in each shell, and pack the shells brim-full with the garlic butter. Arrange them carefully, open ends up, in the hollows of the snail dishes, and heat them in a 450° oven until they are bubbling hot. Serve them in the same dishes, with plenty of French bread for mopping up the melted butter.

LAC DE NANTUA *Bresse*

Shrimp Nantua

Crevettes Sautées Nantua

(Shrimp, mushrooms, tomato paste, cream)

This is an adaptation of an elaborate provincial specialty which is usually made with fresh-water crayfish.

Boil 2 pounds of shrimp for 5 minutes, cool them and shell them. Over a very low flame simmer the shrimp in 4 tablespoons of butter for about 10 minutes, turning each one at least once. Add ½ pound of sliced mushrooms and simmer them another 5 minutes. Sprinkle the mixture with 2 teaspoons of flour and blend it in thoroughly. Dilute 1½ teaspoons of tomato paste with a little heavy cream, add enough cream to make 1¾ cups in all and pour it over the shrimp. Season the sauce with salt and freshly ground white pepper and simmer it gently for a few minutes until it thickens somewhat. Serve *crevettes Nantua* in individual ramekins or scallop shells. Serves six to eight.

148

THE CATHEDRAL OF ST. ETIENNE—AUXERRE   *Burgundy*

Veal Birds à la Française

Paupiettes de Veau

(Veal scallops, sausage meat, bread crumbs, milk, eggs, parsley, white wine, cream)

On a chopping board pound 8 veal scallops quite thin with a wooden potato masher. Trim them to even rectangles and add the scraps, finely minced, to the following stuffing: Mix together ¼ pound of sausage meat, ½ cup of crumbled stale bread soaked in hot milk and squeezed dry, 1 beaten egg, 1 tablespoon of minced parsley, and a little black pepper. Spread the stuffing on the scallops, roll them up and tie them neatly with kitchen thread. Melt 2 tablespoons of butter in a skillet, add the veal birds and simmer them, without browning too much and turning several times, for ½ hour. Then add ½ cup of white wine or stock and braise the *paupiettes* slowly for 1 hour, or until they are glazed brown and tender. Transfer them to a heated platter and cut off the threads. Deglaze the skillet with a little hot stock and ¼ cup of thin cream, and stir this sauce briskly over a good flame for 2 or 3 minutes. Pour the sauce over the *paupiettes* and serve immediately with sautéed mushroom caps. Serves four.

SIDE PORTAL OF THE CATHEDRAL—METZ *Lorraine*

Baked Eggs Lorraine

Oeufs sur le Plat Lorraine

(Eggs, ham, Swiss gruyère, cream)

Butter individual shirred-egg dishes. In each one put first a thin slice of ham, then a thin slice of Swiss gruyère. Break 2 eggs into each dish and pour over them 2 tablespoons of heavy cream. Sprinkle sparingly with salt and pepper. Bake the *oeufs Lorraine* in a 350° oven for 10 minutes, or until the cheese has melted, the whites are set, but the yolks are still soft.

THE FLEET AT ST. VALERY-SUR-SOMME *Picardy*

Lobster Bisque

Bisque de Homard

(Lobster, chicken consommé, white wine, seasonings, cream, egg yolks, sherry)

In a soup kettle heat together 4 cups of chicken stock or consommé, 2 cups of water and 1 cup of dry white wine, with 1 stalk of celery and 1 onion, both cut in pieces, 4 crushed peppercorns, 1 bay leaf, a pinch of thyme and a sprig of parsley. When this *court-bouillon* has simmered for 15 minutes, boil a live 2-pound lobster in it for 20 minutes. Remove the lobster and strain the stock through a fine sieve. Let the lobster cool, remove the meat and set it aside. Discard the large claw shells, and break the rest of the carcass and shell into pieces and reserve it.

Heat 4 cups of the stock in the top of a large double boiler, stir in 2 table-spoons of butter creamed with 3 tablespoons of flour, and add 1 cup of thin cream. Add the reserved shells and cook the bisque over simmering water for 1 hour, stirring occasionally. Shortly before servingtime, strain the bisque again, return it to the double boiler, and add ¼ cup of sherry and ½ cup of heavy cream mixed with 3 lightly beaten egg yolks. Taste the bisque for seasoning, reheat it, stirring until it thickens a little, and garnish it with pieces of claw meat. (See Lobster Canapés in the *Index* for one way to use up the rest of the meat.) Serves six.

151

CHÂTEAU DE PUYGILHEM *Périgord*

Veal Steak Gratiné

Rouelle de Veau au Gratin

(Veal steak, bacon, shallots, parsley, bread crumbs, chicken consommé)

Use a thick veal steak cut from the leg, weighing about 1½ pounds. Put the steak in a shallow well-buttered baking dish and cover it with a mixture of 3 table-spoons of finely chopped bacon, 2 chopped shallots, 2 tablespoons of chopped parsley, pepper and a little salt, and sprinkle these seasonings with fine bread crumbs. Add ½ cup of chicken consommé and bake the steak in a 300° oven for 1¼ hours, or until it is tender and well browned. Baste it occasionally with the juices in the dish, adding a little consommé if necessary. Serve from the baking dish, garnished with parsley and slices of lemon. Serves four.

152

HILLSIDE FARM LANDS   *Guyenne*

Veal Chops with Mushrooms and Cream

Côtes de Veau à la Crème

(Veal chops, butter, button mushrooms, cream, egg yolks, sherry)

In a heavy skillet, over high heat, brown 4 thick loin veal chops well on both sides in 2 tablespoons of hot butter. When they are brown, lower the heat, cover the skillet, and simmer them for 20 to 25 minutes, turning them once and adding butter sparingly if they tend to stick. Five minutes before the chops are done, drain a 2-ounce can of button mushrooms, reserving the juice, and add the mushrooms to the skillet. Then remove the chops to a hot platter and keep them warm. Pour the juice from the mushrooms into the skillet and stir well, scrapping up all the brown scraps. Add ¾ cup of cream mixed with 2 egg yolks and 1 tablespoon of sherry or Madeira, season to taste with salt and pepper, and heat the sauce slowly without letting it boil, stirring constantly, until it thickens. Pour the sauce and mushrooms over the chops and serve them with noodles or rice.

BASQUE VILLAGE—AÏNHOA   *Béarn*

Basque Rice

Riz à la Basquaise

(Rice, butter, chicken stock, onions, sweet pepper, olive oil)

Heat 1 cup of raw rice in 2 tablespoons of melted butter, stirring often, until every grain is coated and it begins to turn golden. Add 1 cup of chicken stock or consommé and bring it to a boil, then lower the flame and cook the rice, covered, for 15 minutes, or until all the liquid has been absorbed. Add another 2½ cups of hot chicken stock and continue cooking the rice very slowly, still covered, until all the liquid has been absorbed. Meanwhile, in a skillet, sauté 3 medium onions, chopped, and 1 sweet red or green pepper, diced, in 3 tablespoons of butter or olive oil until they are cooked through and golden. Mix the vegetables and rice together with a fork and add a little freshly ground pepper. Serves four.

LA MALLERIE, NEAR PLOUBALAY *Brittany*

Caramel Baked Pears

Poires Joséphine

(Anjou pears, sugar, butter, cream)

Arrange 6 firm Anjou pears, peeled, quartered and cored, in one closely packed layer in a shallow baking dish. Sprinkle them generously with granulated sugar and dot them with 4 tablespoons of butter cut in small bits. Put them in the hottest possible preheated oven and bake them until the sugar is brown and caramelized. Then add ¾ to 1 cup of heavy cream, spoon the caramelized juice and the cream over the pears to blend the sauce, and serve them warm, from the baking dish. Serves four to six.

DEAD-END STREET—POUILLY-SUR-LOIRE *Nivernais*

Celery Root with Rémoulade Sauce

Céleri Rémoulade

(Celery root, with a sauce of egg yolks, mustard, vinegar, olive oil, herbs)

This classic of the French hors-d'oeuvre tray is very little trouble if you have a good vegetable shredder. Choose celery roots (celeriac) that are not too large and pare off all the fibrous outside. Cut the roots into chunks and put them through the shredder, using a blade that cuts strips about ⅛ inch wide.

For 2 cups of shredded celery root, mash together 1 hard-boiled and 1 raw egg yolk. Add 1½ teaspoons of strong Dijon mustard (or 1 tablespoon of mild American mustard), salt, pepper, and 2 tablespoons of tarragon vinegar. Work the mixture to a smooth paste and add bit by bit ½ cup of cold olive oil, stirring constantly until the sauce thickens like mayonnaise. Mix the dressing and celery root together, chill, and sprinkle with minced parsley and chives before serving.

MARKET DAY IN TULLE *Limousin*

Sardine-stuffed Tomatoes

Tomates Galloise

(Tomatoes, sardines, hard-boiled eggs, water cress, seasonings)

Cut off the stem ends of tomatoes, remove the center core and the seeds, and let the tomatoes drain, cut side down, for an hour or two. The proportions for the stuffing are about 3 medium sardines to 1 hard-boiled egg to ¼ cup of chopped water cress. Drain the sardines, take off the skin if it is coarse, and mash them with a fork. Chop the whites of the eggs and mash the yolks. Mix sardines, eggs and water cress together and season the mixture well with lemon juice, chives, capers, mustard, pepper, and a little salt and olive oil. Stuff the tomatoes and garnish the tops with a slice of hard-boiled egg and 3 or 4 whole water cress leaves. Serve as an hors-d'oeuvre, with French bread and sweet butter.

ROMANESQUE PORCH—ST. GILLES

Squab with New Peas

Pigeons aux Petits Pois

(Squab, bacon, onions, chicken consommé, green peas, lettuce, bouquet garni)

Squab or Rock Cornish game birds may be used. For 6 tiny birds or 3 larger ones, in a casserole brown lightly 2 strips of diced bacon in 2 tablespoons of hot butter. Remove the bacon and reserve it, and brown 8 to 10 tiny whole onions, or 3 or 4 medium ones, quartered, in the casserole. Remove the onions and reserve them, and in the remaining fat brown the birds evenly on all sides. Take them out, and if there is too much fat in the casserole, pour off all but 2 tablespoons. Blend ½ tablespoon of flour into the remaining fat and when the *roux* is golden brown, add gradually ½ cup of chicken consommé. Bring the mixture to a boil once, stirring constantly, then return the birds, the bacon and the onions to the casserole and add a *bouquet garni*. Cover the casserole and bake it in a 400° oven for 45 minutes to 1 hour, depending on the size of the birds. Thirty minutes before the cooking time is up, add 3 cups of young green peas and 2 or 3 lettuce leaves. To serve, discard the *bouquet garni* and arrange the birds on a deep platter with the vegetables and sauce around them. Serves six.

PLACE DES VOSGES

Paris

Beef Tenderloin with Mushroom Sauce

Filet aux Champignons

(Beef tenderloin, mushrooms, butter, sherry, brandy, cream, mustard)

Sauté ½ pound of sliced fresh mushrooms in 2 tablespoons of butter for 5 minutes or until they are soft. Add salt and pepper and 2 tablespoons of dry sherry. Put a match to 1 tablespoon of warmed brandy and pour it flaming over the mushrooms. Shake the pan until the flame dies out, then add 3 tablespoons of cream blended with 1 teaspoon of flour and 1 tablespoon of mild Dijon mustard. Simmer all together, stirring often, until the sauce is slightly reduced.

Meanwhile, in a skillet over a moderate flame, brown 4 1-inch-thick slices of tenderloin of beef in a little hot butter for 2½ minutes on each side. They should be well browned, but rare inside. Transfer them to a hot platter and pour the mushroom sauce over them. Serves four.

ROMAN ARCH—ST. RÉMY *Provence*

Artichokes Barigoule

Artichauts Barigoule

(Artichokes, mushrooms, onion, garlic, ham, herbs, white wine, stock, olive oil)

Trim the bases of 4 artichokes and cut ½ inch from the tips of the leaves. Parboil them in salted water for 20 minutes, drain them, and remove the thin center leaves and the chokes. Meanwhile, sauté lightly ¼ pound of mushrooms, 1 small onion and 1 small clove of garlic, all minced, in 2 teaspoons of butter and 1 tablespoon of olive oil. When the vegetables are soft, add ¼ cup each of minced ham and fine bread crumbs, 1 tablespoon of stock, 1 teaspoon of minced parsley, and a little pepper. Mix well and fill the centers of the artichokes with this stuffing. Put 3 tablespoons of olive oil in a small casserole, add the artichokes, 1 small sliced carrot, ½ cup each of dry white wine and chicken stock or consommé, and a *bouquet garni*. Pour a few drops of oil into each artichoke and bring the liquid to a boil on top of the stove. Then bake them, covered, in a 300° oven for 40 minutes, basting occasionally. Serve the artichokes with the juice poured over them. Serves four.

160

TOUR DE L'HORLOGE—AUXERRE   *Burgundy*

Duck with Glazed Onions

Canard aux Oignons Brulés

(Duck, onions, butter, sugar, chicken consommé)

   Rub a duck with a little salt and pepper and roast it in a 325° oven for 20
to 25 minutes per pound; prick the skin to release the fat and baste the bird with
the pan juices diluted with a spoonful of chicken consommé. Serve it surrounded
with a dozen or more onions cooked as follows: In a heavy saucepan sauté
whole medium onions gently for 5 minutes in 2 or 3 tablespoons of hot butter,
shaking the pan and turning them often. Sprinkle them with 1½ to 2 tablespoons
of granulated sugar and cook them another 5 minutes, still turning them often,
until they are brown and begin to glaze. Add 1 cup of chicken consommé, and
simmer the onions, covered, for 40 minutes, or until they are soft but still whole.

DELACROIX'S STUDIO, PLACE FURSTENBERG   *Paris*

Flambéed Fresh Figs

Figues Flambées Boulestin

(Figs, Curaçao, brandy, heavy cream)

Peel carefully 12 ripe purple figs, leave them whole, and put them in a chafing dish with 3 tablespoons each of Curaçao and brandy. Light the alcohol lamp and in a few seconds put a match to the liqueurs. Prick each fig with a silver fork and shake the pan gently until the flame dies. The figs will be warm and a little softened and the liqueur reduced. Serve immediately and pass a pitcher of heavy cream separately. Serves six.

THE MOUNTAIN TOWN OF GRASSE *Riviera*

Scrambled Eggs Paul Reboux

Oeufs Brouillés Paul Reboux

(Eggs, orange rind, cream, sherry, butter)

Beat 4 eggs lightly with a fork and add the grated rind of half an orange, salt, pepper, and 1 tablespoon each of heavy cream and sherry. Melt a generous lump of butter in a skillet, add the eggs and cook them slowly, stirring constantly with a wire whisk, not a fork, until they achieve a rich creamy consistency. Serve the eggs on hot buttered toast with just a soupçon of grated orange rind on top.

163

THE GOOD SHIP "BELLE FRANCE"—NICE *Riviera*

Mixed Salad Niçoise with Ravigote Sauce

Macédoine Niçoise, Sauce Ravigote

(Chicken, ham, cheese, herring, eggs, vegetables, French dressing, herbs)

In a wooden salad bowl that has been rubbed with a cut clove of garlic, mix together the following, all cut in thin julienne strips: Enough cold chicken to make about 1 cup; 2 good slices of ham; enough Italian *mortadella* or salami to make ½ cup; 3 herring fillets preserved in oil; the whites of 2 hard-boiled eggs, and 1 medium-sized boiled beet. Then add the following, all diced: 2 cold boiled potatoes, ½ a tart apple, 2 stalks of celery, and 1 green pepper. Finally add the heart of 1 head of lettuce, shredded, and a dozen or more small black Italian or Greek olives.

Just before serving the *macédoine,* pour over it about ¾ cup of *sauce ravigote* —a highly seasoned French dressing made of 1 part wine vinegar, 3 parts olive oil, and salt, pepper, dry mustard, onion and parsley (both minced), orégano, and capers, all added to taste. Mix the salad thoroughly and sprinkle it with the sieved yolks of 2 hard-boiled eggs. Serves four as a salad or eight as an hors-d'oeuvre.

RIVERSIDE ARCHITECTURE IN AURILLAC *Auvergne*

French Boiled Dinner

Pot-au-Feu

(Beef, veal knuckle, carrots, turnips, leeks, onion, herbs, cabbage, potatoes)

In a soup kettle put a 4-pound piece of rump of beef, free of fat, a piece of cracked veal knuckle, a piece of beef shin bone, 5 quarts of water, a few whole peppercorns, and 2 tablespoons of salt. Simmer the meat for 2 hours and skim the surface of the bouillon several times. Then add 4 carrots, 2 medium white turnips and 6 small leeks, all cut in pieces, 1 large onion stuck with 3 whole cloves, 1 bay leaf, ½ teaspoon of dried thyme and several sprigs of parsley. Simmer the *pot-au-feu* over a low fire for another 1½ hours. One half hour before servingtime, ladle out enough bouillon to cook separately a small head of cabbage, cut in serving pieces. Traditionally, the strained *pot-au-feu* bouillon, with the fat skimmed off, is served first as a soup course. Then the beef is served sliced, with the vegetables, boiled potatoes, coarse salt and a pot of French mustard. Serves six to eight.

CHURCH SPIRE AT BRÉZOLLES   *Orléanais*

Grand Marnier Soufflé

Soufflé Grand Marnier Ile-de-France

(Eggs, sugar, Grand Marnier, cream of tartar, butter)

Separate 10 eggs and put 2 of the yolks aside. In the top of a double boiler beat the 8 remaining yolks until they are lemon colored, then beat in gradually ⅔ cup of granulated sugar. Cook the mixture over barely simmering water, stirring constantly with a whisk. As soon as the yolks have thickened, place the top of the double boiler in a bowl of cracked ice and stir in ½ cup of Grand Marnier. Beat the 10 egg whites with a tiny pinch of cream of tartar until they stand in peaks but are not dry. Transfer the yolk mixture to a bowl and with a rubber spatula fold in thoroughly one third of the whites, then fold in the rest very lightly. Pour the batter into a 2-quart soufflé mold first buttered and sprinkled lightly with sugar. Tie a strip of waxed paper around the mold so that it makes a collar standing about 2 inches above the rim of the mold, and butter the inside of the collar. Bake the soufflé in a preheated 450° oven for 15 minutes. Sprinkle the top lightly with sugar, remove the paper collar, and serve immediately. Serves six.

CONVERSATION—LE PUY *Auvergne*

White Wine Rabbit Stew

Lapin en Gibelotte

(Rabbit, bacon fat, stock, white wine, garlic, herbs, tomato paste, sour cream)

Have the butcher cut a 4- to 5-pound rabbit into serving pieces. In a casserole brown the pieces on all sides in 3 tablespoons of bacon fat. Sprinkle them with 2 tablespoons of flour, blend well, and add 2 cups each of stock and white wine. Add 1 clove of garlic, chopped, a *bouquet garni*, 2 heaping tablespoons of tomato paste, and salt and pepper. Simmer the rabbit, covered, over low heat for 1½ hours, or until it is tender. Transfer the meat to a platter; reduce the sauce if necessary, stir in 2 tablespoons of sour cream, and strain it over the rabbit. Serves six.

167

PYRENEES LANDSCAPE

Gascony

Beef in Onion Sauce

Miroton de Boeuf

(Boiled beef, onions, vinegar, stock, garlic, tomato paste, bread crumbs, Parmesan)

This sturdy dish is intended for leftover boiled beef (see French Boiled Dinner in the *Index*) and is also good for serving leftover roasts hot instead of cold.

In a covered iron skillet simmer 3 large onions, finely chopped, in 3 table-spoons of butter, stirring often. When they are cooked through and golden, but not brown, sprinkle on 1 tablespoon of flour, blend it in thoroughly, and add 2 tablespoons of vinegar, 1 cup of beef stock or consommé, and 2 tablespoons of tomato paste. Season the sauce well with salt, freshly ground pepper and a touch of minced garlic, and simmer it for 20 minutes. Pour half the sauce into a shallow baking dish. On it arrange 8 slices of boiled beef, not too thick, cover them with the rest of the sauce, and sprinkle the dish lightly with bread crumbs and grated Parmesan. Put the *miroton* in a moderate oven until the bread crumbs brown. Serve very hot, with small sour pickles. Serves four.

MANOIR DE CAUDEMONE   *Normandy*

Fruit Cup with Sherbet and Champagne

Coupe Jacques

(Pineapple, bananas, strawberries, oranges, grapes, kirsch, sherbet, champagne)

Half fill stemmed sherbet glasses with a *macédoine de fruits* made of diced fresh pineapple, bananas, strawberries, oranges, and seedless grapes which have all been marinated and chilled together with a little sugar and kirsch. On the fruit place a scoop of fruit sherbet, preferably lemon, and decorate it with a tiny sprig of mint. At the table open a bottle of chilled dry champagne and pour a little over each *coupe*. Needless to say, one drinks the rest of the champagne, and probably more, with *coupe Jacques*.

169

MARSEILLES WATER FRONT   *Provence*

Bouillabaisse

Bouillabaisse de Marseille

(Fresh fish and shellfish, olive oil, onion, garlic, tomatoes, herbs, saffron, white wine)

In a soup kettle sauté 1 large onion and 4 cloves of garlic, all minced, in ¾ cup of olive oil until they are golden. Add 2 large ripe tomatoes, peeled, seeded and chopped, 3 tablespoons of chopped parsley, 1 bay leaf, a pinch of thyme, a piece of fennel, 1 teaspoon of dried saffron, and plenty of freshly-ground black pepper. Simmer the mixture for a few minutes and add 2 small lobsters and 3 pounds of fish. Perfection can be achieved only with Mediterranean fish, but a selection of whiting, bass, red snapper, eel, and haddock or cod, or whatever is locally available and absolutely fresh, will nevertheless do very well. Cut the fish, carefully cleaned, and the lobsters, live, into 2-inch pieces, put the coarser-fleshed fish in the kettle first, then the lobsters, then the rest of the fish. Add ¾ cup of dry white wine and boiling water just to cover the fish. Bring the liquid back to a boil and cook the *bouillabaisse*, covered, over very high heat for 15 minutes. If mussels are available, add about 1 pint of them, thoroughly scrubbed, 6 minutes before cooking time is up. Serve in soup plates, from a tureen, with sliced French bread spread with garlic butter and toasted. Or serve the broth poured over the toasted bread and the fish in a separate dish. Serves eight.

170

TOUR DE CHOIZEL, NEAR MENDE   *Languedoc*

Braised Celery

Céleri Ménagère

(Celery, bacon, onion, carrot, herbs, chicken consommé, butter)

Remove the green outside stalks from 2 heads of celery, cut off the tops below the leaves, trim the root end, and split the heads lengthwise into halves or quarters, depending on their size. Wash them thoroughly and parboil them for 10 minutes. In an ovenproof casserole just large enough to hold the celery in one closely-packed layer, place 1 strip of bacon, diced, and 1 small carrot and 1 onion, both thinly sliced. Arrange the celery, well-drained, on top and add a *bouquet garni,* including a few celery leaves. Add enough clear chicken consommé barely to cover and bring it to a boil. Then place the casserole, covered, in a 350° oven for about 1½ hours, or until the celery is tender, basting occasionally. Remove the celery to a hot platter and keep it warm. Strain the juice in the casserole into a small saucepan, add a lump of butter, and reduce it over high heat for a few minutes. Pour this sauce over the celery and garnish it with chopped parsley and the sliced carrot. Serves four to six.

THE BANKS OF THE RIVER ISÈRE—GRENOBLE *Dauphiny*

Trout Grenoble

Truite à la Grenobloise

(Trout, and a sauce of butter, mushrooms, bread crumbs, lemon, capers)

Clean, wash and dry small fresh trout, trim off the fins, but leave the heads and tails. Sauté them *meunière* by dipping them lightly in flour seasoned with salt and pepper, then browning them on both sides in a heavy skillet with a good tablespoon of hot butter for each fish. Remove them to a hot platter. For 4 small trout add another tablespoon of butter to the skillet and in it sauté 4 minced mushrooms and a heaping tablespoon of bread crumbs. Add the juice of half a lemon and a teaspon of drained capers, stir the sauce briskly for a few seconds and pour it over the trout.

SPRINGTIME ROAD NEAR DIE   *Dauphiny*

Guinea Hen Chasseur

Pintade Chasseur

(Guinea hen, herbs, brandy, mushrooms, shallot, garlic, bacon, stock)

Wipe a 2½-pound guinea hen inside and out with a damp cloth and rub the cavity with a mixture of ⅛ teaspoon of dried thyme, 2 or 3 chopped rosemary leaves, ½ teaspoon of olive oil and ½ teaspoon of brandy. Leave these seasonings in the bird and let it stand for several hours.

Make a stuffing with the liver of the guinea hen, 5 large mushrooms, ½ shallot, 1 good sprig of parsley and 6 or 8 fresh rosemary leaves, all chopped, ½ clove of garlic, minced, and salt and freshly ground pepper. Stuff the bird and truss it. Blanch 1 tablespoon of diced bacon in boiling water for 30 seconds and drain it. Melt 1 tablespoon of butter in an iron *cocotte,* add the bacon, and put in the bird. Turn it several times to brown it on all sides, then add ½ cup of chicken stock or consommé. Bake the guinea hen, covered, in a 350° oven for 45 minutes, basting it several times; then remove the cover and let the bird brown for another 15 minutes. Shortly before servingtime, sauté a dozen small mushroom caps in a little olive oil and add a soupçon of shallot and garlic for the last minute of cooking. Season the mushrooms with salt and pepper, sprinkle them with minced parsley and use them to garnish the *pintade.* Serves two or three.

173

FARMHOUSE IN THE MIDI *Languedoc*

Cabbage-stuffed Cabbage
Chou Farci Aristide

(Cabbage, butter, onion, parsley, bread crumbs, eggs, nutmeg)

Discard the wilted outside leaves of a 1½-pound cabbage, and peel off 5 perfect leaves and reserve them. Core the cabbage, and slice and chop the rest of it finely. In a heavy casserole melt 6 tablespoons of butter, add the cabbage and cook it, uncovered, stirring often, over very low heat for 30 minutes, or until it is soft and golden. Add 1 medium onion, minced, and 1 tablespoon of chopped parsley, and simmer all together for 10 minutes. Let the cabbage cool, add 3 tablespoons of bread crumbs, 2 lightly beaten eggs, a pinch of nutmeg, and salt and pepper, and mix well. Put a clean cloth in a bowl, leaving the edges hanging over the side. Arrange the reserved cabbage leaves in the bowl, overlapping and stem ends up, to form a large cup closed at the bottom. Spoon the cabbage into this cup, pull the cloth up around it and tie it tightly, like a pudding in a bag. Drop the "pudding" into boiling salted water to cover generously, and cook it at the lowest possible simmer for 1 hour, turning it once. Unwrap it, drain it, and put it in a serving bowl, stem end down, with a little melted butter poured over it. To serve, quarter the cabbage with a sharp knife. Serves four.

VILLAGE TOOL SHOP *Guyenne*

Rice and Vegetable Salad

Salade de Riz

(Rice, green beans, artichoke bottoms, celery, eggs, radishes, French dressing)

Boil 1 cup of rice in plenty of salted water until it is done but still quite firm. Drain it thoroughly and while it is still hot add ¼ cup of tart French dressing made of 2 parts wine vinegar, 5 parts olive oil, and salt and pepper to taste. When the rice has cooled, mix with it ¾ cup of diced cooked green beans, 3 cooked and diced artichoke bottoms (canned if you wish), 1 small stalk of celery with its leaves, finely chopped, and the whites of 3 hard-boiled eggs, also finely chopped. Turn the salad into a glass bowl, sprinkle the top with the sieved yolks of the 3 hard-boiled eggs, and decorate it with thinly sliced red radishes and a circle of minced parsley. To serve, add another ¼ cup of French dressing and toss the salad again at the table. This is excellent with cold chicken or cold boiled lobster. Serves four.

175

LES SABLES D'OLONNES   *Poitou*

Poached Fish with Black-butter and Caper Sauce

Raie au Beurre Noir

(Fish, onion, herbs, vinegar, capers, butter)

The French use black-butter and caper sauce to glorify the otherwise un-interesting skate, or *raie*. This fish is not often found in our markets, but a sauce *au beurre noir* also improves many other fish that are of sturdy texture and flavor, such as cod, haddock or halibut.

Place a 3-pound piece of fish in a saucepan, sprinkle it with salt and pepper, and add 1 small onion, sliced, 1 bay leaf, a pinch of thyme, ¼ cup of vinegar, and enough water barely to cover. Bring the liquid to a boil and poach the fish, covered, over the lowest possible heat for about 20 minutes, or until it is firm. Put it on a cloth to drain, skin it, and take out the bones that can be removed without breaking it. Transfer the fish to a hot platter and sprinkle it with chopped parsley and 4 teaspoons of drained capers. Meanwhile, melt ¼ pound of butter in a skillet, heat it slowly until it is dark brown, and pour it over the fish. Stir 3 tablespoons of vinegar into the hot skillet, pour this over the butter sauce and serve immediately. Serves six.

176

MOUNTAIN VILLAGE   *Pyrenees*

Stuffed Baked Tomatoes

Tomates Farcies

(Tomatoes, sausage meat, bread crumbs, onion, garlic, parsley, butter)

Slice off and reserve the smooth ends of 4 firm tomatoes. Scoop out the centers of the tomatoes, reserve them, and discard the seeds. Mix together a stuffing of ¼ pound of fresh sausage meat, ½ cup of bread crumbs moistened with 2 tablespoons of consommé, 1 small onion and 1 small clove of garlic, both minced and sautéed together in butter until soft, the tomato centers, chopped, and 2 tablespoons of chopped parsley. Stuff the tomatoes, sprinkle them with fine bread crumbs, dot each one with a small piece of butter, replace the caps, and bake them in a lightly oiled baking dish in a 300° oven for 35 minutes. Serves four.

MALMAISON   *Ile-de-France*

King Henry IV's "Chicken for Every Pot"

Poule au Pot Henri IV

(Fowl, bread, ham, shallots, garlic, herbs, eggs, carrots, turnips, onions, leeks)

Use a plump 5- to 6-pound boiling fowl. Mix together well a stuffing of 5 slices of stale French bread, crumbled and soaked in ½ cup of milk; the liver, heart and skinned giblet of the hen, and 1 slice of ham or bacon, all ground together with the finest blade of a meat grinder; 2 shallots and 2 cloves of garlic, all minced; 2 tablespoons of chopped parsley and a pinch each of rosemary, thyme, nutmeg, salt and pepper; and lastly, 2 small eggs, or 1 large one, lightly beaten. Stuff the hen, sew it up carefully at both ends, and truss it.

Put the hen in a soup kettle and add 3 small carrots and 2 small white turnips, all cut in pieces; 3 whole onions, one of them stuck with 2 cloves; 2 leeks with most of the green part cut off; 1 small stalk of celery with its leaves; and 1 bay leaf, 6 crushed peppercorns, and 1 teaspoon of salt. Add water to cover the hen, but not more than 3 quarts. Cover the kettle and bring the water to a boil, then simmer the hen over very low heat for 2 hours, or until it is tender. To serve, carve the hen and arrange the meat on a hot platter. Break open the carcass, remove the stuffing and slice it. Arrange the stuffing and the vegetables around the meat, pour a little of the broth over the platter, and serve the rest in cups. Coarse salt is passed at the table with *poule au pot*. Serves six.

178

LANDSCAPE NEAR VIENNE

Dauphiny

Hot Apple Mousse

Mousse de Pommes

(Apples, butter, sugar, egg whites, apricot jam, kirsch)

Peel, quarter and core 2 pounds of tart apples. Bake them, covered with a piece of heavily buttered paper, buttered side down, in a 350° oven for 45 minutes, stirring them occasionally. Force the apples through a sieve, add ⅓ cup of sugar, simmer them until they are thick and jamlike, stirring often, and let them cool. Meanwhile, in a saucepan over medium heat melt ½ cup of sugar and heat it, stirring constantly, until it turns golden brown. Coat the inside of a 1½-quart soufflé mold with this caramel and let it harden. Beat 6 egg whites stiff with 3 tablespoons of sugar and fold them into the applesauce. Spoon the apple mousse into the mold and bake it in a pan of hot water, on a low rack in a 350° oven, for 1¼ hours. Let it cool for 15 minutes, then unmold it onto a platter. Serve warm, with a hot sauce made of 1½ cups of apricot jam puréed in an electric blender, thinned with a little water if necessary, and flavored with 2 teaspoons of kirsch. Serves six.

MANOIR DU LIEU-BINET, NEAR LISIEUX   *Normandy*

Normandy Scalloped Potatoes
Pommes Gratinées à la Normande
(Potatoes, leeks, onion, butter, bay leaf, chicken stock)

In a skillet sauté the white parts of 2 leeks and 1 medium onion, all thinly sliced, in 2 tablespoons of hot butter until they are soft and golden but not at all brown. Slice 4 large potatoes thinly, arrange a third of the slices in a buttered baking dish, spread half the sautéed vegetables over them, put in another third of the potatoes, then the rest of the vegetables and 1 bay leaf, and finish with the rest of the potatoes. (Sprinkle a little pepper between layers, but no salt.) Fill the dish just to the level of the top layer of potatoes with chicken stock or consommé, dot the *gratin* generously with butter, and bake it in a very slow oven for 1¼ to 1½ hours, or until the potatoes are done, the liquid is absorbed and the top is delicately browned. Serves four.

180

MONT ST. MICHEL   *Normandy*

Braised Peas and Carrots

Carottes et Petits Pois à l'Etuvée

(Carrots, peas, butter, onion, herbs)

Scrape and dice 6 young carrots. Simmer them in a heavy saucepan, covered, for 10 minutes, with ½ cup of water, a good lump of butter, 1 small onion, sliced, a pinch each of sugar and thyme, and salt and pepper. Then add 2 cups of green peas, ½ cup of water and a sprig of parsley, and cook the vegetables together slowly, still covered, until they are tender, or for about 20 minutes. The water should be almost all evaporated when the vegetables are done. Serves four.

181

CLUNY MUSEUM   *Paris*

Poached Peaches with Raspberry Sauce

Pêches aux Framboises Antoinette

(Fresh peaches and raspberries, sugar, vanilla bean, kirsch)

Parboil 8 ripe peaches, preferably white cling-stone peaches, in boiling water for 1 minute, peel them and leave them whole. In a saucepan boil together 1½ cups of water, ¾ cup of granulated sugar and a piece of vanilla bean for 3 or 4 minutes. Remove the vanilla bean, poach the peaches in the syrup over low heat for 5 minutes, and remove them to a serving bowl. In an electric blender, purée 3 cups of fresh raspberries and strain out the seeds through a fine sieve. Sweeten the sauce to taste with 2 or 3 tablespoons of the peach syrup and add 2 teaspoons of kirsch. Pour it over the peaches, chill the fruit before serving, and garnish it with slivered blanched almonds. Serves four to six.

THE TOWN OF MONTBARD   *Burgundy*

Braised Ham with Mushroom Sauce

Saulpiquet Montbardois Belin

(Half a ham, seasonings, white wine, stock, mushrooms, cream, peas, lemon, brandy)

Trim the fat from a 5-pound half of a processed ham. (Or use half a smoked ham, but simmer it in water first, allowing 15 minutes per pound.) In a heavy saucepan or kettle brown lightly in butter 1 small carrot and 1 onion, both sliced. Put in the prepared ham, a *bouquet garni,* and 2 cups each of dry white wine, chicken stock or consommé, and water. Braise the ham, covered, at the lowest possible simmer, allowing 15 minutes per pound, and turn it once while it is cooking. When it is done, let it rest in the liquid for 15 minutes, then remove it and keep it warm.

Skim all the fat from the broth and simmer it briskly until it is reduced by about one third. Sauté ¾ pound of sliced fresh mushrooms in 2½ tablespoons of butter for 5 minutes. Dissolve 1 tablespoon of potato flour in a little of the reduced ham broth, then add enough broth to make 1¾ cups. Add this to the mushrooms, add 1¼ cups of heavy cream, and simmer the sauce for 5 minutes, stirring often. Then add 1 cup of cooked young green peas, 2 tablespoons of brandy, and the juice of half a lemon, and simmer another 2 or 3 minutes. Serve the ham carved into thin slices with the sauce poured over them. Serves eight.

183

MINIATURE PORT AT STE. MARINE   *Brittany*

Lobster Canapés

Canapés Bretonne

(Lobster, mayonnaise, lemon juice, white bread, parsley, capers)

Carefully remove the tail meat of large boiled lobsters, and remove the coral, if any, and the green tomalley. Save the shells and the rest of the meat for some other purpose, such as a bisque (see *Index*). With a very sharp knife split the tail meat lengthwise and cut it crosswise into neat slices.

Season homemade mayonnaise to taste with plenty of lemon juice, white pepper and the tomalley (about 3 parts mayonnaise to 1 part tomalley). Spread thin 1½-inch circles of firm white bread with the seasoned mayonnaise and top each canapé with a slice of lobster. Decorate with a tiny sprig of parsley and with a scrap of the scarlet coral or a caper. Serve the canapés as soon as possible, but meanwhile cover them with aluminum foil and keep them in a cool place.

184

THE LOWER GARDENS—VERSAILLES   *Ile-de-France*

Pheasant with Endive

Faisan aux Endives

(Pheasant, salt pork, onion, carrot, chicken consommé, endives, lemon)

Tie a strip of salt pork over the breast of a cleaned and trussed 3½-pound pheasant. In a flameproof casserole brown the bird on all sides in 2 tablespoons of hot butter. Add 1 onion and 1 small carrot, both quartered, and ½ cup of chicken consommé, lower the heat, and cook the pheasant for 50 minutes. Put a piece of parchment paper under the lid to catch the steam, discard this liquid occasionally, and add more consommé sparingly to the casserole as needed. Ten minutes before the bird is done, turn it breast side down to finish browning. Meanwhile, slice 8 heads of endive crosswise into ¾-inch sections, separate the leaves, and heat them slowly in a heavy saucepan with 2 tablespoons of melted butter. When they begin to soften, add salt and pepper, the juice of 1 lemon, and ½ cup of water, and simmer the endive until it is cooked through and the liquid is almost evaporated. When the pheasant is done, transfer it to a hot platter and discard the trussing strings and the salt pork. Stir ¼ cup of boiling water into the juices in the casserole, scrape up all the brown scraps, strain this sauce over the bird, and add the endive to the platter. Serves four.

185

LOCKSMITH SHOP—OBERNAI

Alsatian Ham and Beef Broth

Bouillon à l'Alsacienne

(Ham bone, soup beef or canned broth, vegetables, herbs, cabbage, leek, potatoes)

In a soup kettle put a ham bone with a little meat on it, a 1½-pound piece of soup beef, and 2½ quarts of unsalted water. Bring the water to a boil slowly and skim it carefully just before it begins to bubble. Then add 1 stalk of celery with its leaves, 1 onion and 1 carrot, all cut in pieces, 6 crushed peppercorns, 1 bay leaf and a sprig of parsley. Cover the kettle and simmer the broth over the lowest possible heat for 2½ hours, skimming occasionally. Remove the ham bone and meat, strain the broth through a colander lined with a cloth, cool it, then skim off the fat. To serve, add ½ cup each of finely shredded cabbage and leeks, first parboiled until tender but still slightly crisp, and 1 cup of diced boiled potatoes. Reheat the soup and add salt if necessary. This makes 1½ to 2 quarts of bouillon. The same soup can be made by boiling the ham bone alone, with the same seasonings, in 1½ quarts of water. Add 3 cups of canned beef broth 15 minutes before the cooking time is up.

186

SPRINGTIME VALLEY, NEAR MARLENS

Savoy

Strawberries and Cream

Fraises en Vasque

(Strawberries, sugar, cherry brandy, cream, sour cream, pistachio nuts)

Wash and drain very thoroughly 3 pints of large perfect strawberries, hull them and put them in a glass serving bowl. Sprinkle them lightly with granulated sugar, add 2 tablespoons of cherry brandy, and chill them for several hours. Just before servingtime, with a whisk beat 1 cup of heavy cream until it thickens a little, but do not whip it, and blend it with ½ cup of thick sour cream. This will approximate the wonderful *crème fraîche* which is unobtainable in America. Pour the cream over the berries and sprinkle it with chopped pistachio nuts. Serves six to eight.

CHÂTEAU BY THE RIVER—BOURDEILLES　　　　　　　　　*Périgord*

Veal Marengo

Veau Sauté Marengo

(Veal, olive oil, tomatoes, onions, white wine, stock, garlic, mushrooms)

Whether or not Napoleon actually was regaled with *veau sauté Marengo* on the battle fields of Italy, its fame promises to be as lasting as that of the little emperor himself.

In a heavy casserole brown 1½ pounds of tender stewing veal, cut in cubes, in 3 tablespoons of olive oil. Add 4 ripe tomatoes, peeled, seeded and chopped, and 1 dozen tiny whole onions (2 medium onions, coarsely chopped, will do) first browned briefly in butter. Simmer the mixture for 4 or 5 minutes, sprinkle on 2 teaspoons of flour and blend it in thoroughly. Then add 1 cup of dry white wine, 2 cups of chicken stock or consommé, 1 whole clove of garlic, and salt and pepper. Cover the casserole and simmer the veal for 1 hour. Then add 1 dozen mushroom caps, first sautéed for 3 or 4 minutes in butter, and simmer all together for another ½ hour, or until the meat is tender. Serve sprinkled with chopped parsley and garnished with sautéed croutons. Serves four.

188

THE CHÂTEAU AT FLEURY-EN-BIÈRE   *Ile-de-France*

Puréed Apricots and Cream

Abricots Chantilly

(Dried apricots, sugar, almonds, whipped cream)

Rinse a 14-ounce package of dried apricots, put them in a saucepan with water to cover well, and simmer them very slowly, uncovered, for 25 minutes. Then stir in ½ cup of granulated sugar and cook them another 5 minutes. Force the stewed apricots through a colander, or cool them and purée them in an electric blender. Mix ¼ cup of blanched slivered almonds into the purée, spoon it into a glass serving bowl and chill.

Just before servingtime, whip ¾ cup of cream, flavor it with a little sugar and vanilla and spread it over the apricots. Or the whipped cream may be mixed into the cooled apricot purée along with the almonds, making a sort of mousse which should be chilled in individual *pots de crème*.

189

THE LOWER TOWN—DINAN

Brittany

Sole (or Flounder) Meunière

Sole Meunière

(Sole or flounder, flour, butter, lemon juice, parsley)

A small, whole, and very nearly unobtainable Dover sole is the ideal fish to sauté *meunière*. However, the many American varieties of sole and flounder, whole or filleted, are also at their best when treated in this perfectly simple fashion.

Sprinkle the fish lightly with salt and pepper, dip it in flour and shake off the excess. Melt enough butter in a skillet to coat the surface generously, but not an excessive amount. Put in the fish as soon as the butter is hot and sizzling, but before it starts to brown. Lower the heat, cook the fish slowly for 5 minutes, turn it, and brown the other side for 5 minutes. Fillets and small whole fish will then be golden brown and cooked through, but larger pieces will have to be turned again to cook for another 2 or 3 minutes on each side. Remove the fish to a hot platter when it is done, sprinkle generously with lemon juice and chopped parsley, and keep it warm. For each serving add 1 generous tablespoon of butter to the skillet, and heat it until it is dark gold and foaming but not brown. Pour the hot butter over the fish, garnish each piece with a slice of lemon dipped in minced parsley, and serve immediately.

REMAINS OF THE ROMAN THEATER—ARLES *Provence*

Country Roast Pork with Herbs

Rôti de Porc Campagnarde

(Boned pork roast, herbs, white wine)

This is a standard method applicable to any cut of pork suitable for roasting. The piece need not be boned, but the herbs are more effective if it is. Cuts with a heavy layer of fat should be partly trimmed and scored with a sharp knife.

For a roast weighing 2 pounds after boning, crush together to a powder, preferably in a mortar, 2 tablespoons of coarse salt, ½ teaspoon of dried thyme, ½ teaspoon of mixed powdered clove, cinnamon and nutmeg, 1 bay leaf, and a dozen peppercorns. Rub the meat well on all sides and in every crevice with this powder, then roll and tie it if necessary. Let it stand in a cool place for 24 hours. Roast it, uncovered, in a 350° oven for 1½ hours. turning it occasionally and basting it often, first with a little hot water and later with the accumulated pan juices. When the roast is done, remove it to a hot platter and garnish it with water cress. Skim as much fat as possible from the pan juices and stir into them ⅓ cup each of hot water and dry white wine. Scrape up all the brown scraps, simmer the sauce for 2 or 3 minutes, strain it, and serve it in a sauce boat. Mashed potatoes are the natural accompaniment. Serves four.

HILLSIDE STREET—CHAUMONT-EN-VEXIN *Ile-de-France*

Chicken Consommé Velouté

Consommé Velouté

(Chicken consommé, potato starch, egg yolks, fresh tarragon)

Use 7 cups of chicken consommé in all. Bring 6 cups of the consommé just to the boiling point. Blend smoothly 2 tablespoons of potato starch with ½ cup of cold consommé and, with a wire whisk, stir the mixture slowly into the hot soup. Simmer it, uncovered, for 15 minutes, then let it cool. Shortly before servingtime, mix 4 egg yolks with another ½ cup of cold consommé and stir them carefully into the soup with the whisk. Reheat the soup, stirring and being sure not to let it boil, until it begins to thicken. If you can get them, float fresh tarragon leaves on each serving of *velouté*. Serves six to eight.

CANAL BARGE—NEAR BRIENNON   *Lyonnais*

Fish Sauté Romagnole

Poisson à la Paysanne Romagnole

(Fish sautéed in a sauce of olive oil, garlic, tomatoes, white wine, herbs)

In a heavy casserole sauté gently 2 cloves of garlic and 1 tablespoon of parsley, all finely minced, in 4 tablespoons of olive oil. Add 3 pounds of any firm white fish (halibut, haddock, whitefish, carp or pickerel, for instance) cut in 2-inch pieces. Sauté the fish over a low flame for 5 minutes, being careful not to let it stick. Add 4 large, ripe tomatoes, peeled, seeded and chopped (or 1½ cups of drained Italian plum tomatoes), ¼ cup of dry white wine, salt, pepper, and a good pinch of thyme. Cover the casserole and simmer the fish for 20 minutes, or until the tomatoes are reduced to a juicy but flavorful sauce. Serve with boiled new potatoes. Serves six.

CHÂTEAU DE RIGNY-USSÉ *Touraine*

Chicken en Cocotte

Poulet en Cocotte

(Chicken, bacon, butter, onions, carrots, white wine, mushrooms)

In a flameproof casserole brown 1 strip of bacon, finely diced, in 1 tablespoon of hot butter. Remove the bacon, reserve it, and put a cleaned and trussed 4-pound chicken on its side in the casserole. Brown it on one side, then the other, then breast down, for 5 minutes each time. Meanwhile, in a skillet sauté a second strip of diced bacon in 1 tablespoon of butter, remove it and set it aside. To the fat remaining in the skillet add 8 to 10 tiny whole onions, or 3 or 4 medium ones, quartered, and 3 medium carrots, cut in small pieces. Toss the vegetables in the fat, sprinkle them with ½ tablespoon of sugar, and cook them, stirring often, until they are brown on all sides, or about 10 minutes. Then turn the chicken on its back, and add to the casserole the sautéed vegetables, salt, pepper, ½ cup of hot water, and ¼ cup of dry white wine. Place it, uncovered, in a 350° oven and bake the chicken for 45 minutes to 1 hour. Fifteen minutes before it is done, add the reserved bacon and ¼ pound of quartered mushrooms first sautéed briefly in a little butter. Sprinkle the *poulet en cocotte* with chopped parsley and serve it from the casserole with sautéed potato balls.

194

THE LOUVRE FROM THE SEINE   *Paris*

Parisian Madeleines

Madeleines

(Eggs, sugar, flour, butter, lemon rind)

In the top of a double boiler, over barely simmering water, work together with a wooden spoon 4 lightly beaten eggs and ½ cup of fine granulated sugar until the mixture is creamy and lukewarm. Take it from the heat and beat it again until it is cold. Beat in gradually 1⅛ cups of flour, sifted after measuring, ½ cup of lukewarm melted butter, and the grated rind of 1 small lemon. Butter and flour lightly small shell-shaped Madeleine molds, or fluted tartlet molds, and fill them two-thirds full of batter. Bake the Madeleines in a 400° oven for 25 minutes. Makes a dozen or more small Madeleines.

LA ROQUE-GAGEAC ON THE DORDOGNE *Dordogne*

Blanquette of Lamb Gascony

Agneau en Blanquette à la Gasconne

(Lamb, ham, onion, herbs, lemon juice, egg yolks)

In an iron *cocotte* heat 1 tablespoon of butter and in it brown quickly 2 pounds of good lean stewing lamb, cut in cubes. Add 1 cup of finely diced ham, 2 onions, chopped, a *bouquet garni,* and boiling water to cover. Put the lid on the *cocotte* and simmer the stew for 2 hours. Then, in a small bowl, blend 1 tablespoon of flour with ¼ cup of the cooking liquid, add this to the stew and let it simmer another ½ hour.

Shortly before servingtime, drain the cooking liquid into a bowl, discard the *bouquet garni,* and keep the meat hot in a covered dish. In a saucepan mix 2 egg yolks with 2 teaspoons of lemon juice, then stir in slowly 2½ cups of the hot stock. Reheat this sauce cautiously, stirring constantly and not letting it boil, until it is slightly thickened. Pour it over the lamb and serve the *blanquette* with steamed new potatoes. Serves four.

NOTRE-DAME AND THE ILE ST. LOUIS   *Paris*

Parisian Gnocchis
Gnocchis Parisienne

(Butter, flour, eggs, Swiss cheese, dry mustard, cayenne, cream sauce)

Add ¼ teaspoon of salt and 2 tablespoons of butter to 1½ cups of water and bring the mixture to a boil in a small saucepan. Take the pan off the fire and beat in 1½ cups of flour, sifted after measuring. When the mixture is smooth, beat in 3 large eggs, one at a time, and continue beating until the dough is shiny. Then mix in 3 tablespoons of grated Swiss cheese, 1 teaspoon of dry mustard, salt to taste, and a touch of cayenne.

Heat a large saucepan of salted water barely to the boiling point. Dip a teaspoon in the hot water to heat it, scoop up a small piece of the *gnocchi* paste with it and scoop it out again, with another heated spoon, into the simmering, never boiling, water. Poach the miniature dumplings for about 15 minutes, or until they are just firm. Take them carefully from the water with a slotted spoon as they are done, drain them on a clean cloth, and then arrange them in a shallow buttered baking dish. Cover the *gnocchis* with 1½ cups of cream sauce made with thin cream and seasoned with salt, cayenne and 3 tablespoons of grated cheese. Sprinkle the dish with a little more cheese, dot with butter and glaze briefly under a hot broiler. Serves four.

197

ABBAYE DE SOLESMES

Maine

Crème Brulée

Crème Brulée à la Jeanne

(Heavy cream, eggs, dark brown sugar)

Scald 2 cups of heavy cream in the top of a double boiler. In a bowl beat together with an egg beater 4 eggs, a pinch of salt and 3 tablespoons of dark brown sugar. Pour the hot cream slowly into the beaten eggs, stirring constantly, and return the mixture to the double boiler. Cook the custard for exactly 3 minutes over simmering water, beating constantly with the egg beater. Pour the custard into an ovenproof serving dish and let it cool completely. Then cover the top with a ¼-inch layer of finely crumbled dark brown sugar and put the custard under a hot broiler, leaving the door open, until the sugar melts and glazes. Chill the *crème brulée* for several hours and serve it ice cold. Serves six.

THE GRAND' PLACE—ARRAS   *Flanders*

Asparagus with Egg and Butter Sauce

Asperge à la Flamande

(Asparagus, hard-boiled eggs, parsley, lemon juice, butter)

Boil 1 pound of asparagus, washed, scraped and trimmed, in salted water for 20 minutes, or until it is tender but still firm. Drain the asparagus first in a colander, then on a clean cloth. Arrange it on a hot platter and sprinkle the tips with the mashed yolks, still warm, of 4 hard-boiled eggs, 2 tablespoons of minced parsley, and the juice of half a lemon. Pour over this ¼ cup of melted butter, heated until golden but not brown, garnish the platter with quarters of lemon, and serve immediately. Serves four.

CATHEDRAL OF ST. PIERRE—BEAUVAIS *Ile-de-France*

Jellied Beef Tongue

Langue de Boeuf en Gelée

(Beef tongue, veal knuckle, onions, carrots, herbs, spices, white wine, brandy)

Boil a well-scrubbed fresh tongue in lightly salted water to cover for 1 hour, skimming the surface several times. Remove the tongue, skin it and trim off the roots. In an ovenproof casserole brown lightly 2 onions and 2 carrots, all cut in pieces, in 1 tablespoon of bacon fat. Add the prepared tongue, a cracked veal knuckle, a *bouquet garni*, 1 clove of garlic, 6 whole cloves, 6 crushed peppercorns, 1 teaspoon of salt, ½ cup of dry white wine, and 4 cups of the water in which the tongue was boiled. Cook the tongue, tightly covered, in a 250° oven for 2 hours, or until it is tender.

Remove the tongue, cool it, and store it in the refrigerator. Strain the broth through a cloth, reserving the carrots, and simmer it until it is reduced to 3 cups. Cool it and store it also in the refrigerator. Next day, or when the broth has jelled firmly, scrape off all the fat, bring the broth to a boil, add 1 ounce of brandy, simmer it another minute and take it off the heat. Slice the tongue and arrange the slices in a serving dish, sprinkle them with minced parsley and garnish them with slices of the reserved carrots. Pour on the broth, let the dish cool, and chill it until the broth has jelled again.

200

CHÂTEAU DE CHAUMONT, ON THE LOIRE *Orléanais*

Baked Salmon Val de Loire

Saumon Val de Loire

(Salmon, salt pork or bacon, shallots, butter, wine vinegar, white wine)

Skin one side of a 2-pound piece of salmon. Tie a slice of bacon over the skinned side; or better, with a larding needle run a few fine strips of salt pork into the fish. Butter a shallow baking dish, put in 3 or 4 minced shallots and place the salmon on top of them, skin side down. Dot the fish with 4 tablespoons of butter and bake it, uncovered, in a 350° oven for 15 minutes, basting several times with the pan juices. The add ¼ cup each of good wine vinegar and water to the pan, and cook the fish another 15 minutes, still basting. Remove the salmon to a hot platter, discard the bacon, and keep the fish warm. On top of the stove, dilute the pan juices with ½ cup of dry white wine and stir in 1 tablespoon of butter creamed with 2 teaspoons of flour. Simmer the sauce, stirring often, for 2 or 3 minutes, taste it for seasoning, strain it, and pour it over the salmon. Serves four.

VINEGROWN COTTAGE—ALBIGNY *Savoy*

Baked Eggs Savoy

Flan d'Oeufs sur le Plat Savoyarde

(Eggs, cream, nutmeg, butter, grated cheese)

Separate 6 eggs, putting the whites in a bowl and leaving each yolk in half an egg shell. With an egg beater, beat the whites with ¼ cup of heavy cream, a pinch of nutmeg, and salt and pepper, until the mixture is frothy. In a shallow baking dish, over low heat and using an asbestos mat, put 2 tablespoons of butter and add the egg whites as soon as it melts. Cook them, stirring constantly with a whisk, until they are thick and creamy. Take the dish from the fire and drop the yolks one by one in a circle on top of the whites. Cover the baking dish, put it back on the fire, still using the mat, and cook the eggs for about 6 minutes, or until the whites are puffed and set but still soft. Serve the *flan* immediately, from the baking dish, with mild freshly grated cheese to sprinkle over it and accompanied by a crisp green salad with a tart dressing. Serves three or four.

202

STREET CORNER, BAR-SUR-SEINE   *Champagne*

Blanquette of Turkey

Blanquette de Dindon à la Crème

(Cold roast turkey, butter, flour, cream, turkey broth, mushrooms, lemon juice)

Cut cold roast turkey into large dice and remove the skin. For 2 packed cups of turkey meat, blend 1 tablespoon of flour into 1½ tablespoons of melted butter and add gradually ½ cup each of thin cream and turkey broth made from the carcass (or use canned chicken consommé). Add salt and pepper to taste and cook the sauce, stirring often, until it is smooth and slightly thickened. Meanwhile, in a small covered saucepan, simmer ¼ pound of quartered mushrooms for 5 minutes in 3 tablespoons of water and 1 tablespoon of lemon juice. Add the turkey meat and the mushrooms, with their liquor, to the cream sauce, and simmer the *blanquette* slowly until the turkey is heated through. Serves four.

ORNANS ON THE RIVER LOUE   *Franche-Comté*

Lentil Soup Conti

Purée de Lentilles à la Conti

(Lentils, bacon, butter, onion, carrot, herbs, egg yolks, croutons or lemon)

Soak 1 cup of lentils in cold water overnight. Drain them and put them in a soup kettle with 6 cups of fresh water and 1 teaspoon of salt. Bring the water to a boil and skim the surface once or twice. Meanwhile, in a skillet, sauté 2 strips of bacon, diced, in 1 tablespoon of butter. Add 1 onion and 1 carrot, both chopped, and a pinch of thyme. Simmer all together over a low flame for 7 or 8 minutes until the vegetables are golden but not brown. Add 1 bay leaf, 2 sprigs of parsley and the contents of the skillet to the simmering lentils. Cover the kettle and simmer the soup for 2½ hours, or until the lentils are thoroughly cooked. Then remove the parsley and bay leaf and force the soup through a sieve; or cool it and purée it in an electric blender. To serve, mix a little of the soup in the bottom of a tureen with 2 lightly beaten egg yolks. Reheat the soup, taste it for seasoning, and pour it into the tureen. Stir it carefully and garnish it with small croutons sautéed in butter, or with thin slices of lemon. Serves four.

THE PORT—VILLEFRANCHE-SUR-MER *Riviera*

Garlic-broiled Lobster

Homard Grillé à l'Ail

(Lobster, butter, garlic, parsley, mayonnaise, sour cream, lemon juice)

Split live lobsters lengthwise and remove the intestinal veins. Crack the claws, lay the lobsters flat, shell side down, in a broiler pan, and butter the meat with a little Burgundian snail butter (see *Index*). Broil the lobsters under a high flame, but not too close to it, for 15 to 20 minutes depending on their size, and slip a little more snail butter into each shell as soon as the meat pulls away from it. Serve the lobsters immediately, with a chilled sauce made of 3 parts homemade mayonnaise thinned with 1 part sour cream and seasoned with a touch of crushed garlic and lemon juice.

205

SUNSET ON THE RHÔNE *Lyonnais*

Onion Omelette with Croutons

Omelette Lyonnaise aux Croûtons

(Eggs, butter, onions, bread, wine vinegar)

In a skillet sauté 2 medium white onions, thinly sliced, in a generous table-spoon of butter until they are soft and golden. In a second skillet sauté ¼ cup of finely diced white bread in butter, stirring often, until it is brown and crisp. Make a 6-egg omelette and when it is set but still soft, take it off the fire, spread the onions across the center, sprinkle the croutons over the onions, fold the omelette and turn it out on a platter. Melt and brown slightly 1 more tablespoon of butter in one of the skillets, stir in ½ teaspoon of wine vinegar and pour this over the omelette. Serves three or four.

OLD SALTS OF CONCARNEAU *Brittany*

Mussels (or Clams) Marinière

Moules Marinière

(Mussels, white wine, onions, garlic, parsley, thyme, butter)

Though fresh mussels are not as hard to find in the fish markets as they once were, they do remain scarce; clams, particularly the soft-shelled ones, can be substituted with a different but no less worthy result.

Brush, scrape and wash thoroughly 2 quarts of mussels. Put them in a soup kettle with ½ cup of dry white wine, 2 white onions (or 3 shallots) and 1 clove of garlic, all minced, ¼ cup of chopped parsley, a pinch of thyme, and freshly ground pepper, but no salt. Cook them, covered, over a brisk flame, shaking them several times. The mussels are done when the shells have opened, or in about 6 minutes. Remove them and keep them warm, and pour into a saucepan as much of the cooking liquid as you can without taking the sand that will probably be in the bottom. Add 3 tablespoons of butter creamed with 1 teaspoon of flour, and reduce the sauce quickly for 3 or 4 minutes. Serve the mussels in soup plates and pour the sauce over them. Serves four as a first course, two as a main dish.

DRY-GOODS STANDS—ST. FLOUR *Auvergne*

Mushrooms on Toast

Croûtes Bayonnaise

(Mushrooms, bread, butter, ham)

For each serving allow 1 heaping tablespoon of finely diced cooked ham, 4 whole mushrooms and a slice of bread, either good white bread with the crust trimmed off, or a slice of French bread ⅜ inch thick, untrimmed and cut on the diagonal to make it large enough.

Trim the stems from the mushrooms and wash and wipe the caps; do not peel them. In one skillet brown the slices of bread on both sides in plenty of hot butter. Turn the slices at once to coat both sides with butter before browning them; this will keep them from soaking up an exorbitant amount. In another skillet lightly brown the diced ham in a little butter. Remove the ham, add more butter to the skillet and sauté the mushrooms in it. Remove them when they are golden but before they begin to shrivel and arrange them on the croutons. Sprinkle the ham over the mushrooms, season the *croûtes* with freshly ground pepper, and brown them under the broiler for 2 minutes just before serving.

HÔTEL DE VILLE—COMPIÈGNE   *Ile-de-France*

Venison Cutlets with Chestnut Purée

Côtelettes de Chevreuil aux Marrons

(Venison cutlets or loin steaks, marinade, Madeira, cream, chestnuts)

Marinate 4 venison cutlets (loin steaks), cut 1½ inches thick, for at least 6 hours in a mixture of 2 tablespoons each of olive oil, dry white wine and wine vinegar, with 1 bay leaf, ½ an onion and 1 clove of garlic, both chopped, and a little thyme, chopped parsley, salt, and freshly ground pepper. Turn the cutlets occasionally and wipe them carefully before cooking them. In a skillet sauté them quickly in a little hot oil for 3 or 4 minutes on each side. They should be brown, but rare inside. Transfer them to a hot platter and keep them warm. Add 2 tablespoons of butter to the skillet, stir in 2 tablespoons of Madeira and ½ cup of cream, and add salt and pepper to taste. Simmer the sauce, stirring, for 1 or 2 minutes, and pour it over the cutlets. Serve them with a chestnut purée made of 1½ pounds of chestnuts, shelled, boiled in salted water with a stalk of celery until tender, carefully peeled, then forced through a sieve, reheated and beaten with a whisk with cream, butter, and salt and pepper. Serves four.

ANTIQUE SHOP—COLMAR *Alsace*

Mocha Cake

Gâteau Moka

(Eggs, sugar, flour, butter, rum, mocha butter-cream, toasted almonds)

In the top of a double boiler beat together with a whisk 6 eggs and ¾ cup of sugar. Continue beating the mixture over barely simmering water until it is creamy and lukewarm. Take it from the heat and beat again until it is cold. Add 2 teaspoons of rum and beat in, still with the whisk, 1¼ cups of flour, sifted after measuring. Stir in ¼ cup of lukewarm melted butter and pour the batter into a buttered and lightly floured 9-inch cake pan. Bake this *génoise* in a 350° oven for 35 minutes and unmold it onto a cake rack to cool.

With a wooden spoon cream thoroughly ¼ pound of butter. Heat 5 tablespoons of sugar dissolved in 2 tablespoons of extremely strong hot coffee until the syrup spins a light thread. With a whisk beat the syrup gradually into 2 lightly beaten egg yolks, and continue beating until the mixture is cool and thickened. Beat this coffee cream into the butter, spread the *crème au beurre* on the cake, and cover the sides with slivered toasted almonds.

HARAS-DU-PIN *Normandy*

Normandy Potato Salad

Salade Cauchoise

(Potatoes, celery, cream, sour cream, vinegar, lemon juice, ham)

Boil 1 pound of potatoes in their jackets, taking care not to overcook them. Peel them when they are cold and cut them in julienne strips, as for shoe-string potatoes. Cut enough white center stalks of celery, also in julienne strips, to make about half as much celery as potatoes. Whip ¾ cup of heavy cream just long enough to thicken it to the consistency of a thin mayonnaise. Add ¼ cup of sour cream and season well with 2 tablespoons of vinegar, the juice of ½ lemon, or more to taste, and salt and white pepper. Pour this dressing over the salad, mix it in gently so as not to break the potatoes, and turn the salad into a serving dish. Scatter about ½ cup of ham cut in julienne strips over the salad. The incomparable last touch, that is, however, expendable, is 1 or 2 truffles also cut in the same way and added with the ham. Serves four.

211

THE VILLAGE OF ROCHESERVIÈRE *Poitou*

Ground Steak Miremonde

Bifteks Miremonde

(Ground beef, bread crumbs, milk, onion, eggs, cream of wheat, nutmeg, wine)

Mix together ¾ pound of ground beef, 2 tablespoons of minced sautéed onion, ¼ cup of bread crumbs moistened with ¼ cup of milk, 2 beaten eggs, 1 tablespoon of cream of wheat, salt, pepper, and a little grated nutmeg. Let the mixture stand for 1 hour, then form it into cakes 1 inch thick. In a covered skillet sauté them slowly in butter, about 10 minutes on each side. Remove them to a hot platter, and add ¼ cup of white wine and 1 tablespoon of chopped parsley to the pan juices. Simmer the sauce, stirring briskly, for a couple of minutes and pour it over the *bifteks* which should be crisp outside and soft and light inside. Serves four.

ROOFTOPS OF PAU   *Béarn*

Chicken Liver and Mushroom Omelette

Omelette Chasseur

(Eggs, chicken livers, mushrooms, shallot, butter, consommé, white wine)

The correct way to fill this classic French omelette is to slit the top of it within a couple of inches of either end after it is folded and turned out on the platter, and then to spread the filling in the slit and sprinkle it with chopped parsley.

Use two small skillets to make the filling. For a 6-egg omelette sauté in the first skillet 3 thinly sliced mushrooms in 1 teaspoon of butter for 4 or 5 minutes; in the second one sauté ½ a small shallot, very finely minced, and 2 chicken livers, each cut into about 6 little pieces, in 1 tablespoon of butter for less than a minute. Do not let the livers get hard or the shallot scorched. Season the livers with salt and pepper, sprinkle them with ¼ teaspoon of flour, and add 1 tablespoon each of chicken consommé and dry white wine (or 2 tablespoons of either one). Blend the mixture quickly, add the mushrooms, and keep the filling warm until the omelette is ready. Serves four.

213

AFTERNOON LIGHT—LA BÉNISSONS DIEU   *Lyonnais*

Rolled Shoulder of Lamb Boulangère

Epaule de Mouton à la Boulangère

(Boned shoulder of lamb, butter, onions, potatoes, meat glaze, parsley)

Sprinkle the inside of a boned shoulder of lamb lightly with salt and pepper, roll it tightly and tie it. Melt 4 tablespoons of butter in a small roasting pan, put in the rolled lamb and roast it, uncovered, in a 300° oven, allowing 20 minutes per pound. Baste it with the pan juices and turn it often to brown it evenly. Meanwhile, in a skillet, sauté 20 tiny whole onions, or 5 medium ones, sliced or quartered, in 3 tablespoons of butter until they are golden. Add 5 medium potatoes, cut in pieces, and cook the vegetables together, stirring often, for another 5 minutes. Thirty minutes before the lamb is done, arrange them in the pan around the meat, and roast all together, still basting often. Remove the lamb and vegetables to a hot serving platter. Dissolve 1 teaspoon of meat glaze in ¾ cup of boiling water, stir this into the pan juices, and strain the sauce into a sauce boat. Sprinkle the potatoes and onions with chopped parsley. Serves six.

214

WEST PORTAL, ÉGLISE STE.-FOY—CONQUES *Gascony*

Christmas Eve Smothered Beef

Estouffat de Noël à la Gasconne

(Round of beef, ham rind, spices, herbs, bacon, vegetables, brandy, red wine)

The tradition in Gascony is to cook this savory dish on Christmas Eve and serve it after midnight Mass.

Make 6 small incisions in a 3-pound piece of round of beef and insert half a clove of garlic in each one. In an ovenproof casserole place a piece of ham rind about 4 inches square, add the piece of beef and sprinkle it lightly with salt and pepper and a pinch each of nutmeg and cinnamon. Add a *bouquet garni*, 3 whole cloves, 1 slice of bacon, diced, 4 shallots, cut in halves, 2 medium onions, quartered, and 2 carrots, cut in long strips. Then add ¼ cup of brandy, 2 cups of red wine, ½ cup of beef stock, and enough water almost to cover the meat with liquid. Put a piece of heavy parchment paper over the casserole and tie it tightly around the rim. Put the lid on the casserole and cook the *estouffat* in a 250° oven for about 6 hours. To serve, remove the beef to a deep platter, surround it with the vegetables, and pour the juices over it, first skimming from them as much fat as possible. Serves six.

215

THE CHÂTEAU OF ST. GERMAIN-EN-LIVET *Normandy*

French Crêpes with Applesauce and Rum

Crêpes Grandgousier

(French crêpes, applesauce, lemon rind, nutmeg, butter, sugar, rum)

This is a delightful variation on the well-known theme of *crêpes Suzette,* and not quite so much trouble:

Make 24 paper-thin French pancakes according to a standard recipe, but flavor them with rum instead of the usual cognac. Season 2½ cups of homemade applesauce with a little grated lemon rind and nutmeg and 2 teaspoons of butter. Simmer it down to thicken into a sort of apple jam. Spread a heaping teaspoon of applesauce in the center of each *crêpe,* roll them all up, arrange them on a buttered heatproof platter and dust them with extra-fine granulated sugar. Put them in a hot oven to glaze for a few minutes. Warm ¼ cup of rum and take it to the table with the platter of *crêpes.* Set a match to the rum, pour it quickly all over the *crêpes,* and serve them on hot plates as soon as the flame dies. Serves six.

216

PLACE DE LA CONCORDE   *Paris*

Baked Halibut Parisienne

Flétan à la Parisienne

(Halibut, butter, mushrooms, onion, shallot, bay leaf, white wine, cream)

Dry a 2-pound piece of halibut with a cloth, rub it lightly with flour, and season it with salt and pepper. Place it in a buttered baking dish, dot it with 2 tablespoons of butter, and bake it for 10 minutes in a 350° oven. Then surround the fish with ½ pound of mushrooms (slice the caps, peel and slice the stems), 1 sliced onion, and 1 minced shallot. Add a bay leaf and ½ cup of dry white wine. Cover the dish with aluminum foil, return it to the oven, and cook it for 30 more minutes, basting occasionally. Remove the halibut to a hot platter and spread the mushrooms and onions over it. Discard the bay leaf, reduce the pan juices quickly over a hot fire if necessary, and add to them ¼ cup of heavy cream. Taste this sauce for seasoning, reheat it, and pour it over the fish. Serves six.

THE VILLAGE OF AIRVAULT

Poitou

Glazed Carrots and Onions

Carottes aux Oignons Campagnarde

(Carrots, onions, bacon, butter, sugar, parsley)

In a heavy saucepan brown 2 strips of lean bacon, diced, in 1 tablespoon of butter. Remove the bacon scraps, and in the fat remaining in the pan brown 12 tiny whole onions lightly on all sides. Then add 6 young carrots cut in small pieces. Season the vegetables with a little salt, pepper, and ½ teaspoon of sugar, and when the carrots are lightly browned add ½ cup of water. Simmer the vegetables, covered, over a very low flame for about 30 minutes, or until they are tender and the liquid is reduced to a glaze. Sprinkle with parsley before serving. Serves four to six.

PROVINCIAL STREET — SAULIEU *Burgundy*

Mustard Sauce for Roast Pork

Rôti de Porc, Sauce Robert

(Roast of pork, onion, butter, white wine, flour, stock, French mustard)

Season the desired cut of pork and roast it for 35 to 40 minutes per pound in a 350° oven. Meanwhile, simmer 2 chopped onions in 4 tablespoons of butter for about 20 minutes, or until they are completely soft and golden but not browned. In a small saucepan simmer 1 cup of white wine until it is reduced by half. Add 1½ tablespoons of flour to the cooked onions and stir over low heat until the flour is golden. Add 1½ cups of beef stock and the reduced white wine, simmer the sauce for 20 minutes, and season it to taste with salt and pepper.

When the roast is done, transfer it to a hot platter. Skim all the fat from the pan juices and deglaze the pan with a little of the sauce. Blend 1 tablespoon of prepared French mustard with a spoonful of sauce. Then combine the remaining sauce, the pan juices, and the mustard mixture. Add a pinch of sugar, strain the sauce through a fine sieve, and serve it in a sauceboat. Never allow the sauce to boil after the mustard has been added. Serves six.

COUNTRY FARMYARD

Dordogne

Pork Sausage Hunter Style

Saucisses Chasseur

(Sausages, shallots, flour, bouillon, tomato paste, garlic, bay leaf, mushrooms)

For four persons allow 8 large fresh sausages, or more if you must use small ones. Prick the skins here and there and brown the sausages lightly and slowly on all sides, taking care not to overcook them. Remove the sausages to a dish and discard all but 2 tablespoons of the fat they have rendered. Add 2 chopped shallots to the pan and cook them briefly without browning them. Stir in 1 tablespoon of flour and add gradually 1 cup of bouillon into which 1 tablespoon of tomato paste has been blended. Stir well, add 1 small clove of garlic, chopped and mashed, and half a bay leaf, crumbled, and simmer the sauce for 5 minutes. Meanwhile, sauté 6 or 8 sliced mushrooms in 1 tablespoon of hot butter for 5 minutes. Add the mushroom and sausages to the sauce and simmer all together for 10 minutes. Remove sausages and sauce to a hot serving dish, sprinkle with minced parsley, and serve. Serves four.

MOUNTAIN STREAM

Pyrenees

Trout with Almonds

Truites aux Amandes

(Trout, butter, almonds)

Wipe dry 4 cleaned medium-size brook trout, season them with salt and pepper, and coat them lightly with flour. Heat 4 or 5 tablespoons of butter in a large frying pan and, when it has stopped foaming but before it browns, put in the trout and cook them rather slowly, turning them to brown on both sides; be careful not to burn the butter. Remove the fish to a hot platter. Add enough butter to what remains in the pan to make 4 tablespoons in all, and add ¼ cup of slivered almonds. Sauté the almonds slowly in the butter until they are golden. Spoon butter and almonds over the trout, surround with wedges of lemon, and serve at once. Serves four.

221

THE HARBOR AT CASSIS   *Riviera*

Marseilles Fish Soup

Soupe de Poissons Marseillaise

(Fish, olive oil, onion, leek, tomatoes, garlic, herbs, saffron, spaghetti, cheese)

In a soup kettle sauté 1 onion and the white part of 1 leek, both finely chopped, in 3 tablespoons of olive oil until they are transparent. Add 2 ripe tomatoes, chopped, and simmer the vegetables together for 3 or 4 minutes, stirring often. Then add 2 pounds of miscellaneous salt-water fish, including if possible 2 or 3 small crabs. (Do *not* use oily fish such as mackerel or salmon.) Cook all together for 5 minutes, then add crushed garlic (1 or 2 cloves, to taste), a *bouquet garni* (composed of a pinch of thyme, 1 bay leaf, 1 small stalk each of celery and fennel, and several sprigs of parsley), 2 quarts of water, salt, pepper, and ½ thimbleful of saffron. Bring the liquid to a boil, skim the surface, and cook the soup over a moderate flame for 20 minutes. Then strain it and reserve the fish for another dish, such as a mousse (see *Index*). Taste the soup for seasoning, bring it back to the boiling point, and add 4 ounces of very fine spaghetti or vermicelli. Serve as soon as the spaghetti is cooked, with a bowl of grated Parmesan or Romano to sprinkle on top. Serves six.

222

MEDIEVAL FORTRESS — SALSES *Pyrenees*

Tomato Soup with Tapioca
Potage Purée de Tomates

(Tomatoes, onions, butter, herbs, chicken consommé, minute tapioca)

In a large saucepan sauté 2 medium onions, finely chopped, in 2 tablespoons of melted butter until they are soft and golden. Add 3 large ripe tomatoes, chopped, a sprig of parsley, a pinch of thyme, 1 bay leaf, and salt and pepper. Cover and cook the vegetables until most of the juice has evaporated, then force them through a sieve. Return the purée to the saucepan, add 4 cups of chicken consommé and bring the soup to a boil. Add 3 teaspoons of minute tapioca and simmer the soup for 15 minutes. Add a lump of butter just before serving. Serves four to six.

THE PORT — BARFLEUR *Normandy*

Sole (or Flounder) with Normandy Sauce

Filets de Soles, Sauce Normande

(Sole or flounder, hard cider or white wine, herbs, butter, egg yolks, lemon juice)

To serve four, buy enough sole or flounder to make 2 pounds of fillets, and save the heads and back bones. In a covered saucepan simmer the heads and bones for 20 minutes in 2 cups of water and 1 cup of hard cider or dry white wine, with several slices of onion, 1 bay leaf, a sprig of parsley, a pinch of thyme, 4 or 5 pepper corns, and a little salt. Strain the *court-bouillon* and poach the fillets in it for 20 minutes or until they are firm, keeping the liquid just below the boiling point. Transfer the fillets to a heated dish and keep them warm.

Blend 1½ teaspoons of flour into 1 tablespoon of melted sweet butter, and add gradually ½ cup of the fish stock. Season the sauce with salt and pepper, heat it, stirring, until it is slightly thickened, then add 2 egg yolks first beaten with the juice of ½ lemon and 2 tablespoons of the stock. Add 1 tablespoon of butter and stir this *sauce normande* with a whisk until it is hot and thick; do not let it boil. Spoon the sauce over the fish and serve at once.

224

PONT ALEXANDRE III   *Paris*

Broiled Lobsters Chatard

Homards Grillés Chatard

(Live lobsters, court-bouillon, paprika, butter, sour cream, fresh herbs)

For two 1¼- to 1½-pound lobsters, boil together for 15 minutes 1 quart of water and 1 cup of dry white wine, with 1 sliced onion, a *bouquet garni,* 6 crushed peppercorns, and 1 tablespoon of salt. Put in the lobsters, very much alive, bring the *court-bouillon* back to a boil, and cook them for 7 minutes. Remove the lobsters, split them in half lengthwise, and remove the large claws. Crack the claws, take out the meat, and put it in the shells with the tail meat.

Mix together ½ cup of sour cream, 2 teaspoons each of chopped fresh parsley and chervil, 1 teaspoon of chopped fresh tarragon, and a little salt and freshly ground white pepper. Sprinkle the lobster meat with Hungarian paprika and dot it generously with butter. Put the lobsters in a very hot oven for 5 minutes. Then take them out, spread the meat with the sour-cream mixture, and return them to the oven just long enough to glaze the cream. Serves four as a first course, or two as a main dish.

STREET SCENE — RIQUEWIHR *Alsace*

Baked Calf's Liver

Foie de Veau au Four

(Whole calf's liver, salt pork, cloves, butter, red wine, vinegar)

Choose a small whole calf's liver, weighing 3 pounds or less, that is light in color. Roll several strips of salt pork in freshly ground black pepper and run them into the liver with a larding needle. Place the liver in an earthen casserole just large enough to hold it. With a sharp pointed knife cut a slash about ½ inch deep across the top of the liver, sprinkle the cut with salt and pepper, and put in several cloves and a good lump of butter. Add ½ cup of water, cover the casserole, and bake the liver in a 300° oven for 1 hour, more or less, depending on the size of the liver. Fifteen minutes before it is done, add ½ cup of dry red wine and 2 teaspoons of wine vinegar. Serve the liver sliced, with mashed potatoes, and with the juices in the casserole as sauce. Baked liver is also excellent served cold. Serves eight.

CHÂTEAU DE FONTAINEBLEAU *Ile-de-France*

Baked Chicken Montsouris

Poulet Flambé Montsouris

(Chicken, butter, shallots, brandy, tarragon, cream)

Split a 3- to 4-pound chicken as for broiling and brown the halves in a small roasting pan, on top of the stove, in 3 tablespoons of hot butter. When both sides are well browned, put the pan in a 300° oven and roast the chicken for 30 minutes or a little longer, depending on the size of the chicken, basting occasionally with the pan juices. Then transfer it to a hot platter and keep it warm.

In the roasting pan, again on top of the stove, simmer 2 minced shallots briefly in the pan juices. Add 2 tablespoons of warmed brandy, set it aflame, and shake the pan until the flame dies. Dissolve 1 chicken bouillon cube in ¼ cup of hot water, stir this into the pan juices, and pour all this sauce through a strainer into a small saucepan. Add 1 tablespoon of chopped fresh tarragon (or ½ tablespoon of dried tarragon), simmer the sauce for a few seconds, and stir in ¾ cup of cream. Taste for seasoning, reheat the sauce, simmer it briefly and serve it in a sauce boat. Serves four.

MARKET DAY — ST. CÉRÉ

Guyenne

Eggplant Bordelaise

Aubergine Bordelaise

(Eggplant, oil, shallots, garlic, parsley, bread crumbs)

Cut a small eggplant in slices ¼ inch thick; do not peel it. In a skillet brown the slices quickly, a few at a time, in hot oil. Turn them to brown on both sides and transfer them to a hot platter as they are done. Season with salt and pepper. Add oil to the skillet sparingly as needed, and heat it before adding fresh slices. When they are all done, add to the oil left in the skillet a mixture of 4 shallots and 2 cloves of garlic, all very finely minced, 1 tablespoon of chopped parsley, and ½ cup of dry bread crumbs. Stir briskly and sprinkle over the eggplant almost immediately; the mixture will scorch if it is in the pan more than a few seconds. Serve at once. Serves four.

CHURCH YARD

Brittany

Marinated Mackerel for Hors-d'Oeuvre

Maquereaux Marinés

(Baby mackerel, onion, olive oil, white wine, lemon juice, herbs, spices)

Sauté 3 small thinly sliced onions very lightly in 2 tablespoons of olive oil. Add 1½ cups of dry white wine, the strained juice of 1 lemon, salt and pepper, 10 grains of coriander, and a *bouquet garni* composed of parsley, thyme, 1 bay leaf, 1 clove of garlic, and a stalk of fennel, if available. Boil this *court-bouillon* over a good flame for 10 minutes.

Coat the surface of a shallow, flameproof baking dish with olive oil, and in it arrange side by side a dozen whole baby mackerel or other small fish such as herring, fresh sardines or smelts. Sprinkle the fish with salt and pepper, cover them with the hot *court-bouillon*, and poach them gently for 10 minutes. Remove the *bouquet garni* and cool the fish in the *court-bouillon*. Serve chilled, as a luncheon hors-d'oeuvre, with quarters of lemon and French bread and butter.

QUIET PAVILION AT VERSAILLES   *Ile-de-France*

Asparagus and Shrimp Salad

Salade de Pointes d'Asperges

(Asparagus, shrimp, mayonnaise, lemon juice, egg, artichoke bottoms, parsley)

Cook 1 pound of asparagus, reserve 6 of the best stalks, and cut the rest into 1-inch pieces. Cook and shell ¾ pound of fresh shrimp, reserve 6 of them, and dice the rest. (Or cook only 6 large shrimp, and substitute for the diced shrimp 8 ounces of canned miniature shrimp, well drained.) Toss the cut-up asparagus and the diced shrimp together gently with some rather thin mayonnaise, well seasoned with lemon juice, and chill the salad in the refrigerator. Marinate 6 cooked artichoke bottoms (canned ones will do very well) in French dressing.

Just before serving, put the salad in a bowl, sprinkle it with 1 sieved hard-boiled egg, and arrange the reserved asparagus like the spokes of a wheel on top. Drain the artichoke bottoms and garnish each one with a spoonful of mayonnaise, 1 whole shrimp, and a tiny sprig of parsley. Arrange them around the edge of the salad and serve immediately. Serves six.

230

XIITH-CENTURY CHURCH — STE. MAURE   *Touraine*

Stuffed Onions

Oignons Farcis

(Onions, butter, bread crumbs, sausage meat, parsley, nutmeg, chicken stock)

Peel 6 large sweet onions, cut a ½-inch slice from the top of each one, and parboil the onions for 10 minutes. Hollow out the centers, leaving shells ½ inch thick. Chop the centers and sauté them gently in 2 tablespoons of butter until they are soft. Soak ¾ cup of soft bread crumbs in a little cream and press out the excess moisture. Mix together the sautéed onion, ¾ cup of sausage meat, the prepared bread crumbs, and 1 tablespoon of minced parsley, and add pepper, nutmeg, and a little salt to taste. Fill the onions with this stuffing, put them in a baking dish, and pour in enough chicken stock to come half way up the onions. Bake them in a 350° oven for about 1 hour, or until they are almost done, then sprinkle the tops with dry bread crumbs and a pinch of sugar, and dot them with butter. Continue cooking the onions until they are very tender, the pan juices are well reduced, and the tops are golden brown. Serves six.

231

CHURCHES OF SENLIS *Ile-de-France*

Chicken Liver Pâté

Pâté de Foies de Volailles

(Chicken livers, shallots, sweet butter, eggs, brandy, Madeira, herbs, spices)

Cut 1 pound of chicken livers into coarse pieces and cook them slowly in ¼ pound of sweet butter with 4 finely minced shallots. Be careful not to brown the livers and remove them from the heat when they are firm but still very tender. In a bowl cream another ¼ pound of sweet butter and add the cooked livers with all their pan juices, 3 large hard-boiled eggs, finely chopped or forced through a sieve, 1½ tablespoons each of good brandy and Madeira, 2 teaspoons of salt, ⅛ teaspoon of powdered clove, and a scant ¼ teaspoon each of pepper, thyme, marjoram, ginger and cinnamon. Mix all the ingredients together well, then purée the mixture, one third at a time, in an electric blender. Fill four half-pint jars with the pâté, cover the jars, and chill thoroughly before serving.

WHEAT FIELDS

Champagne

Chicken Fricassee Old Style

Fricassée de Poulet à l'Ancienne

(Fowl, veal knuckle, vegetables, herbs, onion, mushrooms, egg yolks, cream)

Have a 5- to 6-pound fowl cut into serving pieces. In a large saucepan place a cracked veal knuckle and the back, wing tips, giblets and neck of the chicken. Add 1 onion, 1 small carrot, 1 small white turnip, all cut in pieces, and 1 bay leaf, a pinch of thyme, a sprig of parsley, and salt and pepper. Add water to cover well and simmer the stock very slowly for 3 hours, skimming occasionally. Then simmer the pieces of chicken for 1½ hours or until they are tender, in enough of the stock, strained, to cover. In two separate saucepans, cook in the remaining stock 12 tiny onions and the caps of ½ pound of mushrooms. Drain the chicken when it is done, put it in a deep serving dish, and keep it warm.

Blend 2½ tablespoons of flour into 3 tablespoons of melted butter and add gradually 2½ cups of the hot chicken stock. Add the cooked onions and mushrooms, and stir in 3 egg yolks mixed with ½ cup of cream. Reheat the sauce, stirring constantly, until it thickens. Pour the sauce over the chicken and serve with boiled rice. Serves six.

THE ESSENCE OF NORMANDY — NEAR LIVAROT   *Normandy*

Carrot Soup

Potage Purée de Crécy

(Carrots, onions, butter, chicken stock, rice, croutons)

Slice 4 or 5 medium carrots very thin and chop 1 medium onion. Sauté the vegetables in a large covered saucepan for 15 minutes, over low heat, in 2 tablespoons of melted butter. Season them with a little salt, pepper, and a pinch of sugar. Then add 1 quart of hot chicken stock or consommé and ¼ cup of rice, and simmer the soup for 35 minutes. Strain it through a sieve and force the vegetables through with the liquid. Add 2 more cups of stock, reheat the soup, add a lump of butter, and garnish it with small croutons fried in butter. Serves six.

CHÂTEAU DE MAINTENON   *Orléanais*

Chocolate Cream

Crème au Chocolat

(Unsweetened chocolate, milk, sugar, unsalted butter, egg yolks)

Warm ¾ cup of milk with 6 tablespoons of sugar and a small pinch of salt, and stir until the sugar is dissolved. In the top of a double boiler, over hot but not simmering water, melt 4 ounces of unsweetened chocolate, coarsely grated, with ¼ pound of unsalted butter, stirring constantly. When the mixture is perfectly smooth, add the sweetened milk and blend well. Then, with a wire whisk, beat in 8 egg yolks, one at a time. Pour the chocolate cream into 6 individual ramekins and chill well before serving. This cream is very rich and the servings should be small. Serves six.

CATHÉDRALE DE SOISSONS   *Champagne*

Cottage-Cheese Fritters

Beignets de Fromage Blanc

(Cottage cheese, egg, salt, flour, frying oil, powdered sugar)

Mash 4 tablespoons of cottage cheese until it is free of all lumps. Stir in 1 lightly beaten egg and a pinch of salt, and add gradually 2 tablespoons of flour. This should be a smooth paste, the consistency of a thick batter. Drop it by small teaspoonfuls into deep hot oil. When the fritters are puffed and golden, remove them to a hot plate and sprinkle them with powdered sugar. Serve at once. Serves two or three.

THE VILLAGE OF OYE   *Burgundy*

Steak Charollaise

Entrecôte Grillée Charollaise

(Steak, butter, onion, flour, red wine, garlic, tomato purée, Madeira)

Broil a good cut of beef steak until rare or medium, and serve it with the following *sauce charollaise:* Sauté 2 tablespoons of finely minced onion slowly in 2 tablespoons of hot butter until it is soft but not brown. Stir in ½ tablespoon of flour, add salt and pepper, and blend in gradually ¾ cup of red wine. Bring this to a boil and add 1 small chopped and mashed clove of garlic and 2 tablespoons of tomato purée. Cover the pan and let the sauce simmer very slowly for 20 minutes. Shortly before removing from the fire, add 1 tablespoon of Madeira. Serves six.

BASQUE FAÇADES — USTARITZ   *Pyrenees*

Basque Stuffed Steak

Entrecôte comme à Ascain

(Steak, shallots, garlic, bacon, ham, mushrooms, parsley, tarragon, egg yolk)

Have the butcher cut for you two ½-inch-thick steaks of identical size and shape. In 2 teaspoons of salad oil sauté briefly 2 shallots and 1 small clove of garlic, all minced, and 1 tablespoon each of finely chopped bacon and ham. Be sure not to let the garlic burn and as soon as the vegetables are soft add 3 tablespoons of minced fresh mushrooms, 1 teaspoon each of minced parsley and tarragon, and salt and pepper to taste. When the water from the mushrooms has evaporated, pour off any excess fat there may be in the pan and put the mixture aside to cool. Then add 1 egg yolk, mix well, spread the stuffing on one of the steaks, and cover with the second steak. In a heavy skillet brown this "sandwich" in a little hot butter over a brisk flame for 4 to 5 minutes on each side.

THE BRIDGE AT AVIGNON *Provence*

Scrambled Eggs with Saffron

Oeufs Brouillés au Safran

(Eggs, cream, butter, meat glaze, saffron)

Beat together with a fork 8 eggs, ¼ cup of cream, and a little salt and pepper. In a skillet melt a generous lump of butter and add ¼ teaspoon of meat glaze and a good pinch of saffron. Blend well and then add the eggs. Cook them slowly, stirring constantly with a wire whisk, until they achieve a rich and creamy consistency. Serves four.

LAC DU BOURGET   *Savoy*

Leeks Savoy

Poireaux à la Savoyarde

(Leeks, bread crumbs, butter, garlic, nutmeg, Swiss cheese)

Cut most of the green tops from 8 medium-large leeks, wash the leeks, and cut them into ½ inch pieces. Drop these into boiling salted water, boil them until they are just tender, drain them well, and pat them dry on a clean towel. Brown 1 cup of coarse bread crumbs in 3 tablespoons of butter. Rub a shallow baking dish with garlic, butter it well, and spread a layer of leeks in it. Sprinkle this with bread crumbs, salt and pepper, a dash of nutmeg, and a little grated Swiss cheese. Repeat the layers, ending with bread crumbs on top. Pour a little browned butter over all, and brown the dish lightly in a hot oven or under the broiler. Serves four.

240

HÔTEL NEGRESCO—NICE   *Riviera*

Zucchini Niçoise

Courgettes à la Mode de Nice

(Zucchini, onion, butter, bread crumbs, garlic, parsley, egg yolks, frying oil)

Scrub 4 young zucchini (Italian squash), cut them in half lengthwise, and make an incision around the inside near the skin. Drop them into boiling salted water, parboil them for 4 or 5 minutes, and drain them. Remove the centers which will have been loosened by the circular cut. Chop this pulp and mix it with 1 medium onion first chopped and sautéed in 1 tablespoon of butter until soft and golden. Add 4 tablespoons of fine bread crumbs, 2 minced cloves of garlic, 2 tablespoons or more of minced parsley, and salt and pepper. Then mix in the yolks of 2 small eggs, or enough to bind the mixture lightly. Fill the zucchini shells with this stuffing, dip in egg yolk beaten with a few drops of water, then roll them in fine bread crumbs. Fry them in deep hot oil until golden brown. Serves four.

241

HÔTEL DE VILLE — COMPIÈGNE   *Ile-de-France*

Apricot Cream

Crème aux Abricots

(Apricots, sugar, almond extract, gelatine, whipped cream)

Purée 1 pound of pitted, very ripe fresh apricots in an electric blender. Rub the purée through a sieve, and add 1 cup of fine granulated sugar and a few drops of almond extract. Soak 1 tablespoon of gelatine in 3 tablespoons of water, add 3 tablespoons of boiling milk, stir until the gelatine is dissolved, and add this to the purée. Whip 1 pint of heavy cream, mix it with the fruit, and pour the mixture into a wet mold. Chill, and unmold just before serving. Serves eight.

HOUSES BY THE CHURCH STEPS — ESTAING   *Guyenne*

Creamed Eggs with Onions

Oeufs Durs à la Tripe

(Hard-boiled eggs, onions, butter, flour, milk, cream, nutmeg, parsley)

In a heavy saucepan simmer 3 medium onions, thinly sliced, in 4 tablespoons of butter for 5 minutes, stirring often. Then cover the saucepan and continue cooking the onions over very low heat for 15 minutes, or until they are soft; stir them occasionally and be sure not to let them brown. Then sprinkle the onions with 3½ tablespoons of flour, blend well, and add gradually 2 cups of hot milk. Season to taste with salt, pepper and nutmeg, and add several sprigs of parsley. Simmer the sauce very slowly for 15 minutes, add ½ cup of cream, and cook another 5 minutes.

Meanwhile cut 9 hard-boiled eggs in half lengthwise, remove the yolks, and cut the whites into julienne strips. When the sauce is ready, remove the parsley, add the halved yolks and the whites, mix together gently, and reheat for 2 or 3 minutes. Transfer the *oeufs à la tripe* to a hot serving dish or individual ramekins, dot with a few tiny pieces of butter, and serve immediately. Serves six.

243

CARCASSONNE   *Languedoc*

Eggs Romaine

Oeufs à la Romaine

(Spinach, eggs, Parmesan, butter)

Spread 4 buttered shirred-egg dishes with about ¼ cup each of hot, seasoned and buttered spinach. Make a hollow with the back of a large spoon in each bed of spinach, and break an egg into each one. Sprinkle the eggs with salt, grated Parmesan, and melter butter. Put them under the broiler, not too near the flame. After 5 minutes, watch them carefully; when the eggs are just set and lightly browned, serve immediately. Serves four.

THE SQUARE AT NOYERS

Burgundy

Carrots Flemish Style

Carottes à la Flamande

(Carrots, butter, sugar, egg yolks, cream, parsley)

Wash and scrape a bunch of young carrots; allow about 2 long carrots per person, or 4 to 6 per person if you can get short baby carrots. Cut them into ¾-inch lengths. To serve six, melt 4 generous tablespoons of butter in a heavy saucepan, put in the carrots, and add ¼ cup of hot water, salt and pepper, and 1 teaspoon of sugar. Cover the saucepan closely and simmer the carrots slowly for 20 to 25 minutes, stirring them often and adding a few drops of hot water occasionally if needed to keep them from sticking. When they are tender there should be no water left, only a buttery but not brown sauce. Beat together 2 egg yolks, ¼ cup of heavy cream, and 1 tablespoon of minced parsley. Stir this into the carrots and reheat until the sauce is just hot; do not let it boil. Serve at once.

CHURCH TOWER — LUCY

Burgundy

Burgundian Cheese Pastry

La Gougère

(Milk, butter, flour, eggs, Swiss cheese, cream)

In a saucepan combine 1 cup of milk, 4 tablespoons of butter, ½ teaspoon of salt, and a little freshly ground pepper. Bring the mixture to a boil, remove the pan from the fire, add ⅞ cup of flour, all at once, and stir well. Return the pan to the fire for one or two minutes, stirring constantly, until the mixture comes away from the sides of the pan. Remove the pan from the fire again and stir in 4 eggs, one at a time and blending well each time. Stir in 2 ounces of finely diced Swiss cheese and 1 tablespoon of heavy cream, and transfer the batter to a buttered tart ring or pie plate. Brush the top with beaten egg, sprinkle it with a little diced cheese, and bake *la gougère* in a 325° oven for 40 to 50 minutes, or until it is puffed and browned. Do not open the oven door for the first 35 minutes of baking. Serve hot as an hors-d'oeuvre, with a bottle of red wine; or cold, with a green salad.

ART GALLERY — MONTMARTRE

Liver and Bacon en Brochette

Brochettes de Foie de Veau

(Calf's liver, bacon, water cress, wine vinegar)

Cut calf's liver into ¾-inch cubes and thread the pieces on skewers alternately with squares of sliced bacon. Cook the *brochettes* under the broiler or in the oven for 10 minutes, or until the liver is firm but still a little pink in the center. Turn the skewers several times to cook the meat evenly. Arrange the *brochettes* on a bed of lightly salted water cress, sprinkle with a little wine vinegar, and serve immediately.

CHÂTEAU DE CHENONCEAUX   *Touraine*

Grilled Devilled Chicken
Poulet Grillé à la Diable

(Chicken, oil, cayenne pepper, mustard, bread crumbs, butter)

Split a large broiler in half and brush the pieces on both sides with oil. Season the chicken with salt and a little cayenne pepper and cook it for 25 minutes in a 350° oven, turning it once. Then spread the under sides of the two pieces quite generously with a good, strong mixed mustard, coat them with fine bread crumbs and baste them with the pan juices and melted butter. Put the chicken in the broiler under a moderate flame for 5 minutes. Then turn it, coat the skin sides with mustard, bread crumbs and butter as before, and broil it for another 5 minutes. Serve with shoe-string potatoes and garnished with water cress. Serves four.

NOTRE-DAME FROM THE ILE ST. LOUIS *Paris*

Bananas in Cream

Bananes Baronnet

(Bananas, sugar, cream, sour cream, kirsch)

Slice thinly 3 ripe bananas and sprinkle them with sugar. With a wire whisk beat ½ cup of heavy cream until it thickens a little, but do not whip it. Stir in 4 tablespoons of thick sour cream and 1 tablespoon of kirsch. Combine the cream and the bananas and serve very cold. Serves four.

VINEYARDS IN THE MACONNAIS *Burgundy*

Shrimps in White Wine and Cream

Crevettes à la Cluny

(Shrimp, shallot, herbs, brandy, white wine, cream, egg yolks)

In a heavy saucepan sauté 1 minced shallot in 3 tablespoons of butter until it is golden. Add 1½ pounds of raw shrimp, shelled and deveined, a pinch of thyme, 1 bay leaf, and a little salt and pepper, and simmer the shrimp for 7 or 8 minutes, turning them occasionally. Then warm 2 tablespoons of brandy, light it and pour it flaming over the shrimp. Shake the pan back and forth until the flame dies, then add ¾ cup of dry white wine. Simmer the shrimp for 5 minutes, transfer them to a heated serving dish, and keep them warm. Reduce the pan juices to about one third their original quantity. Mix together 1 cup of cream, 2 egg yolks, 1 teaspoon of lemon juice, and 1 teaspoon each of chopped parsley, chervil and tarragon. Add this to the saucepan, stir well, and pour the sauce over the shrimp as soon as it is hot and slightly thickened; do not let it boil. Serves four.

ABBAYE DE MARMOUTIER   *Touraine*

Hot Cheese Hors-d'Oeuvre

Croûtes au Fromage

(French bread, white sauce, cayenne, eggs, cheese)

These *croûtes* can be made tiny for cocktail canapés or larger to serve as a simple first course. To serve as a first course for four, make a thick white sauce with 2 tablespoons of flour blended into 1 tablespoon of butter and ¾ cup of milk added gradually. Season with salt, white pepper, and a pinch of cayenne, and cool the sauce. Stir in 1 egg and ¼ cup of grated cheese, blend well, and chill the mixture in the refrigerator. Cut eight ⅜-inch-thick slices from a loaf of French bread (or cut eight 2-inch circles from slices of plain white bread). Spread the slices with the cheese mixture, dip them on both sides in beaten egg, and fry them, a few at a time, in hot oil about ½ inch deep. Drain them on paper as they are done, and serve them very hot, with a bottle of chilled dry white wine.

GATE TO THE CHÂTEAU — GASTON   *Guyenne*

Roast Leg of Lamb with Green Beans Landaise

Gigot aux Haricots Verts à la Landaise

(Leg of lamb, garlic, beans, onion, tomato paste, cream, herbs, egg yolks, ham)

Roast a young leg of lamb, with a few slivers of garlic inserted near the bone. Transfer it to a hot platter when it is done, and keep it warm. Skim all the fat from the pan juices and reserve it. Deglaze the roasting pan with a little white wine and a few drops of lemon juice, and serve the pan juices very hot in a sauceboat.

Shortly before the roast is done, boil 1 pound of string beans and prepare the following sauce: Sauté 1 minced onion lightly in 1 tablespoon of butter. Add 2 minced and crushed cloves of garlic and 1 bay leaf, stir in 3 tablespoons of tomato paste and 1¼ cups of heavy cream, and add salt, pepper, and 1 teaspoon each of minced fresh parsley, chives and tarragon. Then add 2 egg yolks lightly beaten with 1 tablespoon of vinegar. Heat the sauce, stirring constantly with a whisk, but do not thicken it. At the last minute, briefly sauté the cooked beans, well drained, in a little of the fat from the roasting pan. Add ¾ cup of julienne strips of ham, combine with two thirds of the sauce, and transfer the mixture to a baking dish. Pour the rest of the sauce over the top, and put the dish in a hot oven for 2 or 3 minutes, or just long enough to thicken the sauce and glaze the top. Serves four.

CHAPEL AT MONDERMONT *Champagne*

Stuffed Eggs in Cream

Oeufs Farcis à la Crème

(Eggs, butter, shallots, parsley, cream, sour cream)

Shell 8 hard-boiled eggs and cut them in half lengthwise. Remove the yolks and force them through a sieve. In a skillet sauté 2 minced shallots in 2½ tablespoons of hot butter until they are golden. Take the skillet off the fire, add the sieved yolks and 1 tablespoon of minced parsley, and with a wooden spoon work the mixture to a smooth paste. Fill the egg whites with this stuffing and arrange them, cut side down, in a buttered heat-proof serving dish. Blend ¾ cup of sour cream with ¾ cup of sweet cream, and add a little salt, pepper and cayenne to taste. Heat the cream without letting it boil and pour it over the eggs. Put the dish in a moderate oven for about 5 minutes and serve immediately.

FARMHOUSE — ST. JULIEN   *Burgundy*

Tomato and Pepper Salad

Salade Algérienne

(Tomatoes, sweet peppers, French dressing, onion, shallots, parsley)

Peel sweet red or green peppers by putting them under a hot broiler flame for several minutes and turning them often to blister the skins on all sides; then wrap them in a dish towel, let them cool, and scrape off the skins. Core and seed the peppers and cut them into thin rings. Peel the same number of ripe tomatoes as you have peppers and slice them thinly. Arrange the vegetables in an hors-d'oeuvre dish, and pour over them a French dressing made of 1 part wine vinegar, 3 parts olive oil, and salt, pepper and prepared mustard to taste. Sprinkle them generously with finely chopped onion, shallots and parsley. Serve as one of a group of cold luncheon *hors-d'oeuvre variés*.

VALLEY ROAD NEAR DIE   *Dauphiny*

Tomatoes Stuffed with Mushrooms

Tomates Farcies aux Champignons

(Tomatoes, mushrooms, butter, tomato sauce, egg yolk, bread crumbs)

Slice off the stem ends of 6 large tomatoes, cut out the cores, and remove the seeds. Wash 1 pound of mushrooms and trim the stems. Chop the mushrooms and toss them in a bowl with the juice of ½ lemon. Then sauté them in a skillet with 6 tablespoons of hot butter until all the liquid has evaporated and they are lightly browned. Take the skillet off the fire and add ¾ cup of fresh tomato sauce (see *Index*) or canned Italian *marinara* sauce. Add 1 egg yolk, blend the mixture well, and season to taste with salt and pepper. Stuff the tomatoes and arrange them in a shallow buttered baking dish. Sprinkle the tops with fine bread crumbs, dot them with butter, and bake them in a 300° oven for 35 minutes. Serves six.

CHÂTEAU AT ETOGES   *Champagne*

Duchess Potatoes

Pommes de Terre Duchesse

(Potatoes, egg, egg yolks, butter)

The name of this dish refers to the basic mixture which can be used in several ways. Peel 2 pounds of potatoes, cut them in pieces, and boil them in salted water to cover until they are done but not mushy. Drain them, rub them through a sieve, and dry out the purée by shaking it in a saucepan over a medium flame until all the moisture has evaporated. Beat in 4 tablespoons of butter, then add 3 egg yolks and 1 egg, first lightly beaten together. Season the mixture to taste with salt, pepper and nutmeg, and beat it well until it is smooth and fluffy.

Hot *pommes duchesse* may be dropped from a large kitchen spoon into a buttered baking dish to form individual servings; or, with a pastry bag and large tube, they may be formed into a decorative border for meat or fish dishes. In either case they are lightly brushed with egg and browned in the oven or under a broiler just before serving. For croquettes, spread the *pommes duchesse* on a buttered baking sheet, brush them lightly with butter, and chill them in the refrigerator. Cut the chilled potatoes into small oblongs and sauté them in butter until golden brown on all sides. Or shape them into larger croquettes, dip these in beaten egg and fine bread crumbs, and fry them in hot deep fat. Serves six.

LAC D'ANNECY   *Savoy*

Salmon Trout in Red Wine

L'Omble Chevalier au Chambertin

(Salmon trout, shallots, onion, garlic, herbs, red wine, mustard, cream)

The *omble chevalier* is a succulent fish to be found only in the deep lakes of the Savoie. Our salmon trout will take its place gracefully.

Sauté briefly 3 shallots, ½ onion, and 1 clove of garlic, all finely minced, in 3 tablespoons of melted butter. Spread the vegetables in a shallow baking dish and on them place a fine whole salmon trout weighing 1½ to 2 pounds. Add 2 teaspoons of minced parsley, 1 bay leaf, a pinch of thyme, salt and pepper, and 1 to 1½ cups of good red Burgundy, or enough almost to cover the fish. Cook the fish in a preheated 350° oven for 20 to 30 minutes, then drain off all the juice and keep the fish warm. Blend 1½ teaspoons of potato starch with 1 tablespoon of prepared French mustard and ¼ cup of heavy cream. Add gradually 1 cup of the red-wine juice, and stir the sauce over gentle heat until it is slightly thickened. Pour it over the trout and sprinkle with minced parsley. Serves two or three.

PONT DE L'ARCHE   *Normandy*

Normandy Vegetable Soup
Soupe Normande

(White turnips, leeks, potatoes, shell beans, stock, milk, butter, cream, herbs)

Sauté slowly in 2 tablespoons of hot butter 2 small white turnips, peeled and cut in small slices, and the white parts of 3 leeks, also sliced. When the vegetables are softened, add 2 medium potatoes, peeled and sliced, ½ cup of fresh shell beans (or partly cooked dried white beans), 1 quart of beef or chicken stock, and 2 cups of milk. Cook the soup at a slow simmer for 1 hour. Taste for seasoning, stir in 2 tablespoons of sweet butter and ¾ cup of thin cream, reheat, and serve sprinkled with minced chervil or parsley. Serves six.

ROOFTOPS OF ST. TROPEZ

Spinach Italian Style

Epinards à l'Italienne

(Spinach, butter, olive oil, onion)

Wash 2 pounds of tender young spinach, remove the stems, break the leaves in 2-inch pieces, and dry them well in a cloth. Melt 3 tablespoons of butter in a large heavy saucepan, and add 3 tablespoons of olive oil and 1 small whole onion. When the oil and butter are hot, put in the spinach, several handfuls at a time, turning and stirring the leaves to coat them, and adding more as they wilt. Simmer the spinach over low heat, uncovered, stirring occasionally, until all the liquid is absorbed. Season to taste with salt and pepper, and remove the onion before serving. Serves four.

MARCHÉ VERT—SELESTAT   *Alsace*

Alsatian Salad

Salade Alsacienne

(Chicken, ham, beet, potatoes, anchovies, French dressing, gherkins, parsley)

Dice or cut into julienne strips the wing and breast meat of half a small cooked chicken, 1 slice of ham, 1 cooked beet, and 3 medium-size cold boiled potatoes. Chop 3 anchovy fillets. Combine all the ingredients except the beet. Make about ⅓ cup of French dressing (1 part wine vinegar, 3 parts olive oil, salt, pepper, and ½ teaspoon of prepared mustard). Marinate the beet in 1 tablespoon of the dressing, and add the rest of the dressing to the mixed ingredients, stirring well; let them stand for an hour or more. Just before serving, combine all the ingredients, add 1 or 2 chopped sour gherkins, stir the salad well, and sprinkle it with finely minced parsley. Serve with other assorted hors-d'oeuvre, or alone as a first course or salad course for four.

CHÂTEAU DE DISSAY   *Poitou*

White Turnip Soup

Potage aux Navets Blancs

(White turnips, onion, butter, bread, egg yolks, cream, parsley)

Peel, slice, and chop coarsely 4 medium-size white turnips and 1 large onion. Melt 3 tablespoons of butter in a large saucepan or casserole, add the vegetables, and sauté them slowly over a low fire for 5 minutes. Add 6 cups of boiling water, salt and pepper, and 3 slices of bread first dried out in a slow oven and crumbled. Simmer the soup for about half an hour, then press it all through a fine sieve. Reheat the soup and add, off the fire, 2 egg yolks beaten well with ½ cup of cream. Stir the soup until it is well blended but do not let it boil. Serve at once with a little finely minced parsley sprinkled on top. Serves six.

CHÂTEAU DE PIERREFONDS   *Ile-de-France*

Braised Rump or Round of Beef

Culotte de Boeuf Braisée

(Rump or round of beef, bacon, carrot, onion, stock, white wine, brandy)

Line the bottom of an ovenproof casserole with several slices of bacon. Add 1 carrot and 1 onion, both sliced, and place a 4-pound piece of round or rump of beef on the vegetables. Season the meat with coarsely ground black pepper and a little salt, and add ½ cup of beef stock or bouillon. Place the casserole, uncovered, in a 450° oven to reduce the liquid and brown the surface of the roast. Then add 1½ cups of dry white wine and ½ cup of brandy, and tie a piece of heavy parchment paper tightly over the top of the casserole. Put the lid on the casserole, lower the oven temperature to 250°, and braise the meat for about 4 hours, adding a little beef stock if the juices become too much reduced. When the meat is done and very tender, remove it to a platter and keep it hot. Skim the excess fat from the juices in the casserole, strain them into a small saucepan, and reduce them over a brisk fire if necessary. There should not be very much sauce and it should be quite thick. Pour it over the roast and serve with buttered noodles. Serves six.

262

THE CATHEDRAL SQUARE — STRASBOURG   *Alsace*

Lemon Soufflés Suzanne

Oeufs Mousseline Suzanne

(Eggs, butter, sugar, lemon, macaroon crumbs)

Tie strips of buttered paper around 12 small ramekins so that each "collar" comes up ½ inch beyond the edge of the ramekin. Separate 4 eggs, and put the yolks in one bowl and the whites in another. To the yolks add 4 tablespoons of butter cut in small pieces, 4 tablespoons of sugar, the juice of 1 lemon, and the grated rind of ½ the lemon. Fit the bowl into the top of a pan of barely simmering water, and cook the mixture, stirring constantly, until it begins to thicken like hollandaise. Then remove it from the heat, and beat it well with a wooden spoon for 2 minutes. Beat the egg whites until they are stiff but not dry, fold them into the egg-yolk mixture, and pour the batter into the ramekins. Put them in a large roasting pan with a lid, and pour enough boiling water into the pan to come half way up the ramekins. On top of the stove, reheat the water until it just reaches the boiling point. Then turn off the heat, put the lid on the pan, and leave the soufflés to set in the steam for 12 minutes. Take them out, remove the paper collars, sprinkle the soufflés with fine macaroon crumbs, and serve immediately.

CATHÉDRALE DE ST. CYR ET STE. JULITTE—NEVERS *Nivernais*

Chicken-Liver Foie Gras

Purée de Foies de Volailles

(Chicken livers, chicken stock, butter, pepper, salt, brandy, Madeira, truffle)

Cut ½ pound of chicken livers in halves, cover them with chicken stock, and bring it to a boil; simmer the livers for about 10 minutes. Drain and chop the livers and force them through a fine sieve; or put them in an electric blender and blend until smooth. Mix the purée with ½ cup of soft butter. Add a little pepper, a pinch of salt if needed (this is not to be a highly seasoned pâté), a few drops of brandy, 1 tablespoon of Madeira, and 1 very finely minced truffle. Blend the mixture very thoroughly with a small wooden spatula, and pack it in an earthen jar or small bowl. If it is to be kept for some time, pour a thin layer of bacon or chicken fat over the surface. Chill well in the refrigerator. Serve with assorted hors-d'oeuvre or as a spread with cocktails.

FARM NEAR COULANGES   *Orléanais*

Cucumber Salad with Cream

Salade de Concombre à la Crème

(Cucumber, herbs, cream)

Peel a cucumber, cut it in half lengthwise, and remove the seeds with a spoon. Slice the two halves very thinly, put the slices in a bowl, sprinkle with salt, and place a weighted saucer on them. Let them stand this way under slight pressure for 2 hours, then drain off the water they have rendered. Season them with a little vinegar, chopped chervil or tarragon, and enough heavy cream or sour cream to coat them well. Serve as one of a group of assorted hors-d'oeuvre.

THE PORT — ST. JEAN-CAP-FERRAT   *Riviera*

Mackerel with Sweet Peppers
Maquereaux à l'Algerienne
(Mackerel, sweet peppers, tomatoes, oil, paprika, bread crumbs, lemon, parsley)

Seed a large sweet red or green pepper and cut it in thin strips. Simmer it in a covered skillet with 2 tablespoons of salad oil and a little salt and pepper until it is soft. In another skillet simmer 3 tomatoes, peeled, seeded and chopped, with salt, paprika and 2 tablespoons of oil until they are partly reduced.

Split 4 small whole mackerel, remove the backbones, and stuff the fish with the simmered pepper. Spread the tomato sauce in a shallow baking dish and arrange the mackerel close together upon it. Sprinkle the fish with fine bread crumbs, pour a few drops of oil over them, and bake them in a 350° oven for about 25 minutes. Serve the mackerel from the baking dish, garnished with slices of peeled lemon and chopped parsley. Serves four.

FAIR GROUNDS — CHARTRES   *Orléanais*

Veal Chops Charmille

Côtes de Veau Charmille

(Veal chops, butter, bread crumbs, onion, Parmesan, parsley, white wine, sour cream)

Brown 4 thick veal chops quickly on both sides in 1 tablespoon of hot butter. Arrange the chops side by side in a shallow buttered baking dish. Combine ½ cup of fine bread crumbs, 1 finely minced onion, ¼ cup of grated Parmesan cheese, and 2 teaspoons of minced parsley. Add salt and pepper and just enough dry white wine to bind the mixture. Spread it on the chops, dot them with butter, and bake them, uncovered, in a 300° oven for 45 minutes, basting occasionally with a few spoonfuls of white wine. When they are almost done, baste them one last time with 2 tablespoons of chicken consommé; when the chops are done, the juices should be reduced to a very small amount. Drop a spoonful of sour cream on each chop and serve as soon as the cream is hot. Serves four.

ENTRANCE TO THE PLACE DES VOSGES   *Paris*

Potatoes Anna

Pommes de Terre Anna

(Potatoes, butter, salt, pepper)

Peel 6 large potatoes and trim the sides slightly so they can be cut into more or less even slices; makes the slices *less* than ⅛ inch thick. Spread a good quantity of soft butter in the bottom of an iron skillet. Place a layer of potatoes, overlapping in even rows, over the butter, covering the bottom of the skillet completely. Season with salt and pepper and coat with more butter. Continue making layers in this manner to a depth of about 2 inches. Cover the skillet closely and cook the potatoes in a 325° oven for about 1 hour. To serve, place a serving dish upside down over the potatoes and, holding it firmly, turn the whole thing over so that the bottom crust of potatoes comes out on top. Serves six.

CHÂTEAU DE BLOIS *Orléanais*

Fruit Compote

Compote de Fruits

(Pears, apples, grapes, vanilla sugar, cloves, lemon)

In a saucepan combine 2½ cups of water, 1 cup of vanilla-flavored sugar, and 3 cloves. Quarter, core, and peel 4 red apples and add the peels of two of the apples to the syrup. Sprinkle a little lemon juice on the apples for flavor and to keep them from darkening. Simmer the sugar syrup for about 8 minutes. Meanwhile, quarter, core, and peel 2 large or 3 medium pears. Poach the pears in the syrup at a very low simmer until they are just tender. This takes about 3 minutes for ripe juicy pears, longer for firm green ones; they must not be too ripe or the pieces will break. With a slotted spoon remove the pears carefully to a bowl. Put the apples in the syrup and simmer them slowly for 4 minutes, more or less, depending on the type of apple. Lift them out when they are tender and add them to the bowl. Then simmer 20 large black grapes in the syrup for 8 minutes and add them to the other fruit. Strain the syrup over them and chill before serving. Serves six. In season, black bing cherries, small prune plums, and apricots may be used in this compote.

ALSATIAN SILHOUETTE — ST. HIPPOLYTE *Alsace*

Kidney-bean Purée Ali-Bab

Purée Ali-Bab

(Kidney beans, red wine, herbs, bacon, butter)

Wash 1 pound of dried kidney beans and soak them overnight in water to cover well. Bring them slowly to a boil in the same water and simmer them for 1½ to 2 hours, or until they are tender. Add salt shortly before they are done. Drain the beans, reserving the cooking water, and force them through a sieve.

Meanwhile, simmer 1½ cups of dry red wine with a few slices of carrot and onion, 1 bay leaf, a sprig of parsley, a pinch of thyme, and salt and pepper, until the wine is reduced by half; strain it and discard the vegetables. In a skillet brown 3 slices of bacon until they are crisp. Drain on absorbent paper and pour off all but 1 tablespoon of the fat in the skillet. Blend 2 teaspoons of flour into the remaining fat and gradually add the red wine. Simmer this sauce, stirring often, until it thickens, then stir it into the puréed beans. Add a good lump of butter and salt and pepper, and add a little of the cooking water, if necessary, to give the purée a good consistency. Serve the purée with the bacon crumbled over it. This is a good accompaniment for grilled meats, particularly game.

270

BRETON COTTAGES — ROCHEPORT-EN-TERRE *Brittany*

Flambéed Pears

Poires Flambées

(Pears, applesauce, butter, sugar, vanilla bean, apricot jam, rum)

Simmer 2 cups of homemade applesauce with 1 teaspoon of butter until it is rich and thick. Peel 6 firm ripe pears, leaving them whole and leaving on the stems. Boil together 2 cups of water and 1 cup of sugar for 3 or 4 minutes with a piece of vanilla bean. Remove the vanilla bean and poach the pears in the syrup, 2 or 3 at a time, for 5 to 8 minutes, or until they are just tender. Spread the hot applesauce in a heated serving dish and arrange the pears standing in a circle on top. Mix 1 cup of the syrup with ½ cup of strained apricot jam, simmer stirring often, until the sauce is smooth and somewhat reduced, and pour it over the pears. Put a match to 2 tablespoons of warmed rum, pour it flaming over the fruit, and serve as soon as the flame goes out. Serves six.

LOW TIDE — DOUARNENEZ *Brittany*

Lobster in Madeira Sauce

Homard à la Duchesse

(Lobster, butter, Madeira, cream, egg yolks)

Slice the meat of a 2-pound boiled lobster and sauté the pieces briefly in 2 tablespoons of hot butter. Add ¾ cup of Madeira, and salt and a pinch of cayenne pepper. Simmer the lobster for about 5 minutes, or until the pan juices are well reduced. Mix 1 cup of cream with 3 egg yolks and pour this over the lobster. Keep the flame low, stir well, and tilt the pan back and forth so all the lobster will be coated with sauce. Serve as soon as the sauce is hot and just beginning to thicken; do not let it boil. Serves two or three.

WASH DAY — MARTIGUES   *Riviera*

Potato and Mussel Salad Dumas
Salade Japonaise Dumas

(Mussels, white wine, shallots, new potatoes, herbs, truffles, French dressing)

This salad is expensive, because of the truffles, and not easy to shop for, because of the fresh mussels. But if you can manage to collect the ingredients it is incomparable:

Brush, scrape and wash thoroughly 3 quarts of fresh mussels. Put them in a soup kettle with ½ cup of dry white wine and 2 minced shallots, and cook them, covered, over a brisk flame until the shells have opened, or for about 6 minutes. Remove the mussels from their shells when they are cool enough to handle. Peel and slice 2 pounds of small boiled new potatoes while they are still warm. Combine the mussels and potatoes and add ¾ cup of French dressing made with 2 parts white wine vinegar, 5 parts olive oil, and salt and pepper to taste. Add 2 teaspoons each of minced fresh parsley and chives, toss the salad gently so as not to break the potatoes, and put it in a serving bowl. Drain a 2- or 3-ounce can of truffles (save the juice to flavor the sauce of some other dish), slice them thinly, and spread them over the salad. Cover the serving dish and chill the salad for 1 hour, or serve it warm. Serve as a luncheon hors-d'oeuvre or at a cold buffet.

273

LARROQUES-LES-ARCS

Guyenne

Leg of Lamb Diplomate
Gigot Diplomate

(Leg of lamb, salt pork, marinade. stock)

Remove the skin and most of the fat from a leg of young lamb, and run a few strips of salt pork through the meat with a larding needle. Marinate it for 48 hours, turning it occasionally, in a mixture of ¾ cup of dry red wine and ¼ cup each of olive oil and wine vinegar, with 1 small onion and 1 small carrot, both sliced, 1 bay leaf, a sprig of parsley, a pinch of thyme, 2 cloves, and salt and pepper. Braise the leg of lamb with its marinade in a covered casserole. Allow 15 minutes per pound in a 300° oven; the meat should be pink near the bone.

Remove the leg to a hot platter and keep it warm. Strain the casserole juices, through a sieve lined with cheese cloth, into a small saucepan. Skim off all the fat and reduce the juice, over a brisk flame, to about ½ cup. Blend 1 teaspoon of potato starch with a little hot stock, add enough stock to make 1 cup, and add this to the reduced juices. Simmer the sauce for 10 minutes, season it well to taste with a little salt and plenty of pepper, and serve in a sauceboat.

CATHÉDRALE ST. JÉRÔME — DIGNE   *Provence*

Chicken with Saffron Rice

Poule au Riz Provençale

(Fowl, bacon, vegetables, herbs, stock, white wine, rice, onion, saffron)

Truss a 6-pound fowl and put it in a soup kettle with 1 teaspoon of diced bacon, 1 onion stuck with 4 cloves, 1 carrot, cut in pieces, 1 stalk of celery with its leaves, 2 cloves of garlic, 1 bay leaf, a pinch of thyme, several sprigs of parsley, and 4 crushed peppercorns. Add 4 cups of water (or 2 cups each of chicken stock and water), 1 cup of dry white wine, and 1 teaspoon of salt. Add less salt if the stock is seasoned. Bring the liquid to a boil, then lower the heat and cook the chicken at a very slow simmer for 1½ to 2 hours.

Thirty minutes before the chicken is done, in a heavy saucepan sauté 1 minced onion in 1 tablespoon of butter until it is soft and golden. Add 1 cup of raw rice and stir well to coat every grain with butter. Add 1 cup of chicken stock from the kettle, strained and skimmed of fat, and simmer the rice, covered, for about 10 minutes, or until the liquid is absorbed. Then add ½ teaspoon of saffron and 2½ cups more chicken stock. Cook the rice for another 20 minutes, or until all the liquid is absorbed. Carve the chicken, discarding the skin, and arrange it on a hot platter, around the rice piled in a mound in the center. Serve the remaining bouillon, strained and skimmed, in soup cups at the same time. Serves six.

SMALL CHÂTEAU AT SENLISSE   *Ile-de-France*

Roast Duck with White Turnips

Canards aux Navets

(Duck, onions, white wine, stock, white turnips, butter, sugar)

Put a young duck in a roasting pan with 2 whole onions, sprinkle it with salt and pepper, and roast it in a 350° oven for 20 to 25 minutes per pound. Prick the skin to release the fat and, after the duck has begun to brown, add ¼ cup each of dry white wine and chicken stock to the pan juices and baste it several times with them.

Meanwhile, peel and cut in pieces 1 pound of young white turnips. Brown them on all sides in 2 or 3 tablespoons of butter, then sprinkle them with 1 teaspoon of sugar. Forty-five minutes before the duck is done, put them in the roasting pan with the duck to finish cooking. Transfer the duck to a hot serving platter and put the turnips and onions around it. Skim the fat from the pan juices, deglaze the pan with a little white wine, reheat the juices, stirring briskly, and serve them in a sauceboat.

RIVERSIDE ARCHITECTURE — TONERRE   *Burgundy*

"Wine-Merchant" Sauce for Steak
Entrecôte Marchand de Vin Select
(Steak, shallots, butter, flour, stock or meat glaze, red wine, vinegar, cream)

In a small saucepan sauté 1 tablespoon of minced shallots in 1 teaspoon of hot butter until pale gold. Blend in 1 teaspoon of flour, add 2 tablespoons of rich stock (or ½ teaspoon of meat glaze dissolved in 2 tablespoons of hot water), 1 cup of red wine, ½ teaspoon of vinegar, and salt and pepper. Simmer the sauce until it is reduced to ½ cup, then stir in 1 tablespoon of extra-heavy cream and simmer a few seconds more. Meanwhile, pan broil a thick, juicy steak with a good lump of butter. Transfer it, with all the pan juices, to a hot platter, pour the sauce over it, and sprinkle it with chopped parsley. Makes enough sauce for a steak for four.

WINDING STREET — ST. COME   *Gascony*

Fried Eggs Gascony

Oeufs Frits à la Gasconne

(Eggplant, eggs, ham, oil, tomato sauce, parsley)

Sprinkle six ⅜-inch-thick slices of peeled eggplant with salt, and let them stand under pressure for 1 hour. Meanwhile, make a fresh tomato sauce with 4 chopped tomatoes simmered, covered, for about 20 minutes with 2 tablespoons of butter, ½ medium onion, sliced, 1 clove of garlic, minced, 1 teaspoon of chopped parsley, 1 bay leaf, a pinch of thyme, and salt and pepper. Rub the sauce through a sieve and keep it hot. Drain and dry the eggplant, season the slices with salt and pepper, and brush them lightly on both sides with salad oil. Grill them in the broiler under a moderate flame until they are tender and lightly browned. Meanwhile fry 6 eggs. Arrange the grilled eggplant on a hot platter, top each slice with a fried egg, and sprinkle a few julienne strips of ham on the eggs. Pour the tomato sauce over all and sprinkle with chopped parsley. Serves six.

278

ST. JEAN-PIED-DE-PORT   *Béarn*

Green Beans Béarnaise

Haricots Verts Béarnaise

(Green beans, tomatoes, ham, garlic, butter or chicken fat)

Drain well 1 pound of freshly cooked young green beans and combine them with 3 tomatoes, peeled, seeded and chopped, ½ cup of ham cut in julienne strips, 1 small clove of garlic, minced and crushed, and a good lump of butter. In the Béarn, pork or goose fat is used instead of butter; chicken fat is an excellent substitute. Add salt and pepper, and simmer all together for a few minutes, until the tomatoes are somewhat reduced. Serves four.

279

ROMANESQUE CHAPEL — LE PUY   *Auvergne*

Stuffed Ham Rolls au Gratin

Paupiettes de Jambon Gayole

(Ham, cream sauce, cheese, butter, shallots, mushrooms, white wine)

Have ready 6 large, thin slices of cooked ham. Make a cream sauce with 3 tablespoons of flour blended into 4 tablespoons of melted butter and 2 cups of rich milk, added gradually. Add ½ cup of grated mild American cheese and salt and pepper, and stir over medium heat until the cheese melts and the sauce is thickened.

In a skillet sauté briefly 2 minced shallots in 1½ tablespoons of hot butter. Add ¼ pound of minced fresh mushrooms, and cook together gently for 5 minutes, or until the liquid has evaporated. Add ¾ cup of finely diced ham (and, for a perfect dish, 1 minced truffle), stir in 3 tablespoons of dry white wine, and simmer until the wine is well reduced. Take the skillet off the fire and add 3 tablespoons of the prepared cream sauce, or enough to bind the mixture. Let it cool and add ¼ cup of finely diced cheese. Spread a strip of this stuffing across the center of each slice of ham, roll them up, and arrange them side by side in a shallow baking dish. Pour the rest of the sauce over the rolls, sprinkle lightly with grated cheese, fine bread crumbs, and melted butter, and put the dish in a hot oven for 5 minutes, or until the top is lightly browned. Serves six.

VILLAGE TRAFFIC — ST. PAULIEU *Languedoc*

Goose and Bean Casserole

Cassoulet

(Goose, dried beans, onion, garlic, herbs, salt pork, garlic sausage, tomatoes)

Soak 1 pound of dried white beans in water overnight, drain them, and cover them with 1½ quarts of fresh water. Add 1 onion stuck with 2 cloves, a *bouquet garni*, and a little salt, and simmer the beans over very low heat for 1½ hours, or until they are three quarters done. Drain them and reserve the cooking liquid. Dice coarsely and blanch ½ pound of lean streaky salt pork. In a skillet brown the salt pork and 1 garlic sausage, cut in pieces, in 3 tablespoons of hot butter. Remove the meat, and in the remaining fat brown well on all sides ½ a small young goose, cut in serving pieces. (Roast the other half for another meal, or substitute for the goose a whole duck cut in pieces.) Remove the pieces of goose and in the same pan sauté 1 minced onion. Then add 2 chopped cloves of garlic, a *bouquet garni,* 2 tomatoes, peeled and chopped, salt, pepper, and ½ cup of the reserved bean stock. Simmer this sauce, covered, for 20 minutes.

In a large earthen casserole put half the cooked beans, then the salt pork, sausage and goose, and add half the tomato sauce. Add the rest of the beans, the rest of the sauce, and enough bean stock to come just to the surface. Bake the *cassoulet,* covered, in a 275° oven for 2 hours, adding more bean stock occasionally if necessary. Then sprinkle the top with buttered crumbs, and bake, uncovered, for 1 hour or more, until a good brown crust has formed. Serves six.

281

NAPOLEON'S TOMB *Paris*

Chocolate Truffles

Truffes au Chocolat

(Bittersweet chocolate, milk, unsalted butter, egg yolk, Dutch cocoa)

In the top of a double boiler, over boiling water, melt ¼ pound of bittersweet chocolate with 3 tablespoons of milk, stirring constantly. Add 3 tablespoons plus 2 teaspoons of unsalted butter, blend well, and set the mixture aside to cool for a few minutes. Then stir in 1 egg yolk and chill the mixture until it is firm. Form it into balls the size of small cherries, roll them in Dutch cocoa, and store them in the refrigerator. Makes about 18 truffles.

CHÂTEAU D'ESCUMONT *Orléanais*

Chilled Melon Bowl

Melon en Surprise

(Melon, fresh fruit and berries, frozen strawberries, kirsch, almonds)

Cut a circle out of the stem end of a ripe melon. Remove all the seeds, scoop out about two thirds of the flesh with a melon-ball cutter, and take out the rest with a spoon. Turn the shell upside down to drain.

Add enough miscellaneous ripe fresh fruit to the melon balls to fill the shell (such as seedless grapes, pitted black cherries, sliced peaches and apricots, diced fresh pineapple, and all kinds of berries). Make a sauce of frozen strawberries puréed in an electric blender. Add a little kirsch and a few split blanched almonds, combine the sauce with the mixed fruit, and fill the melon shell. Fit the lid back on and chill well before serving.

CAFÉ AT LONGNY   *Normandy*

Roast Duck Rouennaise

Canard Rôti, Sauce Rouennaise

(Duck, red wine, peppercorns, herbs, shallots, meat glaze, brandy, duck liver)

Roast a 5½- to 6-pound duck for about 1¾ hours in a 325° oven. Carve the duck and pass the following sauce with it.

Sauce Rouennaise: Remove most of the fat from the roasting pan in which the duck was cooked. Add ½ cup of red wine to the pan, stir up all the good brown juices, and pour this into a small saucepan. Add 3 or 4 crushed peppercorns, ½ a bay leaf, a pinch of thyme, 1 chopped shallot, and ½ teaspoon of meat glaze dissolved in ½ cup of hot water (or ½ cup of good rich brown stock if you have it). Simmer the sauce to reduce it by about half, then add 1 tablespoon of brandy and simmer briefly to evaporate the alcohol. Now add the duck's liver, raw and finely chopped, and heat the sauce but do not let it boil again. Strain and press the sauce through a fine sieve into a heated sauceboat. This is also good with wild duck. Serves four.

CHARTRES

Orléanais

Easy Mousseline Sauce

Sauce Mousseline

(Egg yolks, cream, butter, lemon juice)

Beat the yolks of 2 eggs well with ½ cup of heavy cream. In a saucepan, melt 4 tablespoons of butter without letting it boil or brown. Stir in the egg-and-cream mixture, and add the juice of half a lemon and salt to taste. Heat the sauce, still without letting it boil and beating it continually with a whisk, until it thickens. Serve with salmon mousse (see *Index*) or any poached fish. Serves four.

PORT-EN-BESSIN *Normandy*

Fish Mousse

Mousse de Poisson

(Cooked fish, egg whites, nutmeg, cream, Normandy sauce)

Use 2 cups of boned and skinned cooked white fish. Purée it, one quarter
at a time, in an electric blender. Return the fish to the blender, one third at a
time with the white of 1 egg each time, and blend until the purée is very smooth.
Season with salt, pepper and a good dash of nutmeg, and chill the mixture for
1 hour. Then add gradually 1 cup of heavy cream and beat the mousse with a
wire whisk until it is light and well blended. Pour it into a generously buttered
fish mold and cover with a piece of buttered waxed paper. Place the mold in a
baking pan containing about 1 inch of boiling water, and cook the mousse in a
350° oven for 20 minutes, or until it is firm to the touch. Let it stand a few
minutes, then unmold and cover with Normandy sauce (see *Index*). Serves four.

FARM NEAR MOUGIN   *Riviera*

Smothered Beef Provençal
Boeuf en Daube Provençale

(Stewing beef, vegetables, garlic, herbs, spices, calf's foot, orange rind, red wine)

In a heavy casserole brown lightly ½ cup of diced bacon in 1 tablespoon of extra bacon fat and 1 tablespoon of salad oil. Add 4 pounds of lean stewing beef cut in 2-inch cubes, and brown the meat quickly on all sides. Then add 6 medium onions and 4 small carrots, all quartered, 1 small onion stuck with 4 cloves, and a piece of calf's foot or a cracked veal knuckle. When the vegetables have taken on a little color, add 3 large quartered tomatoes, 4 shallots, 1 minced clove of garlic, 2 sprigs of parsley, a few celery leaves, 3 bay leaves, a pinch each of thyme, summer savory, cinnamon and ginger, a dozen crushed peppercorns, salt, and the thin outer rind of ½ an orange cut in fine julienne strips. Add 2 cups of good red wine and 1 cup of beef stock or bouillon, and bring the liquid to a boil. Then cover the casserole, put it in a very slow oven, 250° or less, and cook the *daube* at the slowest possible simmer for 5 hours. Add a little stock if necessary. Serve with buttered macaroni with grated cheese. Serves eight.

CHÂTEAU VAUX-LE-VICOMTE

Ile-de-France

Sliced Roast Lamb with Piquante Sauce

Salmis de Pré-Salé, Sauce Piquante

(Lamb, shallots, garlic, white wine, vinegar, stock, meat glaze, pickles)

Roast a small leg of lamb (saddle or shoulder may also be used) for about 12 minutes per pound, leaving it quite underdone and rare. In the meantime make the following sauce.

Sauce Piquante: In 2 tablespoons of hot butter sauté slowly 2 tablespoons of chopped shallots and 1 minced clove of garlic without letting them brown. Add 2½ tablespoons of flour and cook, stirring, until it takes on a pale golden color. Add gradually 1 cup of dry white wine, 1 tablespoon of wine vinegar, and 2 cups of good consommé or stock, and let the sauce simmer for 20 minutes. Strain it through a fine sieve, return it to the saucepan, and add a dash of freshly ground pepper, a pinch of cayenne, and 1 teaspoon of meat glaze. Simmer it very slowly for about 45 minutes, skimming it carefully from time to time. Then remove the fat from the pan in which the lamb was cooked and combine the brown juices with the sauce. Carve the lamb and arrange the slices overlapping in rows in an ovenproof dish. Add 2 to 3 tablespoons of chopped sour pickled gherkins to the sauce and spoon it over the lamb. Let the meat "poach" in the lowest possible oven for 15 minutes, but be sure not to let the sauce boil. Serve in the baking dish, with buttered rice. Serves six.

UTAH BEACH   *Normandy*

Loin Lamb Chops on Skewers

Quartier de Pré Salé à la Broche

(Loin lamb chops, lamb kidneys, thyme, onion, oil, tomatoes, green pepper, lemon)

Rub 8 not-too-thick loin lamb chops with salt, pepper, thyme, and a little grated onion. Coat them with oil and let them marinate, covered, for 3 hours. Thread them on individual skewers, two to a skewer, with a lamb kidney between each two chops. Cook them over a charcoal or wood fire, turning often. Serve them well-browned but still pink in the center. When they are two-thirds done, add a small tomato and a piece of green pepper to each skewer. Serve on the skewers and sprinkled with lemon juice. Serves four. If the chops are large and thick, one apiece is plenty.

THE CHÂTEAU — VERSAINVILLE   *Normandy*

Eggs with Tomatoes and Chicken Livers

Oeufs Isoline

(Eggs, butter, tomatoes, oil, garlic, chicken livers, Madeira, parsley)

Melt 2 tablespoons of butter in a shallow baking dish, carefully break 4 eggs into it, and bake them in a 350° oven for 10 minutes, or until the whites are set and the yolks are still soft. Spoon the hot butter back over the eggs and season them with salt and pepper.

Meanwhile, have ready 2 small halved and seeded tomatoes and 2 quartered chicken livers. In one pan sauté the tomatoes lightly on both sides in 2 tablespoons of hot olive oil; then add ½ a minced clove of garlic and salt and pepper, and cook for another 2 minutes. In another pan sauté the chicken livers in 1 tablespoon of hot butter for 2 minutes; then season them with a little salt and pepper, add 1 tablespoon of Madeira, and simmer them for another minute. Arrange the tomatoes around the baked eggs, and pour any oil remaining in the pan over them. Put the pieces of chicken liver on the tomatoes, spoon their juice over them, and sprinkle with chopped parsley. Serves four.

VINEGROWN CHÂTEAU — HARCOURT *Normandy*

Turnips in Cream

Navets à la Crème

(White turnips, butter, cream)

Peel and slice 6 young white turnips. Put them in a saucepan with barely enough water to cover, cover the pan, and simmer them until they are half done. Then add 4 tablespoons of butter and cook the turnips, uncovered, until the water is all absorbed and they begin to fry a little in the butter. Add salt and pepper, stir in ½ cup of heavy cream, and reheat the turnips for about a minute. These are very good with veal. Serves four.

MONTMARTRE AND SACRÉ COEUR   *Paris*

Turnips Bordelaise

Navets à la Bordelaise

(White turnips, butter, garlic, shallot, bread crumbs, parsley)

Peel 2 pounds of young white turnips and cut them into pieces each about the size of a walnut. Melt 3 tablespoons of butter in a heavy pan, and add the turnips, salt and pepper, and a very small amount of water. Cover the pan and cook the turnips very slowly; from time to time remove the lid and shake the pan to turn the turnips and cook them evenly on all sides. When they are done and tender, the liquid should be almost entirely absorbed. Mix together 2 cloves of garlic and 1 shallot, all very finely minced, ½ cup of coarse dry bread crumbs, and 1 tablespoon of minced parsley. Add 1 tablespoon of butter to the pan, sprinkle the bread-crumb mixture over the turnips, and brown briefly over moderately high heat, shaking the pan often. Serves six.

UMBRELLA PINES   *Provence*

Stewed Celery and Tomatoes

Céleri à la Bonne Femme

(Celery, onion, carrot, butter, tomatoes, herbs, stock)

Wash and string a bunch of celery. Discard all but the smallest yellow leaves in the heart. Split the stalks and cut them into 2½-inch lengths. Drop them into boiling salted water and parboil them for 2 minutes. Chop 1 medium onion and grate ½ a carrot, and soften these over moderate heat in 2 tablespoons of butter. Add salt and pepper, 2 large peeled and coarsely chopped tomatoes, a pinch of thyme, and the celery. Moisten with ¼ cup of stock, cover the pan, and simmer the mixture slowly for about 1 hour, or until the celery is tender and the tomato sauce is reduced to a good consistency. Add 1 teaspoon of finely minced parsley before serving. Serves four.

ROMAN MONUMENT — ST. RÉMY   *Provence*

Cream of Turnip Soup

Potage Crème de Navets

(White turnips, butter, leeks, cream-sauce base, cream)

Peel and slice thinly 1 pound of white turnips. Drop them into boiling water, boil them for 3 minutes, and drain. Then stew them gently until soft in 3 tablespoons of butter, together with the white parts of 2 leeks, well washed and thinly sliced. Make 4 cups of cream-sauce soup base (see *Index*). Combine the cream sauce and the vegetables in the top of a double boiler, and cook the soup for 45 minutes. Then purée it, 1 cup at a time, in an electric blender, or force it through a fine sieve. Reheat the soup, taste it for seasoning and, just before serving, add ½ cup of heavy cream. Serves six.

LANDSCAPE NEAR ALBOUSSIÈRE *Languedoc*

Grandmother's Pork Chops

Côtes de Porc Grandmère

(Pork chops, butter, onion, nutmeg, egg, bread crumbs)

Remove the meat from 6 pork chops. Clean off the bones, remove most of the fat, and put all the clear meat through the fine blade of a meat grinder. For each ½ pound of clear meat add 3 tablespoons of softened butter, ½ a small onion, finely minced and cooked until soft in 1 teaspoon of butter, salt, a good dash of pepper, a little freshly grated nutmeg, and 1 beaten egg. Shape the mixture into six patties, dip these in flour, and fit each one against a chop bone, giving the appearance of the original chops, slightly flattened. Dip the chops in beaten egg, then in bread crumbs, sprinkle them with a little melted butter, and broil them rather slowly under a moderately low flame until they are well browned on both sides and thoroughly cooked. Serve with mashed potatoes. Serves six.

TOWN FOUNTAIN—RIOM   *Auvergne*

Poached Eggs Régal

Oeufs Pochés Régal

(Potatoes, butter, ham, eggs, cream sauce, grated cheese)

Bake 4 large potatoes in a 450° oven for 40 minutes, or until done. Slice a section lengthwise off each one. Remove the pulp and beat it well with 4 tablespoons of butter, a little milk, and salt and pepper. Make ¾ cup of cream sauce (add 1½ tablespoons of grated cheese to the sauce); mince enough ham to make ¼ cup; and poach 4 eggs. Fill each potato shell half full with mashed potato, spread with minced ham, top with the eggs, and over each egg pour 2 to 3 tablespoons of cream sauce. Sprinkle the sauce with a little more grated cheese, and brown lightly in a hot oven or under the broiler. Serves four.

CHURCH AND CUSTOMS HOUSE — BARFLEUR   *Normandy*

Cream of Oyster Soup

Crème aux Huîtres

(Oysters, butter, flour, milk, onion, cream, parsley)

Over low heat poach 24 oysters (1 pint) in their liquor until the edges just begin to curl. Drain them, reserve the liquid, and trim off the outer "beards," reserving these also. Cut the soft centers into two or three pieces each. Make a cream sauce by blending 6 tablespoons of flour into 3 tablespoons of melted butter and adding gradually 3½ cups of hot milk. Sauté 1 finely minced onion slowly in 1 tablespoon of butter until it is soft and transparent but not brown. Combine the cream sauce, the onion, and the reserved oyster liquor and beards. Season the soup with a little salt to taste and pinch of cayenne. Cook it over boiling water for 15 minutes, then strain it and discard the oyster beards. Just before serving, add 1 cup of cream and the reserved oysters. Reheat the soup without allowing it to boil, and serve sprinkled with finely minced parsley. Serves six.

THE ROMAN ARENA — NÎMES

Languedoc

Macaroon Cream Omelette

Omelette aux Macarons à la Crème

(Eggs, butter, macaroons, apple jelly, cream)

With a fork beat together for 30 to 40 seconds 6 eggs, 3 teaspoons of cold water, and a very small pinch of salt. You may also add 2 or 3 teaspoons of sugar, though this is not absolutely necessary. Make the omelette in a pan coated with 1 generous tablespoon of melted butter; before folding it, spread the following filling across the center: With a rolling pin crush 3 large dried macaroons, and combine the crumbs with 3 tablespoons of apple jelly and a spoonful of whipped cream. Turn out the omlette onto an ovenproof dish, sprinkle it with sugar, and glaze it briefly under a hot broiler. Serve it with more whipped cream if desired. Serves three or four.

EZE, ABOVE CAP FERRAT *Riviera*

Lamb à la Poulette

Agneau à la Poulette

(Lamb, butter, flour, herbs, onions, mushrooms, lemon, egg yolks)

Have 2 pounds of good tender lamb cut into 1½-inch cubes. Cover them with salted boiling water and let them stand, covered, for 10 minutes. Drain the lamb and dry it. Put it in a heavy saucepan with 2 tablespoons of butter, and when the butter has melted (do *not* brown the meat) stir in 1½ tablespoons of flour. Blend it in well, then add gradually enough boiling water (or half water and half stock) to cover the meat. Add salt, pepper, a *bouquet garni,* and 6 or 8 very small onions. Cover the pan and simmer the lamb for 1 hour. Then add 10 or 12 mushrooms and continue cooking for ½ to 1 hour, or until the meat is tender. During this time, add a little hot liquid if the sauce reduces too fast; or, remove the lid and raise the heat if it stays too thin.

When the meat is done, taste the sauce for seasoning and add the juice of half a lemon. Mix 2 egg yolks with a little sauce, add this to the stew, and cook gently, stirring, until it is well blended and slightly thickened. Do not let it boil and transfer to a serving dish as soon as it is ready. Serves six.

PONT NEUF   *Paris*

Fillets of Sole Véronique

Filets de Sole Véronique

(Sole, white wine, lemon, parsley, onion, cream, butter, flour, grapes)

Season 2 pounds of fillets of sole with a little salt and pepper, fold each fillet over once, and arrange them in one layer in a well-buttered earthen or glass baking dish. Have the fish market give you the trimmings, heads, and bones of the fish. With these make a stock by simmering them for 15 minutes in ½ cup each of water and dry white wine, with a few drops of lemon juice, a sprig of parsley, a slice of onion, and salt and pepper. Strain the stock over the fillets, cover the dish with buttered paper, and poach the fish in a 375° oven for about 15 minutes. Remove all the liquid from the dish with a basting syringe. Keep the fish warm while you reduce the juices, over a brisk fire, down to about ⅓ of a cup. Add to this ½ cup of heavy cream, and reheat. Taste the sauce for seasoning, and stir in 2 teaspoons of butter creamed with 1 teaspoon of flour. Cook and stir gently until the sauce is somewhat thickened, then pour it over the fish. Heap ¾ cup of cold seedless white grapes in the center of the dish, and serve immediately. Serves six.

FIELDS NEAR MONTÉLIMAR   *Dauphiny*

Poached Chicken Mère Brazier

La Poularde Pochée à la Mère Brazier

(Chicken, chicken stock, carrots, turnips, celery, leeks, bacon, herbs)

Heat 2 quarts of chicken stock with 2 carrots, cut in pieces, 2 small white turnips, quartered, 2 stalks of celery, cut in pieces, 4 leeks with most of their green tops cut off, a cube of lean bacon 1 inch square (or 2 slices), a pinch of thyme, a bay leaf, and 2 sprigs of parsley. Simmer this court-bouillon for 10 minutes, then add a trussed 3-pound chicken, young, tender, and plump. *(Chez* la Mère Brazier the chicken would have numerous slices of truffle inserted under the skin over the breast and leg meat.)

Simmer the chicken, covered, for 20 minutes after the stock comes back to a boil, then turn off the heat and let the chicken stand and continue to poach in the hot stock for 20 minutes. Remove it to a hot platter, pour a little of the stock over it so it will not dry out, and keep it warm. The vegetables should be tender by this time, but if they are not, continue cooking them while you make the sauce: In a small saucepan, over a brisk fire, reduce 1¼ cups of the stock to ½ cup. Taste it for seasoning and whip in 2 tablespoons of creamed sweet butter at the last minute, off the fire. Serve the chicken surrounded by the vegetables and pass the sauce separately. Serves three or four.

301

HARBOR AT BEAULIEU   *Riviera*

Zucchini au Gratin

Gratin de Courgettes

(Zucchini or summer squash, butter, cream sauce, cheese)

Scrub thoroughly (but do not peel) 5 or 6 small zucchini, and cut them into 1-inch pieces. Drop these into boiling salted water and parboil them for 2 to 3 minutes. Drain them thoroughly, then sauté them on both sides in 4 tablespoons of hot butter. When they are lightly browned, place them in rows and in one layer in a shallow baking dish. Cover them with a cream sauce made of 2½ tablespoons of flour blended into 2½ tablespoons of melted butter and 1½ cups of rich milk, added gradually. Season the sauce with salt and pepper, simmer it for 2 or 3 minutes, and pour it over the zucchini. Sprinkle generously with grated cheese (Parmesan or American Cheddar) and with a little melted butter, and brown in a hot oven for 5 to 6 minutes. Serves four.

CHÂTEAU DE CLOS DE VOUGEOT *Burgundy*

Steak Bercy

Entrecôte Bercy

(Steak, shallots, white wine, butter, lemon juice, parsley)

Grill a thick steak for four according to your taste, which we hope is rare. Meanwhile, make the following *sauce Bercy:* Simmer together ¼ cup of finely minced shallots and 1 cup of dry white wine until the mixture is reduced to about ⅓ cup. Off the fire, stir in 3 tablespoons of butter and the juice of half a lemon. Strain the sauce, add 2 tablespoons of finely minced parsley, and reheat it without boiling. When the steak is done, put it on a hot platter, salt and pepper it, and pour the sauce over it. As you carve the steak, the juices will mingle with the sauce and, spooned over each serving, will add a delicious and savory flavor.

CHÂTEAU DU DONJON — BEAUGENCY *Orléanais*

Baked Eggs Héloïse

Oeufs sur le Plat Héloïse

(Eggs, ham, butter, mushrooms, cream, Parmesan or Cheddar)

Sauté 4 slices of cooked ham briefly in butter, on both sides. When they are hot but not really browned, place each one in an individual buttered shirred-egg dish. Chop 6 to 8 mushrooms and sauté them in 1 tablespoon of butter for 3 to 4 minutes. Spread the mushrooms over the ham, season lightly with salt and pepper, and break an egg carefully into each dish. Salt the eggs lightly, pour 2 tablespoons of cream over each one, and sprinkle with a little grated Parmesan or American Cheddar cheese. Bake the eggs in a 350° oven for about 10 minutes, or until the whites are set, but the yolks are still soft, and the cheese has melted. Serves four.

LES RICEYS   *Champagne*

Lemon Mousse

Mousse au Citron

(Lemon, gelatine, white wine, sugar, eggs)

Soak 1 tablespoon of gelatine in 2 tablespoons of water. Combine ¼ cup of sweet white wine, ½ cup of sugar, the juice of 1½ lemons, and the grated zest of the skins. Heat this mixture over hot water, add the gelatine, and stir until the sugar and gelatine are dissolved. Beat 4 large egg yolks until they are very thick and light, and stir in the lemon-gelatine mixture. Beat 4 egg whites stiff and fold them into the yolk mixture. Pour this mousse into a glass serving bowl, and chill it until it becomes firm but is still light and foamy. Serves four.

CLIFFS NEAR DIE   *Dauphiny*

Scrambled Eggs Fines Herbes

Oeufs Brouillés aux Fines Herbes

(Eggs, shallots, olive oil, butter, mushrooms, parsley, cream, croutons)

Chop 3 shallots fine, and sauté them over gentle heat in 1 tablespoon of olive oil and 1 tablespoon of butter combined. When they are pale gold add 4 or 5 chopped mushrooms and cook together slowly until lightly browned. Stir in 1 tablespoon of finely chopped parsley. Drain off the extra fat, and add the vegetables to 6 beaten eggs. Add salt, pepper, and ¼ cup of heavy cream. Melt 3 tablespoons of butter in a skillet and, before the butter is really hot, stir in the egg mixture. Continue stirring, with a wooden spoon, over moderate heat, until the eggs are cooked but still creamy. Serve them on a small platter surrounded with triangles of bread fried in butter. Serves three or four.

SAILBOATS AT LA ROCHELLE *Aunis*

Puffed Ham Croutons

Croûtes au Jambon à la Ménagère

(Bread, butter, flour, milk, ham, egg whites)

Cut stale white bread into 9 slices one half inch thick; trim off the crusts, and divide the slices into quarters or halves. Blend 1½ tablespoons of flour into 1 tablespoon of melted butter, add gradually ½ cup of milk, and season with salt, pepper, and a dash of nutmeg. Cook, stirring with a whisk, until the sauce is very thick and smooth. Add about ¾ cup (3½ ounces) of chopped ham, and let cool. Beat 2 egg whites stiff and fold them very gently into the ham mixture. Spread each piece of bread with this mixture, in a layer about one half inch thick, covering well to the edges. Fry the *croûtes*, a few at a time, in deep fat until the bread is golden and the ham paste has puffed; drain them as they are done on absorbent paper. Serve at once, as hot cocktail hors-d'oeuvre or as a first course for six.

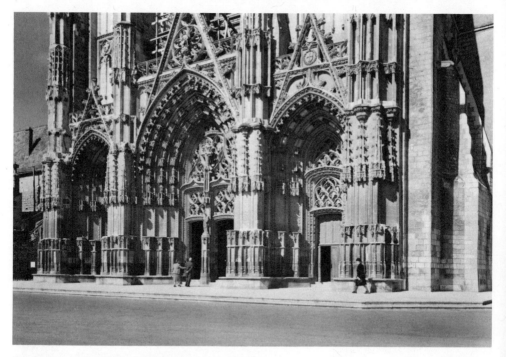

FAÇADE OF THE CATHEDRAL—TOURS *Touraine*

Fresh Green Pea and Chicken Soup

Potage Dame Edmée

(Chicken, stock, peas, butter, onion, lettuce, spinach, herbs, egg yolks, cream)

The next time you boil a chicken for a fricassee, reserve some of the white meat and stock for this delectable soup. (Or you may use left-over roast chicken and canned chicken consommé.) In a large saucepan put 4 cups of fresh peas, 6 tablespoons of butter, 1 finely minced onion, a tender head of garden lettuce cut in julienne strips, about 15 leaves of fresh spinach, a sprig of parsley, a few sprigs of chervil if you have it, 2 teaspoons of sugar, ½ teaspoon of salt, and 1¾ cups of water. Cover the saucepan, bring the soup to a boil, and cook it over a moderate fire until the peas are tender. Meanwhile, boil 1 cup of fresh peas, in a separate pan, to add to the soup later.

Pass the soup through a strainer, or a vegetable mill, pressing the vegetables through with the liquid. Return the soup to the saucepan, add 3 cups of chicken stock, stir well, and simmer over a low fire for about 15 minutes. Then add the extra cup of peas, drained, and ¼ cup of cooked white meat of chicken, cut into very fine julienne strips. Mix 3 egg yolks with 1½ cups of thin cream, and add this gradually to the soup, stirring constantly. Continue cooking until the soup thickens to a creamy consistency, but do not let it boil. Serves eight.

LANDSCAPE NEAR MILLAU   *Guyenne*

Chicken Limousin

Poulet à la Limousine

(Chicken, chestnuts, celery, stock, sausage meat, mushrooms, parsley, onion)

Slash a cross-cut on the flat side of the shells of 2 dozen chestnuts and heat them in a little oil in a heavy frying pan until the shells begin to open. Peel the chestnuts, and cook them slowly for about 20 minutes in enough chicken stock to cover them, with 1 celery stalk, 1 teaspoon of butter, a pinch of salt, and ½ teaspoon of sugar. Meanwhile, mix together ¼ pound of sausage meat, 4 or 5 minced mushrooms, 1 teaspoon of minced parsley, and 1 chopped onion first cooked until soft and transparent in 1 tablespoon of butter. Stuff a 4- to 4½-pound chicken with this mixture, and truss it. In a heavy casserole, on top of the stove, brown the chicken on all sides in 1½ tablsepoons of butter. Place the casserole in a 350° oven and cook the chicken, uncovered, for 20 minutes. Drain the chestnuts, reserving their stock, and place them around the chicken. Add ½ cup of the strained chestnut stock, and continue cooking the chicken, still uncovered, for 1 hour or until it is brown and tender. During this time add more stock if necessary so that the dish will not dry out; you should have a condensed but adequate sauce to serve with the bird. Serves four.

FARM NEAR ST. RÉMY-EN-L'EAU   *Ile-de-France*

Guinea Hen with Tarragon

Pintade à l'Estragon

(Guinea hen, tarragon, butter, bacon, stock, white wine, potato starch)

In the cavity of a guinea hen place a branch of fresh tarragon and 1 tablespoon of butter. Truss it, season it with salt and pepper, and tie strips of bacon over the breast and legs. In a small heavy casserole brown the hen on all sides in 1 tablespoon of hot butter. Then add ¾ cup each of chicken stock and dry white wine, or enough liquid to half cover the bird, and another good-sized branch of fresh tarragon. Cover the casserole and cook the guinea hen in a 350° oven for about 1 hour, or until it is tender; for the last 15 minutes of cooking, remove the bacon and leave the casserole uncovered. Strain the sauce into a small saucepan, skim off the fat, and reduce the sauce over high heat to about ¾ cup. Blend a scant teaspoon of potato starch with a little cold stock or water, add this to the sauce, and add a few fresh tarragon leaves. Simmer until it is slightly thickened and serve with the bird. Serves four.

310

MONTBRISON   *Lyonnais*

Shirred Eggs with Mushrooms

Oeufs Bergère

(Eggs, mushrooms, butter, lemon juice, parsley)

Chop ½ pound of mushrooms, and cook them in 2½ tablespoons of melted butter, with a few drops of lemon juice, for 5 minutes or more, until most of their juice has evaporated. Let them cool, then stir in 2 tablespoons of softened butter, 1 teaspoon of minced parsley, and salt and pepper. Line the bottoms and sides of 4 individual shirred-egg dishes with this mixture. Break an egg into each dish, and bake them for 10 minutes in a 350° oven, or until the whites are set but the yolks are still soft. Serves four.

THE LOWER TOWN—AURAY

Brittany

Shrimp Canapés

Canapés aux Crevettes

(Shrimp, white bread, Green Butter, mayonnaise, capers)

Spread small rounds of thinly sliced white bread or toast evenly with Green Butter (see Classic Flavored Butters in the *Index*). Split cooked shrimp in half lengthwise and place a half on each canapé. Place a small dab of mayonnaise in the centers and a caper on the mayonnaise.

THE LOIRE NEAR SAUMUR   *Anjou*

Asparagus with Normandy Sauce

Asperges, Sauce Normande

(Asparagus, flour, butter, nutmeg, cider or white wine, cream, lemon juice)

Clean a 2-pound bunch of fresh asparagus, reassemble the bunch, and tie it with string in two places. Boil the asparagus in salted water, or steam them, for about 20 minutes or until tender. Drain well, and serve with the following sauce: Blend 1 tablespoon of flour into 1 tablespoon of melted butter, add salt, pepper, and a dash of nutmeg, and stir in gradually ⅓ cup of cider or white wine. When this is well blended, add ⅔ cup of heavy cream and a few drops of lemon juice, and simmer for 2 minutes. Serves four or more.

313

THE CHÂTEAU WALLS — ANGERS *Anjou*

Asparagus Polonaise

Asperges à la Polonaise

(Asparagus, hard-boiled-egg yolks, parsley, bread crumbs, butter)

Wash, trim, and scrape 1 pound of asparagus. Tie it in a bunch in two places, put it in boiling salted water, and cook it rather slowly for 20 minutes, or until tender but not limp. Remove the asparagus, drain it, cut off the strings, and drain the stalks again on a cloth. Place them in overlapping rows on a long heatproof platter so that all the tips are exposed. Sprinkle the tips with a mixture of 4 chopped hard-boiled-egg yolks and 2 teaspoons of minced parsley. Then sprinkle with 2 or 3 tablespoons of bread crumbs mixed with 4 tablespoons of melted butter, and brown briefly under a hot broiler. Serves four.

314

CATHÉDRALE DE ST. PIERRE — ANGOULÊME   *Angoumois*

Roast Pork with Apples

Rôti de Porc

(Loin of pork, herbs, spices, garlic, stock, potatoes, apples)

Have a loin end of pork roast boned; a piece that weighs 3 pounds after boning will serve eight. Remove most of the fat, and rub all the surfaces well with a mixture of 2 to 3 teaspoons of salt, ⅜ teaspoon of freshly ground pepper, ½ teaspoon each of thyme and rosemary, a good pinch of allspice, and ½ clove of garlic, chopped and mashed. Let the meat stand in a covered bowl for 12 hours. Before roasting, wipe off the seasonings with a cloth; roll and tie the meat if necessary. Roast the pork for about 1½ hours, or about 30 minutes per pound, in a 325° oven; a meat thermometer should read 185°. Add small amounts of hot stock to the pan juices to baste with from time to time.

Peel and slice lengthwise the desired number of rather small potatoes, and add them to the roasting pan when the pork is half cooked. About ½ hour before it is done, add 2 tart apples, peeled, cored, and quartered. Serve the roast on a hot platter, surrounded by the potatoes and apples. Skim the fat from the pan juices, add a little stock if needed, and serve in a sauceboat.

315

COUNTRY CHAPEL IN MOURRET *Provence*

Cream Soup Andalusian

Crème Andalouse

(Leeks, buttter, tomatoes, potatoes, cream, croutons)

Clean 4 leeks, slice the white parts thinly, and sauté them slowly in 3 table-spoons of butter until they are soft and golden. Add 8 medium tomatoes, cut in pieces, and simmer the mixture for 10 minutes. Add 2½ quarts of water, 6 medium peeled and quartered potatoes, salt, and a pinch of cayenne. Simmer all together for 45 minutes to 1 hour. Pass through a strainer, pressing the vegetables through with the liquid. Reheat the soup and simmer it down to medium-thick con-sistency. Then add ½ cup of heavy cream and taste for seasoning. Serve with diced bread croutons fried in butter. Serves eight.

316

VERSAILLES

Easy French Crêpes

Crêpes

(Eggs, milk, flour, oil, butter)

Beat 2 eggs, add ¾ cup of milk, then add ½ cup plus 1 tablespoon of flour, 1 teaspoon of oil, and a pinch of salt. (Use these ingredients for unsweetened crêpe dishes; for dessert crêpes, add 1½ teaspoons each of kirsch and sugar.) Beat well with a rotary beater until the batter is perfectly smooth. Or put everything in an electric blender and you have a perfect batter in an instant. These amounts will make 8 to 10 crêpes, serving three, and are the maximum you should mix in the blender at one time; to make about 18 crêpes, serving six, double the quantities, mixing half at a time in a blender, or all at once with a rotary beater. Let the batter stand at least 1 hour before using.

Heat a 6-inch frying pan, grease it with a few drops of oil and ⅛ teaspoon of butter for each crêpe, and pour in 2 to 2½ tablespoons of batter for each crêpe. Cook over a moderate flame until the bottom is lightly browned and the top is dry. Turn, and brown the other side. Spread the crêpes on a board as they are done. A simple way to use plain crêpes is to roll them around a stuffing of creamed chicken or seafood. There are many recipes for finishing dessert crêpes, though they are delicious simply spread with jelly, rolled or folded, and sprinkled with sugar.

PALAIS JACQUES COEUR — BOURGES *Berry*

Duck with Cherries

Caneton aux Cerises

(Duck, herbs, onion, carrot, cherries, sugar, Port, stock, cherry brandy)

Season a 5- to 6-pound duck with salt, pepper, and a pinch of thyme, and add ½ an onion and a sprig of parsley. Put the duck in a roasting pan with the rest of the onion and a small carrot, both sliced. Brown it in a 425° oven for 15 minutes, then lower the heat to 350°, prick the skin, and roast for 1 hour (or 1¼ hours in all for medium-rare, 1 hour and 35 minutes for well-done). Remove the fat in the pan occasionally, and baste with the following cherry juice:

Pit 1½ pounds of tart red cherries and heat them, covered, with ¼ cup each of Port and water and 2½ tablespoons of sugar. Let them stand for 10 minutes off the fire, then drain over a saucepan. Remove two thirds of the cherries, reserve, and force the juice of the remaining cherries through the strainer; use a little of this to baste the duck. Fifteen minutes before the bird is done, remove it from the pan. Skim almost all the fat from the juices, stir in the remaining cherry juice and ¼ cup of strong stock, and strain this sauce. Return the duck to the pan, salt it lightly, add the cherries and sauce, and roast for 15 minutes more. Serve the duck on a hot platter, surrounded by the cherries and with a little sauce poured over it. Thicken the remaining sauce with potato starch (1 teaspoon dissolved in a little water per cup of sauce); add 1 teaspoon of cherry brandy, and pass separately. Serves four to six.

318

NEVERS ON THE LOIRE *Nivernais*

Stuffed Pineapple with Strawberries

Ananas à la Belle de Meaux

(Pineapple, strawberries, sugar, kirsch, cream)

Cut a pineapple in half lengthwise, cutting through the fronds also, which are left on for their decorative effect. Hollow out the shells and dice the fruit, removing the hard core. Combine the pineapple cubes with about the same amount of ripe strawberries, hulled and halved, and add sugar to taste and 1 tablespoon of kirsch. Let the fruits marinate in the refrigerator until they are well chilled. To serve, place the pineapple shells end to end on a long platter. Fill them with the fruit, mound sweetened whipped cream on top, and decorate with a few perfect whole strawberries. Serves four to six.

CHURCH AT LONGPONT   *Ile-de-France*

Leg of Lamb en Daube

Gigot en Daube

(Lamb, red wine, oil, carrot, onion, garlic, herbs, bacon, stock, olives)

Have 2 pounds of boned leg of lamb cut into 2-inch cubes. Remove all the fat. Combine ½ cup of red wine, ¼ cup of oil, 1 carrot and 1 small onion, both sliced, 1 cut clove of garlic, a *bouquet garni,* salt, pepper, and a pinch of nutmeg. Put the meat in a bowl, add this marinade, and let it stand in the refrigerator, covered, for 24 hours, turning it from time to time.

Drain off the marinade and reserve it. In a heavy casserole brown the meat lightly on all sides in 1 tablespoon each of butter and diced bacon. Then add the marinade, 1½ cups of stock, or enough almost to cover the meat, and a strip of orange peel. Cover the casserole, bring the liquid just to the boiling point, then put the casserole in a 325° oven for 2 hours, or until the meat is tender. Remove the lamb to a hot serving dish and keep it warm. Skim the fat from the sauce, and strain the sauce through a fine sieve, forcing the vegetables through with the liquid. Place a dozen black Italian olives on the meat, surround it with 6 croutons of bread rubbed with garlic and buttered and toasted on both sides, and add the sauce. Serve with boiled potatoes. Serves four.

VÉZELAY   *Burgundy*

Poached Eggs in Red Wine

Oeufs Pochés au Vin Rouge

(Eggs, red wine, shallots, herbs, butter, flour, croutons)

Boil together 1 cup of red wine, 1 cup of water, 2 chopped shallots, 1 bay leaf, a pinch of thyme, a sprig of parsley, and salt and pepper to taste. After the liquid has boiled for about 7 minutes, lower the heat, and poach 6 eggs in it. This should take about 1¼ minutes for each egg; poach them one or two at a time, and as each one is done, remove it with a slotted spoon to a warm platter, and keep the platter covered. Have ready 6 slices of bread fried in butter until they are crisp and brown on both sides. When all the eggs are done, reduce the cooking liquid over a brisk fire to about one third its original quantity, and strain it into a small saucepan. Whisk in 1 tablespoon of butter well-creamed with 2 teaspoons of flour. Place an egg on each fried crouton, spoon the sauce over the eggs, and serve at once. Serves six.

CATHEDRAL FAÇADE — MEAUX

Champagne

Classic Flavored Butters for Canapés

Beurres Composés

(Sweet butter with herbs, or mustard, or anchovy paste)

One quarter pound of butter is enough to spread 3 dozen or more small canapés. Use unsalted butter and cream each quarter pound well with your choice of the following ingredients. To make Green Butter (*Beurre Printanier*): 1½ generous tablespoons of very finely minced parsley, 1 teaspoon of very finely minced chives, and 1 tablespoon of cooked, puréed, and well-drained spinach; add a little green food coloring if you wish. Mustard Butter (*Beurre de Moutarde*): 1½ tablespoons French mixed mustard. Anchovy Butter (*Beurre d'Anchois*): 2 tablespoons of anchovy paste, or to taste. Store all butters in the refrigerator, but let them soften somewhat at room temperature before spreading. (See *Index* for canapé recipes.) These same butters are used to season sauces, and *Beurre Printanier* and *Beurre de Moutarde* are both delicious on broiled steaks.

CHÂTEAU DE TOUFFOU, NEAR POITIERS   *Poitou*

Brussels Sprouts in Cream

Choux de Bruxelles à la Crème

(Brussels sprouts, milk, butter, cream)

Clean 1 quart of Brussels sprouts, and boil them in salted water for 10 minutes. Drain them and return them to the saucepan. Add 2 cups of milk and simmer the sprouts on a very low fire for about 30 minutes, or until they are tender and have absorbed most of the milk. Watch carefully that the milk neither boils over nor scorches. Add salt and pepper, 1 tablespoon of butter, and ⅜ cup of heavy cream. Reheat briefly, shaking the pan, and serve. Cooked in this way Brussels sprouts have a very sweet and delicate flavor. Serves four.

WAR MEMORIAL—VILLERS-COTTERETS *Ile-de-France*

Country Vegetable Soup

La Garbure

(Beans, potatoes, onions, carrots, turnips, herbs, garlic, cabbage, bacon)

Soak 1 cup of dried white beans overnight. Drain them and put them in a soup kettle with 3 or 4 peeled and halved potatoes, 2 onions, 2 or 3 carrots, scraped and cut in pieces, 1 white turnip, peeled and quartered, a *bouquet garni* (thyme, bay leaf, and parsley), and 1 mashed clove of garlic. Add 2 quarts of cold water, or enough generously to cover the vegetables, and pepper. Bring the soup slowly to a boil, skim it once or twice, then simmer it as slowly as possible for 1½ hours. Then add 1 young cabbage, cut into very thin strips, and a ½-pound piece of lean bacon.

In France the *garbure* always contains some sort of pork product or, in certain regions of the southwest, preserved fat goose meat. You may also use a ½-pound piece of lean salt pork first blanched for 4 minutes in boiling water to remove some of the salt; or a ham bone with some meat on it; or a piece of good smoked sausage. After adding the cabbage and pork, simmer the soup for another hour; taste for seasoning. They say it should be "so thick a ladle will stand up in it," but add a little boiling water if it reduces too fast, or cook it a little longer if it is not thick enough. Ladle the soup into hot soup plates, over thin slices of toasted French bread. Slice the meat and serve it in the soup. Serves six as a main course.

THE PORT AT ST. JEAN DE LUZ   *Béarn*

Basque Salad

Salad Basquaise

(Sweet peppers, oil, vinegar, tomatoes, olives, onion, tarragon)

Clean and cut into strips 2 sweet peppers, green, red, or yellow; one green one with one red or yellow one makes a colorful salad. Sauté them slowly in ¼ cup of oil until they are somewhat softened, drain them on paper toweling, then marinate them for half an hour in a dressing made of 1 tablespoon of wine vinegar, 3 tablespoons of olive oil, and salt and pepper. Peel, seed, and slice 2 medium-sized ripe tomatoes and add them to the peppers. Add 8 black Italian or Greek olives, 4 slices of sweet onion, and 1 teaspoon of minced fresh tarragon. Mix all together gently. Serves four.

VIEW FROM THE RAMPARTS—ANGOULÊME   *Angoumois*

Chopped Egg and Anchovy Canapés

Canapés aux Anchois

(Anchovies, hard-boiled eggs, bread, Green Butter, parsley or water cress)

Spread rectangles of thinly sliced bread or toast evenly with Green Butter (see Classic Flavored Butters in the *Index).* Cut anchovy fillets into very thin strips and place two of these diagonally in a cross on each canapé. Cover one of the triangles thus formed with sieved yolk of hard-boiled egg. Cover the opposite triangle with finely chopped egg white. The classic version of this canapé goes on to sprinkle the two remaining triangles with minced parsley (or water cress), though the plain green butter is really sufficient.

326

COUNTRY HOTEL — BÉRARDIER   *Dauphiny*

Roast Pork Lyonnaise

Rôti de Porc comme à Lyon

(Pork roast, onion, carrot, bouquet garni, white wine, cream, mustard)

Rub a roast of pork with salt and pepper, put it in a roasting pan, place several slices of onion and carrot on the meat, and add a *bouquet garni*. Brown the roast in a 500° oven for 20 minutes, then turn the heat down to 300° and roast until well done: Allow 25 to 30 minutes a pound for roasts with bone, 45 minutes a pound for boned roasts. When it is done, remove the roast to a hot platter, discarding the vegetables, and keep it hot. Skim all the fat from the pan juices, and deglaze the pan with ¾ cup of white wine. Transfer this sauce to a small saucepan, and reduce it over a brisk fire to about half its original quantity. Meanwhile, in a small skillet brown lightly 2 tablespoons of finely minced onion in 1 teaspoon of butter, and add this to the sauce. Add also 1 tablespoon of Dijon mustard blended with 2 tablespoons of heavy cream, and season with salt and pepper if necessary. Heat the sauce, stirring, until it is well blended and smooth, and strain it through a fine sieve. Serve in a sauceboat. A purée of chestnuts is delicious with roast pork.

CANAL AT TANCARVILLE *Normandy*

Grilled Salmon with Anchovy Butter

Saumon Grillé au Beurre d'Anchois

(Salmon steaks, flour, oil, butter, parsley, anchovy paste)

Wipe four ¾-inch-thick salmon slices with a cloth, dip them lightly in flour and then in oil. Place them on a greased grill and broil them, under medium heat, for about 10 minutes on each side. Place the salmon on a hot platter, and put a teaspoon of butter blended with finely chopped parsley on each slice. Decorate the platter with sprigs of parsley, and pass separately a sauce made of 6 tablespoons of melted butter blended with 1 to 2 tablespoons of anchovy paste or to taste. Serves four.

COTTAGE BY THE SEA—PRIMEZ-TRÉGASTEL   *Brittany*

Veal Stew Robinne

Veau à la Robinne

(Veal, butter, flour, onion, herbs, bouillon, tomato sauce, mushrooms)

Melt 2 tablespoons of butter in a heavy pan, and in it brown lightly on all sides 1½ pounds of veal cut in 1½-inch cubes. Add 1 medium onion, finely minced, and 1 tablespoon of minced parsley. When the onions are lightly colored, sprinkle with 1 tablespoon of flour and blend well. Add gradually 2 cups of warm bouillon and water combined, salt and pepper, and a *bouquet garni.* Simmer the veal, covered, over a low fire for 1 hour, then add 1 cup of fresh tomato sauce. (By this time the juices should be somewhat reduced.) Continue simmering for 45 minutes or more, until the veal is tender and the sauce is reduced, well blended, and smooth. Raise the heat and remove the cover during this time if the sauce is still very thin. Add a small can of button mushrooms, drained, shortly before serving. Sprinkle with finely minced parsley and serve with rice, buttered noodles, or steamed potatoes. Serves six.

HALF-TIMBERING IN KAYSERSBERG   *Alsace*

Quail or Partridge on the Spit

Cailles ou Perdreaux à la Broche

(Quail, grape leaves, bacon; or partridge, black olives, pine nuts; croutons)

The classic and proper way to roast quail (or partridge) is one of the simplest and dates from the earliest French cookbooks: Clean and pluck fat little quail, singe them, and truss them. Even if it makes you nervous, you should really leave on the heads and feet. Wrap each one in a grape-vine leaf, then in wide thin strips of bacon so that only the feet show. Tie them, skewer them on a long spit, and roast them, turning often, over a good bed of glowing coals. A rotating electric spit is ideal for this. Remove the wrappings and serve each quail on a slice of French bread fried in butter. Allow 1 or 2 quail per person, depending on their size or the length of the dinner menu.

Partridge may be done almost the same way: Do not use grape leaves, and the heads and feet may be removed; season the cavities of the birds with salt and pepper, fill them with 2 or 3 black olives and a few pine nuts or broken walnut meats, then wrap in bacon and roast as you would the quail.

THE DUCAL PALACE — NEVERS   *Burgundy*

Chicken Breasts with Mushrooms

Suprêmes de Volailles aux Champignons

(Chicken breasts, mushrooms, stock, lemon juice, butter, flour, cream)

Remove the skin from 2 pairs of chicken breasts, split them, remove the bones, and flatten the fillets a little by pounding them gently between sheets of waxed paper. Simmer 8 large mushroom caps in ¼ cup of chicken stock with 2 teaspoons of lemon juice for 5 minutes; drain, and reserve mushrooms and stock. Season the chicken with salt and pepper and a few drops of lemon juice. Melt 4 tablespoons of butter in a skillet and, when it foams, put in the chicken fillets and turn them to coat both sides with butter. Cover the pan, put it on an asbestos mat over a low fire, and poach the fillets for 8 to 10 minutes; they should feel elastic when pressed with your finger, not hard or dry. This way of cooking is called *à blanc* — poached, rather than browned, in the butter. Remove them to a hot platter and cover them. Into the butter remaining in the pan, blend 1 tablespoon of flour, stir in gradually ¼ cup of the reserved mushroom stock and ¾ cup of cream, and taste for seasoning. Simmer the sauce, stirring, for 3 minutes, or until it is smooth and a little thickened. Place 2 mushroom caps on each *suprême*, spoon the sauce over all, and serve at once. Serves four.

331

YACHTS AT CANNES *Riviera*

Devilled Crab

Crabe à la Diable

(Crabmeat, butter, onion, shallot, brandy, mustard, cream, bread crumbs)

In 2 tablespoons of melted butter sauté lightly, over low heat, 1 small onion and 1 shallot, both finely minced, until they are soft and transparent. Stir in 1 teaspoon of brandy and 1 teaspoon of Dijon mustard, and remove from the heat. Make a cream sauce with 2 tablespoons of butter, 2 tablespoons of flour, and 1 cup of thin cream. Season with salt and pepper. Add the cream sauce to the first mixture, and then add 1¼ cups of cooked flaked crabmeat. Mix all together and spoon the mixture into 4 small individual casseroles (or crab or scallop shells, or ramekins). Sprinkle with bread crumbs, dot with butter, and bake in a 350° oven for about 15 minutes, or until the crumbs are delicately browned. Serves four.

AMBOISE *Touraine*

Braised Beef with Brandy

Boeuf Braisé Maîtresse de Maison

(Rump of beef, butter, brandy, onions, bacon, herbs, garlic, mushrooms, olives)

Melt 1 tablespoon of butter in a heavy casserole, and in it brown on all sides a 2½-pound piece of good rump or round of beef for roasting. Brown it slowly so the butter will not burn, add ¼ cup of brandy, cover the casserole, and simmer the beef on a low fire for 30 minutes. Add 6 small whole onions and a good tablespoon of diced bacon. When these have browned, add ½ cup of warm water, a *bouquet garni*, a clove of garlic, and salt and pepper. Cover the pot, and when the juices begin to simmer place it in a 300° oven. Cook the meat for 2½ hours, or until the meat is very tender, turning it over occasionally. Watch the liquid, add a little if necessary, or remove the lid for a while if there is too much. Thirty minutes before the roast is done, add 6 to 8 mushroom caps and a dozen green Italian olives; pit the olives and blanch them briefly in boiling water first. Serves six to eight.

THE LAVOIR — LA TURBIE *Riviera*

Stuffed Mushrooms

Champignons Farcis

(Mushrooms, butter, garlic, parsley, bread crumbs, olive oil)

Wash 1 pound of large fresh mushrooms and drain well. Remove the stems from the caps, slice off the bottom ends, and chop the stems. Sauté them briefly in 2 tablespoons of hot butter. After 2 or 3 minutes, add ½ clove of garlic, chopped and mashed, and salt, pepper, and 1 teaspoon of minced parsley. Cook together for another 2 minutes, remove from the fire, and mix in about 2 tablespoons of seasoned bread crumbs, or enough to make a light stuffing. Fill the mushroom caps with this, and put them in a shallow well-oiled baking dish. Pour 1 teaspoon of olive oil over each mushroom, and bake them in a 375° oven for 10 to 15 minutes or until done but still firm (they should not be overcooked). Serves four as a first-course hors-d'oeuvre, six as a garnish for roast or broiled meats.

ST. NECTAIRE   *Auvergne*

Leek Salad

Poireaux en Salade

(Leeks, vinegar, oil, seasonings, parsley)

Clean a bunch of leeks, cut off most of the green parts, and wash the leeks very thoroughly under cold running water. If they are large, split them lengthwise; each piece should be about the size of a large stalk of asparagus. Tie them into a bundle in two places, put them in boiling salted water, and cook them slowly for 25 minutes, or until they are tender but not limp. Drain them well. Serve them either hot or cold, with a French dressing made of 1 part wine vinegar to 2 or 3 parts olive oil to taste, salt, pepper, a little mustard, and minced parsley. This dish makes an excellent salad course, though the French usually serve it as an hors-d'oeuvre. Serves two.

THE STEPS OF ST. JÉRÔME—DIGNE *Provence*

Celery Provençale

Céleri à la Provençale

(Celery, tomatoes, olive oil, garlic, parsley, anchovies, black olives)

Clean about 6 stalks of celery, cut them into sticks 4 inches long, and split these lengthwise into pencil-size sticks. Drop the celery into boiling salted water, and boil it for 10 minutes, or until it is cooked but still firm. Peel, seed, and cut up 3 large ripe tomatoes. Cook them slowly in 3 tablespoons of olive oil, with a little salt and pepper and a minced clove of garlic. When the tomatoes are reduced to a purée, add 1½ teaspoons of minced parsley and 3 anchovy fillets, cut in small pieces. Stir and cook the mixture a moment longer.

Drain the celery and arrange it in a small serving dish. Pour the tomato purée over it, sprinkle with a little olive oil, and decorate with a few anchovy fillets and small black olives. Chill well before serving. Serves four as a cold luncheon hors-d'oeuvre; or more if you include other things such as sliced salami, radishes and French bread and butter, and quartered hard-boiled eggs with mayonnaise in this course.

CHENONCEAUX   *Touraine*

French Chocolate Bavarian Cream

Bavaroise au Chocolat

(Milk, flour, sugar, eggs, chocolate, cream)

Measure out 1 cup of milk. Blend 2 tablespoons of the milk with 1 teaspoon of flour, and reserve. Beat 4 egg yolks until they are thick and pale, adding the reserved flour mixture and 3 tablespoons of fine granulated sugar. In the top of a double boiler, over hot water, melt 4 ounces of semisweet chocolate in the remainder of the milk, stirring until well blended. Let this cool somewhat, then combine it with the egg-yolk mixture. Return this custard to the top of the double boiler and cook it, still over hot water, stirring constantly, until it thickens. Then pour it immediately into a cold bowl and let it cool. Whip ½ cup of cream, and beat 4 egg whites stiff. Combine the cream and egg whites carefully, and fold this into the chocolate custard. Spoon the cream into 8 custard cups, and chill for at least 6 hours before serving. Serves eight.

VIEW OF SAINTES *Saintonge*

Fresh Fruit Salad

Macédoine de Fruits Rafraîchis

(Peaches, pears, apples, bananas, strawberries, sugar, white wine or kirsch)

In a glass serving bowl arrange layers of fresh fruits, peeled and sliced rather thin, sprinkling each layer with sugar before adding the next. To serve six use 4 peaches, 3 pears, 2 apples, 2 bananas, and a pint of strawberries, or any combination of fruits in season. Pour ¾ cup of white wine over the fruit, and chill it for 2 hours before serving. In place of the sugar and white wine, you may use ¾ cup of cold sugar syrup (made by boiling together equal quantities of sugar and water for 5 minutes) and 1 tablespoon of kirsch.

THE RECONSTRUCTION OF ST. MALO *Brittany*

Cauliflower Gratiné

Chou-fleur Gratiné

(Cauliflower, butter, flour, nutmeg, cream, bread crumbs, cheese)

Trim a medium cauliflower, removing the leaves and heavy part of the stem. Make a cross cut in the stem end (to allow for easier cooking of the base) and soak the cauliflower in salted water for half an hour (to encourage the departure of unwanted guests within!). Then put it in boiling salted water and boil it, uncovered, for about 20 minutes. Test the base with a pointed knife; it must not be overcooked or the flowerets will fall apart. Drain it well, and put it in a round 2-inch-deep baking dish. Cover it with 1½ cups of rich béchamel sauce (below), sprinkle this with 2 tablespoons of fine bread crumbs mixed with 2 tablespoons of grated Swiss or Parmesan cheese, and sprinkle melted butter over all. Bake the cauliflower in a 375° oven for 10 minutes, or until lightly browned.

Béchamel sauce: Melt 2 tablespoons of butter, blend in 3 tablespoons of flour, add salt, pepper, and a dash of nutmeg, and stir in gradually 1½ cups of thin cream or rich milk. Cook the sauce for 3 minutes, stirring with a whisk to keep it smooth. Serves four to six.

TALLOIRES ON THE LAC D'ANNECY   *Savoy*

Braised Salmon Trout

Truite Saumonée Braisée, Sauce Genevoise

(Salmon trout, carrot, onion, parsley, butter, red wine, meat glaze)

Butter an oval baking dish and in it place 1 carrot and 1 onion, both sliced, and a sprig of parsley. On this bed of vegetables place a 2-pound cleaned and dressed salmon trout. Season the trout with salt and pepper and dot it generously with butter. Bake it, uncovered, in a 375° oven until the vegetables are a little browned. Then add 1 cup of red wine and ½ cup of water, lower the heat to 325°, and continue cooking the fish, still uncovered, until done. This will take 30 to 40 minutes cooking time in all. Lift it out with care, place it on a heated platter, and keep it warm.

Strain the juices into a saucepan and reduce them over a brisk fire to about half their original quantity. Blend in ½ teaspoon of meat glaze and 1 tablespoon of butter creamed with 1 teaspoon of flour, stirring briskly with a sauce whisk. Taste the sauce for seasoning. Serve the trout with steamed potatoes and pass the sauce separately. Serves four.

SURF NEAR HENDAYE *Béarn*

Haddock Basque

Haddock à la Basquaise

(Haddock, onions, olive oil, French bread croutons)

Cut 1½ pounds of haddock fillets, whitefish, or other fish of your choice into serving pieces. Chop 2 onions rather fine and cook them slowly in 3 tablespoons of olive oil. When they are soft and pale gold, add ¾ cup of hot water and salt and pepper. Pour onions and liquid into a casserole, and add the fish. Cover the casserole and cook the fish very slowly, over the lowest possible heat for about 30 minutes. Meanwhile, sauté slices of French bread in olive oil until they are golden on both sides. Arrange the croutons on a hot platter, place the slices of fish on them, and pour the onions and juices over all. Serves four.

HARBOR AT LA CIOTAT *Riviera*

Fish Pudding

Pain de Poisson

(Fish, bread crumbs, milk, seasonings, eggs, cream)

Use 1 pound of a delicate white fish, poached, filleted, and skinned, such as flounder or halibut. Put the cooked fish twice through the finest blade of a meat grinder, and work it to a smooth paste in a mortar (or purée it in an electric blender). Remove the crust from 3 slices of bread, break the bread into crumbs, and put them in a saucepan with 1⅓ cups of milk, or enough to soak them well. Cook this mixture, stirring often, for 8 minutes, or until it is thick. You should have a little less than 1 cup of bread paste. Mix it well with the fish, and add salt, pepper, a pinch of cayenne, ½ cup of heavy cream, and 4 beaten egg yolks. Fold in 4 egg whites, stiffly beaten. Pour the mixture into a deep buttered baking dish and cover it with buttered paper. Put the dish in a pan containing about 1 inch of hot water, and bake it in a 350° oven for 35 minutes, or until nearly firm. Serve with a cream sauce made partly with a fish-stock base and enriched with egg yolk, or with a fresh tomato or mushroom sauce. Serves six.

THE LAVOIR—CHARTRES *Orléanais*

Veal Scallops Beauceronne

Escalopes de Veau Beauceronne

(Veal cutlets, butter, Port, cream)

To serve four, buy ¾ pound of thinly sliced veal scallops (cutlets). Pound them even thinner between sheets of waxed paper, and divide them into smaller pieces if they are very large. Salt and pepper the slices, dip them lightly in flour, and brown them on both sides, over a moderate fire, in 2 to 3 tablespoons of hot butter. Remove them to a hot platter. Deglaze the pan with 3 tablespoons of Port, simmer for a few seconds, then stir in ¼ cup of heavy cream and add salt and pepper. Simmer the sauce, stirring, for about a minute, pour it over the veal scallops, and sprinkle with finely minced parsley.

343

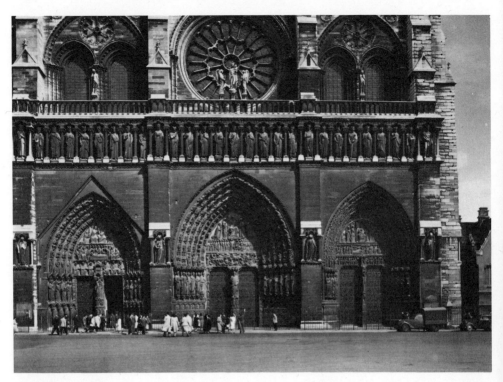

NOTRE DAME *Paris*

Chicken Breasts Supreme

Suprêmes de Volailles

(Chicken breasts, flour, egg, bread crumbs, butter, oil, stock, cream, mushrooms)

Remove the breasts of 2 chickens from the bones and take off the skin. Separate the small fillets from the large ones, and pound them all flat between sheets of waxed paper. Season the fillets with salt and pepper, dip them lightly in flour, then in 1 egg yolk beaten with 1 teaspoon of water, then in fine bread crumbs. Heat together 6 tablespoons each of butter and oil, and brown the chicken breasts in this rather slowly, over moderate heat, for about 3 minutes on each side, or until they are golden brown. Remove the chicken to a platter and keep it warm. Pour the fat in the skillet into a small bowl, wipe the skillet clean, and return to it 2 tablespoons of the clear fat. Blend in 1½ tablespoons of flour and add gradually ¾ cup of chicken stock and ½ cup of cream. Simmer, stirring, until the sauce thickens somewhat. Add a dash of nutmeg, and salt and pepper if necessary. Add a 4-ounce can of button mushrooms, drained. Mix 1 egg yolk with a spoonful of the sauce, add this to the sauce, and reheat it, stirring, without letting it boil. Pass this *sauce suprême* in a sauceboat. Serves four.

POSTWAR LE HAVRE

Normandy

Mushroom Croutons

Croûtes Grandgousier

(Bread, butter, onion, mushrooms, ham, eggs, flour, milk, bread crumbs, Parmesan)

Cut rounds of bread from slices ½ inch thick. These may be small (24 of them) or large (6 of them to serve six), depending on whether you want to serve the *croûtes* with cocktails or as a small luncheon dish. If large, toast them lightly on one side, butter the other side and toast it lightly. If small, toast them on one side only. Cover with the following mixture:

Sauté slowly 1 small onion, chopped, in 2 tablespoons of butter for 3 minutes. Add ¼ pound chopped mushrooms and continue cooking slowly for 5 to 6 minutes. Add 3 tablespoons of ham, minced finely with a knife (not put through a grinder), 2 finely chopped hard-boiled eggs, and salt and pepper to taste. Blend in 1 tablespoon of flour and add gradually ⅜ cup of milk. Heat and stir until thickened. Mound the mixture rather high on the buttered sides of the croutons (on the *un*toasted side if these are cocktail canapés.) Sprinkle with fine bread crumbs, grated Parmesan cheese, and a little melted butter; brown under the broiler and serve hot.

PUISAC, NEAR SOUILLAC *Guyenne*

Potato and Egg Salad

Salade de Pommes de Terre aux Oeufs Durs

(Potatoes, eggs, onions, anchovies, oil, vinegar, parsley)

Boil 1 pound of potatoes in their skins until done but not too soft. Cool, peel, and slice them. Remove the yolks from 4 hard-boiled eggs, and chop the whites rather coarsely. Make a dressing of the yolks creamed with 2 tablespoons of wine vinegar, mixing in afterwards 5 tablespoons of oil, salt and pepper to taste, and 1 teaspoon of minced parsley. To the potatoes add the egg whites, 2 thinly sliced young spring onions, and 2 or 3 anchovy fillets cut in small pieces. Add the dressing and mix all together gently. Serves six as one of several cold luncheon hors-d'oeuvre; three as a salad.

HOTEL IN BESANÇON *Franche-Comté*

Pheasant Champaubert

Faisan à la Champaubert

(Pheasant, pork, chicken liver, herbs, brandy, apple, bacon, meat glaze, Madeira)

Mince ½ pound of cooked fresh pork (lean and fat combined), 1 chicken liver, and the liver of the pheasant. Mix together and add a pinch each of thyme and rosemary, ½ teaspoon of brandy, 1 tart apple, peeled and diced, and salt and pepper. Stuff the bird with this mixture, truss it, and tie 1 or 2 strips of bacon over the breast. Roast the pheasant in a 350° oven for 1 hour or until it is browned and tender, basting often with the pan juices. Remove it to a warm platter and discard the bacon. Deglaze the roasting pan with ½ cup of stock made of ½ teaspoon of meat glaze dissolved in ½ cup of hot water. Pour these juices into a small saucepan and skim the fat from the surface. Add 1 small minced truffle (optional) and 1 teaspoon of Madeira. Reheat the sauce and serve it with the bird. An average-size pheasant serves four.

347

AUXERRE   *Burgundy*

Kidney Parisienne

Rognon Parisienne

(Kidney, white wine, herbs, garlic, butter, mushrooms, flour)

Remove all the fat from 1 beef kidney (or 2 veal kidneys), split it in half, and remove the hard core. Slice the kidney thinly and drop it into boiling salted water. Cover and let stand, off the fire, for 3 minutes. (This removes the strong taste from all kidneys, whether beef, veal, or lamb.) Drain and dry the slices. Simmer together ¾ cup of white wine, ½ teaspoon minced parsley, ½ clove of garlic, 1 bay leaf, and a pinch of thyme. Let this sauce reduce to about ½ cup, then strain it. Sauté the kidney slices and 4 sliced mushrooms in 2 to 3 table-spoons of hot butter for about 2 minutes on each side, or not more than 4 minutes in all. Sprinkle with 1½ teaspoons of flour, add salt and pepper, and stir in the strained white wine. Reheat just until the sauce thickens; do not let the kidneys cook too much or they will toughen. Serves with buttered rice. Serves two or three.

348

TOUR SOLIDOR—ST. SERVAN *Brittany*

Lobster Pilaff Pont-Aven

Pilau de Homard à la Pont-Aven

(Lobster, white wine, herbs, olive oil, onion, rice, tomatoes, saffron, mussels)

Bring 1½ quarts of water and 1 cup of dry white wine to a boil, adding also a slice of onion, a sprig of parsley, salt, freshly ground pepper, a pinch of thyme, and a bay leaf. Plunge a live 1½-pound lobster into the boiling liquid and cook it for 15 minutes. Remove the lobster, cool it, and remove all the meat from the shell and cut it into large dice.

In a casserole sauté 1 medium onion, chopped, in 3 tablespoons of olive oil and 1 tablespoon of butter combined, until it is soft and pale gold. Add 1 cup of raw rice and stir together with a fork until all the grains are coated with oil. Add 1 cup of the hot liquid, strained, in which the lobster was cooked, cover the casserole, and cook the rice over a low fire for 10 to 20 minutes, or until all the liquid is absorbed. Then stir with a fork, add 2 peeled and chopped tomatoes, ¼ teaspoon of saffron dissolved in 2 tablespoons of the lobster stock, and another 2¼ cups of the hot stock. Cover the casserole and cook the pilaff over the lowest possible fire, stirring occasionally, until all the liquid is absorbed and the rice is done. Five minutes before the pilaff is done, add the lobster meat and a dozen steamed mussels or soft-shell clams, removed from their shells. Serves six.

349

PALAIS ROYAL *Paris*

Sliced Egg Canapés

Canapés aux Oeufs Durs

(Hard-boiled eggs, bread, Anchovy Butter, mayonnaise, parsley)

Spread rounds of thinly sliced bread or toast evenly with Anchovy Butter (see Classic Flavored Butters in the *Index*). Place a center slice of hard-boiled egg on each, then a small dab of mayonnaise on the egg, and a tiny sprig of parsley on the mayonnaise.

CHAPEL OF ST. HERBOT

Brittany

Creamed Crabmeat Omelette

Omelette au Crabe à la Crème

(Eggs, butter, crabmeat, cream, Madeira)

Beat together lightly with a fork 6 eggs, 1 tablespoon of cold water, and a pinch each of salt and pepper. Heat the omelette pan, put in 1½ tablespoons of butter, and when the bubbles have subsided but before the butter browns, pour in the eggs. When the omelette is done but still creamy, spread the following filling across the center: In 2 tablespoons of butter gently heat ¾ cup of cooked and flaked crabmeat. Add a pinch of salt and a few grains of cayenne pepper. Blend in 1 teaspoon of flour, then stir in 3 tablespoons of heavy cream and 1 tablespoon of Madeira (or sherry). Simmer the mixture, stirring, for 1 minute. Fold the omelette out on a platter, and serve at once. Serves four.

EGLISE ST. MICHEL—BORDEAUX

Braised Guinea Hen

Pintade de Blanchamp

(Guinea hen, carrot, onion, bacon, herbs, orange liqueur, mushrooms, garlic)

In a heavy skillet, brown a trussed guinea hen on all sides in 1 tablespoon of hot butter. In a casserole of suitable size for the bird, melt another tablespoon of butter and in it sauté slowly half a carrot, sliced, 1 medium onion, chopped, and 1 tablespoon of diced bacon; add salt, pepper, and a *bouquet garni*. When the vegetables are lightly browned, put in the guinea hen, pour over it 2 tablespoons of orange liqueur (such as orange curaçao, Grand Marnier, or Cointreau), and set it aflame. Add 1 cup of hot stock, made ahead by boiling together the wing tips, neck, and giblets, with a slice of onion, a *bouquet garni,* and salt and pepper. Cover the casserole and cook the bird in a 350° oven for about 1 hour, or until done; remove the lid of the casserole for the last 10 minutes of cooking to brown the hen. Place the bird on a hot platter and keep it warm. Skim the fat from the juices, strain them through a fine sieve and force the vegetables through also (or blend together in an electric blender). Add 1 teaspoon of cornstarch first dissolved in a little cold stock. Reheat the sauce, stirring, until it thickens, and stir in 2 teaspoons of orange liqueur.

With the hen, serve sliced mushrooms sautéed briefly in hot olive oil with a little minced garlic; add salt, pepper, and minced parsley before serving. Pass the sauce separately. Serves four.

CHÂTEAU DE GROS BOIS   *Ile-de-France*

Roast Pork with Prunes

Rôti de Porc aux Pruneaux

(Roast of pork, prunes, butter, white wine)

Choose a cut of pork for roasting that may be boned and rolled. It should weigh 2 to 2¼ pounds when boned. Place a row of pitted dried prunes across the center of the meat, and roll and tie it. In an iron pot, brown the roast on all sides in 1 tablespoon of hot butter. Cover the pot and cook the pork over moderate heat for 30 minutes. Then add 15 prunes, not pitted, salt and pepper, and ¾ cup of white wine. Cover, and cook the meat for another 50 minutes, watching the level of the liquid. If necessary add a little hot water or stock from time to time; or remove the cover and turn up the heat a little if the juice is too plentiful. When it is done, remove the meat, which will have lost its brown surface, wipe it, and brown it again briefly on all sides in a little butter in a frying pan. Serve surrounded with the prunes. Skim the excess fat from the sauce and serve it in a sauceboat. Serves six to eight.

353

THE RIVER AT ESPALION   *Guyenne*

Ham Canapés

Canapés Bayonnaise

(Ham, white bread, Mustard Butter, parsley)

Spread small squares of thinly sliced white bread or toast evenly with Mustard Butter (see Classic Flavored Butters in the *Index*). Top with squares of thinly sliced ham or *prosciutto* cut to identical size, and garnish each canapé with a tiny sprig of parsley.

FARMHOUSE NEAR LISIEUX

Chicken Normandy

Poulet Sauté à la Normande

(Chicken, butter, mushrooms, truffles, Madeira, brandy, cream, potato starch)

Have a 2½- to 3-pound chicken cut in serving pieces. Wipe them dry and brown them a little on all sides in 3 tablespoons of butter, heated but not browned, in a casserole. Season them with salt and pepper, cover the casserole, and place it in a 325° oven. Cook the chicken for 30 minutes, or until it is about three quarters done. Add ½ pound of sliced mushrooms, and cook for another 10 or 15 minutes, until the mushrooms are softened and most of their liquid has evaporated. Then add 1 or 2 thinly sliced canned truffles, with a little of the Madeira in which they are preserved; if you have no truffles, add 1 tablespoon of Madeira. Then pour on 2 tablespoons of warmed brandy and flame it. Add ½ cup of heavy cream and more salt if needed, simmer briefly, and stir in 1 tablespoon of butter blended with ½ teaspoon of potato starch. Simmer, stirring, until the sauce thickens slightly. Serves four.

FISHING FLEET—LES SABLES-D'OLONNE   *Poitou*

Baked Fish Steaks

Tranches de Colin sur le Plat

(Codfish steaks, white wine, lemon juice, butter)

Use about 1½ pounds of young cod steaks, sea perch, or similar fish of your
choice to serve four. Butter a shallow baking dish generously and arrange the
slices of fish in it. Pour a tablespoon of dry white wine over each slice, season
them with salt and pepper, add a few drops of lemon juice, and dot them generously with butter. Bake the fish in a 350° oven for 15 minutes, or until the fish
flakes easily at the touch of a fork and is somewhat glazed. Baste often, and add
a little hot water to the dish if it dries out before the fish is done. Serve in the
baking dish.

THE VIADUCT—MORLAIX *Brittany*

Fish Roes on Toast

Croûtes aux Laitances

(Fish roes, white wine, bread, butter, lemon)

Remove the crusts from ½-inch-thick slices of white bread. Fry the bread in plenty of hot butter until golden brown on both sides. Poach the roes of carp, haddock, or shad very gently in dry white wine until they are just firm. Place them on the fried croutons, season with a little salt, paprika, and lemon juice, and pour melted butter over all.

FERME DES ROCHES — BIEVILLE-EN-AUGE   *Normandy*

Baked Trout with Cream

Truites Cauchoise

(Butter, shallots, herbs, butter, white wine, cream, lemon juice)

Butter a shallow baking dish, sprinkle 2 chopped shallots over the bottom, and on these place 2 good-sized fresh trout. Season with salt and pepper, a pinch of thyme, and a bay leaf, and pour 2 tablespoons of melted butter over them. Bake them in a 375° oven for 20 to 30 minutes, depending on their size. Baste them several times with the butter in the dish. Remove them carefully to a hot platter. Deglaze the dish with 3 tablespoons of white wine and ¼ cup of heavy cream. Pour this sauce through a strainer into a small saucepan and boil it for a few minutes to reduce it a little. Add salt and pepper, if needed, and a few drops of lemon juice. Pour the sauce over the fish and serve at once. Serves two.

CHÂTEAU DE BUSSY-RABUTIN   *Burgundy*

Broiled Chicken Languedoc
Poulet Grillé à la Languedocienne
(Chicken, butter or oil, bread crumbs, ham, parsley, garlic)

Have a young chicken split for broiling, season it with salt and pepper, brush it well with melted butter or oil, and broil it under a moderately hot broiler for 10 to 12 minutes on each side, or until it is almost done. Combine ½ cup of dry bread crumbs, 1 tablespoon of finely shredded ham, 1 teaspoon of finely minced parsley, and about ¼ clove of garlic, chopped and mashed. Coat the chicken well on both sides with the bread-crumb mixture, sprinkle it with a little more melted butter or oil, and broil it again until it is well browned on both sides. Serve with mushrooms sautéed in oil, fried eggplant, and tomato sauce served from a sauceboat. The mushrooms used in France for this dish are *cèpes*, available in cans in this country. Serves four.

359

PLACE DE LA CONCORDE   *Paris*

Eggs and Artichokes Fine Bouche

Oeufs Mollets Fine Bouche

(Artichoke bases, foie gras or liver pâté, eggs, ham, aspic, Madeira)

Cook briefly in butter 4 canned or freshly boiled artichoke bases. Season with a pinch each of salt and pepper. Cool them and fill them with purée of *foie gras* or a good liver pâté mixed with a little cream. Boil 4 eggs for 6 minutes, cover them at once with cold water, and peel off the shells, being careful not to break the whites. Place an egg on each artichoke base, and on each egg place a thin circle of boiled ham or tongue.

Soak 1 teaspoon of gelatine in 2 tablespoons of cold water. Heat a can of clear jellied consommé, stir in the gelatine, and when it has dissolved add 1 tablespoon of Madeira or sherry. Cool this aspic in the refrigerator. When it just begins to thicken, spoon a little over and around each egg. Cool in the refrigerator until the aspic is set, and repeat the process until you have a good coating over each serving. Or, if you have small molds of suitable size, arrange the artichoke bases and eggs in these, and fill them with the cooled but not yet set aspic. Chill, unmold just before serving, and serve egg side up. Serves four.

RESTAURANT LA PETITE CHAISE   *Paris*

Veal Patties

Fricadelles de Veau

(Veal, sausage meat, bread crumbs, onions, butter, herbs, nutmeg, egg, stock)

Grind together 1 pound of lean veal, free of all tendons and gristle, and ¼ pound of sausage meat (or ¼ pound of fresh pork which includes a little fat). Combine the meats with: 1 cup of fresh bread crumbs, first soaked in milk and squeezed almost dry; 2 small onions, finely minced and cooked slowly in 2 tablespoons of butter until soft; and 1 tablespoon of minced parsley, a pinch of thyme, a dash of nutmeg, salt and pepper, and 1 beaten egg. Mix thoroughly together and form into 6 half-inch-thick patties. Heat together 2 tablespoons of butter and 1 tablespoon of oil, and in this brown the patties for 2 minutes on each side over moderately high heat. Then lower the heat, cook the patties for about 10 minutes, and remove them to a hot platter. Add ½ cup of good rich stock to the pan and boil it down to about ¼ cup, stirring in all the brown juices. Off the fire add bit by bit 1 tablespoon of softened butter, blending it into the sauce by rotating the pan horizontally. Spoon a little of this over each patty. Good accompaniments are creamed spinach purée and broiled tomatoes. Serves six.

THE HARBOR AT ST. TROPEZ

Riviera

Braised Veal Roast

Rôti de Veau en Cocotte

(Veal roast, bouquet garni, stock, onions, carrots)

Have a piece of rump or loin of veal, weighing 1½ pounds without bone, tied to form a small roast. In an iron or enameled casserole brown it slowly and well on all sides in 1 tablespoon each of butter and oil, together with 1 small onion. Add salt, pepper, a *bouquet garni,* and ¼ cup of hot stock or water. Cover the casserole and let the veal cook over a very low fire for 45 minutes. Then add 2 carrots, cut in large pieces, and 4 small white onions. Cook the veal for another hour, or until it is tender; turn it from time to time and add a little hot water or stock if needed to prevent scorching or sticking. The juices should be rich and brown and not too plentiful. Serves four.

THE LOIRE AT GIEN

Orléanais

Broiled Shad with Sorrel

Alose à l'Oseille

(Shad, herbs, lemon juice, oil, butter, Braised Sorrel)

Place a 1½-pound piece of shad in an oiled dish, and add salt and pepper, a sprig of parsley, 1 bay leaf, a pinch of thyme, and the juice of 1 lemon. Pour a little salad oil over all and let the fish marinate for an hour. Remove the parsley and bay leaf, transfer the shad to a broiling pan, and dot it with butter. Broil it under high heat for 12 to 15 minutes, basting it with the marinade. When it is done and golden brown, serve it with Braised Sorrel (see *Index*), which is the classic accompaniment. Serves four.

ROMAN ARCHES — AUTUN   *Burgundy*

French Chicken Fricassee

Fricassée de Poulet Ménagère

(Chicken, butter, white wine, herbs, onions, flour, mushrooms, egg yolks)

Have a 3- to 4-pound roasting chicken cut in serving pieces. Put them in a casserole with 1½ tablespoons of butter and ½ cup of dry white wine. Cover it tightly and simmer the chicken over very low heat until the liquid has almost all evaporated. Then add 3½ cups of boiling water, salt and pepper, a *bouquet garni* (a sprig of thyme, parsley, and a bay leaf, tied together), and 6 or 8 small white onions first parboiled for 10 minutes in boiling salted water. Boil everything together for 10 minutes, then add a mixture of 3 tablespoons of flour and ¼ cup of cold water blended together until perfectly smooth. Cover the casserole partially, leaving a small space for escaping steam, and simmer the chicken over low heat for 30 to 40 minutes, or until it is very tender; add a little more boiling water if needed. Five minutes before the chicken is done, add the caps of ½ pound of mushrooms first sautéed for 5 minutes in 2 tablespoons of butter. Just before serving, remove the *bouquet garni* and finish the sauce: Beat 3 egg yolks, stir in 3 tablespoons of the liquid from the casserole, and return the mixture to the casserole, stirring well. Reheat without boiling, and stir in 1 tablespoon of minced parsley. Serve with buttered rice, or noodles, or boiled potatoes. Serves four to six.

PORTAL OF THE CATHEDRAL — LE MANS   *Maine*

Beef and Chicken Stockpot

Petite Marmite

(Beef, fowl, ox tail, stock, carrots, turnips, celery, leeks, onion, herbs)

In France, this famous dish, which is a soup and main dish in one, is served directly from the earthen soup pot (*marmite*) in which it is cooked:

In a soup pot put a 2-pound piece of chuck beef, a small boiling fowl, and 1 pound of ox tail. Add 3 pints of stock and 1 quart of water, or enough liquid to cover the meats. Heat slowly, skimming well. When it begins to simmer, add: 3 medium carrots, cut in pieces; 2 small white turnips, quartered; 2 leeks, white parts only, cut in large pieces; 1 stalk of celery, cut in pieces; and 1 onion, stuck with 2 cloves. Add a *bouquet garni* tied in cheesecloth and salt and pepper, cover the pot, and simmer the soup very slowly, skimming often. (Fast boiling produces a cloudy consommé.) The meats should be tender in 3 to 3½ hours; if the chicken is done before the beef, remove it and reheat it in the pot at the end.

When the *marmite* is done, remove the *bouquet garni,* let the soup stand a moment until the fat rises, and skim. For each large hot soup plate have ready 2 thin slices of French bread well dried out in the oven; sprinkle them with grated Swiss cheese. Over them place 2 thin slices of the beef, bits of ox tail, a slice of chicken, and a few assorted vegetables. Ladle the consommé over all generously. Serves eight.

FLEURY-EN-BIÈRE   *Ile-de-France*

Cold Lemon Soufflé

Soufflé Froid au Citron

(Eggs, sugar, lemons, currant jelly)

Separate 6 eggs. Beat the whites until stiff but not dry. In the top of a double boiler beat the yolks well with ¾ cup of fine granulated sugar, and stir in the juice of 2 lemons. Heat this over simmering water, stirring constantly with a whisk, until it thickens. Remove it from the heat, let it cool slightly, and fold in the beaten whites. Pour the mixture into a serving bowl and chill it. Beat a small jar of red currant jelly with a fork until it is fairly smooth and drop it in a decorative pattern on the soufflé. Serves six.

ANTIBES   *Riviera*

Broiled Marinated Quail

Cailles Grillées

(Quail, herbs, spices, onion, lemon, oil, bread crumbs, butter, croutons)

Clean and singe 6 quail and split them down the backs; press lightly to spread them flat. Marinate them for 6 hours with a little salt and pepper, a tiny pinch each of powdered ginger and clove, 1 crumbled bay leaf, a sprig of parsley, a pinch of thyme, 1 slice of onion separated into rings, the juice of 1 lemon, and ¼ cup of oil.

Drain the marinade from the quail but do not dry them. Dip them in dry bread crumbs seasoned with salt and pepper, and sprinkle them with a mixture of 2 tablespoons of melted butter and 1 tablespoon of oil. Broil them on each side under a moderately hot broiler, basting them several times with the pan juices; eight to 10 minutes in all should be enough. Serve the quail on bread croutons fried in butter. Serves three or six, depending on the size of the quail and the size of the dinner.

BOULES GAME AT VERNEUIL

Chicken in Casserole Bonne Femme

Poulet en Cocotte Bonne Femme

(Chicken, sausage meat, bread crumbs, herbs, bacon, onions, potatoes)

Rub the cavity of a 4-pound chicken with salt and pepper. In a frying pan, heat ¼ pound of sausage meat to render some of the fat and pour this off. Combine the sausage meat, the chopped liver of the bird, 2 or 3 tablespoons of coarse stale bread crumbs, and 1 teaspoon of minced parsley. Stuff the bird with this, truss it, and tie a strip of bacon over the breast. In a heavy (enameled iron) oval casserole in which the chicken will fit comfortably, heat 3 tablespoons of butter and 1 tablespoon of oil. Brown the bird in this on all sides, over moderate heat, being careful not to let the butter burn. In about 15 minutes, add 8 small peeled white onions and continue cooking the bird, still over moderate heat. When it is half cooked, or in about 30 minutes, surround the chicken with 1½ cups of potatoes cut in ½-inch dice and 1 slice of bacon cut in squares. Stir the potatoes to coat them with the fat, and add a *bouquet garni.* Cover the casserole with a piece of parchment paper or foil, put on the lid, and put the casserole in a 300° oven to finish cooking, which will take about 45 minutes. Remove the *bouquet garni.* Serves four.

CHÂTEAU DE TALMAY · *Burgundy*

Baked Vanilla Custards

Petits Pots de Crème à la Vanille

(Milk, sugar, vanilla bean, eggs)

In a saucepan combine 2¼ cups of rich milk, ½ cup plus 2 tablespoons of fine granulated sugar, and a vanilla bean. Bring to the boiling point and stir until the sugar is dissolved. Let the milk cool and remove the vanilla bean. Beat together 4 egg yolks and 1 whole egg until light, and gradually add the milk to the eggs, stirring well with a whisk (but do not beat to a froth). Add a small pinch of salt. Line a sieve with two thicknesses of cheesecloth and pour the custard through it. Fill *petits pots*, ramekins, or custard cups carefully and completely with the custard. Place them in a broad pan or roasting pan with a lid, and pour boiling water into the pan to two thirds the depth of the custard cups. Cover the pan and place it in a preheated 325° oven for about 20 minutes; do not let the water boil again and do not overcook the custards. They are done when a knife inserted in the center comes out clean. Cool the custards before serving. Makes about six *petits pots*.

RAMPARTS OF AVIGNON

Provence

Ham in Cream with Mushrooms

Jambon à la Crème

(Ham, white wine, mushrooms, butter, cream, tomato paste, Port, brandy)

Heat four ¼-inch-thick slices of cooked ham in ¼ cup of white wine until almost all the wine has evaporated. Sauté ⅛ pound of sliced mushrooms in 2 teaspoons of hot butter for 5 minutes. Measure out 1 cup of cream. Blend ½ teaspoon of potato starch with 1 tablespoon of the cream until perfectly smooth. Stir in the rest of the cream, 1 teaspoon of tomato paste, 1 teaspoon of Port, ¼ teaspoon of brandy, and salt and pepper. Add the mushrooms, heat, and simmer together for about 2 minutes. Put the ham on a hot platter and spoon this rose-colored sauce over it. Serves four.

CHÂTEAU DE VALENÇAY   *Touraine*

Veal Kidneys Bordelaise

Rognons de Veau à la Bordelaise

(Veal kidneys, shallots, herbs, red wine, mushrooms, butter, tomato paste, stock)

Remove the fat and membranes from 3 veal kidneys, split them, remove the hard fiber at the core, and rinse them well under cold running water. Cut them into ½- to ¾-inch cubes, drop these into boiling water, and let them stand, off the fire, for 2 minutes. Drain and dry them.

Make a Bordelaise sauce as follows: In a saucepan combine 2 chopped shallots, a good pinch each of thyme and marjoram, 1 bay leaf, a pinched each of salt and pepper, and 1 cup of red wine. Simmer the mixture, covered, over a low fire until it is reduced by one half. Meanwhile, sauté ¼ pound of mushrooms, sliced, in 1½ tablespoons of butter for 5 minutes, and reserve them. Combine 1 teaspoon of potato starch, 2 teaspoons of tomato paste, and ¾ cup of stock, and blend until smooth. Strain the reduced red wine, add it to the stock mixture, and simmer this sauce again until it is reduced to a little over 1 cup.

Over a brisk fire, sauté the kidneys for 2 to 3 minutes in 3 tablespoons of hot butter. Add them and the mushrooms to the Bordelaise sauce, and reheat all together without boiling. Pour into a hot serving dish, sprinkle with minced parsley, and serve with fluffy boiled rice. Serves four.

371

FORT ST. ANDRÉ — VILLENEUVE-LES-AVIGNON   *Provence*

Celery Hearts à la Grecque

Céleris à la Grecque

(Celery hearts, olive oil, lemon juice, seasonings, spices, herbs)

Cut 2 celery hearts in quarters lengthwise and trim them evenly. Drop them into boiling salted water to which you have added a tablespoon of vinegar or lemon juice, and parboil them for 4 minutes; drain and cool them. Meanwhile, in an enamel saucepan, combine 1½ cups of water, ¼ cup of olive oil, the juice of 2 lemons, salt to taste, a few whole peppercorns and coriander seeds, a pinch each of fennel seeds, celery seeds, and thyme, and a bay leaf. Bring the mixture to a boil and add the celery. Cover the saucepan and simmer the celery for about half an hour, or until it is tender but not too soft; cool it in the liquid. Drain the pieces and arrange them nicely on an hors-d'oeuvre dish of suitable shape and depth. Spoon some of the cooking liquid over them. Serve chilled with assorted hors-d'oeuvre.

EGLISE NOTRE DAME LA GRANDE—POITIERS *Poitou*

Chicken Livers en Brochette

Brochettes de Foies de Volailles

(Chicken livers, mushrooms, bacon, butter, bread crumbs, shallot, wine, stock, herbs)

Cut a dozen chicken livers in halves, remove the stringy parts, and season the livers with salt and pepper. Sauté them for about a minute in 2 tablespoons of hot butter, turning each piece once. Remove them to a dish and sprinkle them with minced parsley. Cook about 20 small mushrooms (or 10 large ones cut in halves horizontally) in ½ cup of water with a few drops of lemon juice for 3 or 4 minutes. Cut bacon strips into about 20 squares. Thread the chicken livers on 4 small skewers, interspersed with the mushrooms and pieces of bacon. Sprinkle the filled skewers with melted butter and roll them in fine bread crumbs. Broil them under moderate heat, turning them to brown lightly on all sides. Serve with the following sauce.

Sauce Diable: In the butter left in the pan in which the chicken livers were cooked, sauté 1 chopped shallot slowly for 2 minutes without browning it. Stir in ½ cup of white wine and boil it to reduce it by about half. Add ¼ teaspoon of meat glaze dissolved in ½ cup of good hot stock, and season with freshly ground pepper. Simmer the sauce to reduce it again by about half, and strain it. Just before serving, add 2 teaspoons of combined minced parsley and tarragon and stir in, off the fire, 2 teaspoons of soft butter. Serves four.

RIQUEWIHR *Alsace*

Veal Chops in Cream

Côtes de Veau Flambées à la Crème

(Veal chops, butter, oil, brandy, white wine, potato starch, cream)

For 4 veal chops in a heavy skillet heat together 1½ tablespoons of butter and 1 tablespoon of oil. Wipe the chops dry and brown them in the fat, over a brisk fire, for about 3 minutes on each side; be careful not to burn the fat. Season the chops with salt and pepper, cover the skillet, lower the heat, and continue cooking for 15 minutes, or until tender. Then pour 2 tablespoons of warmed brandy over the chops, set it ablaze, and shake the pan back and forth until the flame dies. Remove the chops to a hot serving dish and keep them warm. Add 1 tablespoon of white wine to the pan and stir in all the brown juices. (If the fat has burned, pour it off and melt 1 tablespoon of fresh butter in the pan.) Blend 1 teaspoon of potato starch with 1 tablespoon of cold water, and stir in 1 cup of heavy cream. Add this to the pan, season the sauce, simmer it, stirring, until it is slightly thickened, and pour it over the chops. Serves four.

CALVAIRE AT ST. THÉGONNEC *Brittany*

Beef Consommé

Consommé Simple

(Shin of beef, beef liver, onion, carrot, turnip, celery, leek, herbs)

In a large soup kettle put a section of shin of beef with at least 2 pounds of meat on the bone and a ½-pound piece of beef liver. Add 4 quarts of water, bring it gradually to a boil, and skim well. Lower the heat to keep the liquid at the lowest possible simmer, and continue skimming until no more scum rises. Then add 1 large yellow onion, unpeeled and stuck with 1 clove; 1 carrot, well-scrubbed; 1 white turnip, peeled; ½ stalk of celery with its leaves; and 1 well-cleaned leek with most of the green cut off. Add also 1 large sprig of parsley, 2 bay leaves, ¼ teaspoon of thyme, 6 peppercorns, and ¾ tablespoon of salt. Cover the kettle partially, leaving a small space for steam to escape, and simmer the consommé very, very slowly for about 5 hours; boiling makes it cloudy. Strain it through a sieve lined with a damp cloth. You will have about 3 quarts.

Skim the fat from the surface before serving; or cool the consommé, chill it in the refrigerator, and then remove the hardened fat. If a stronger flavor is desired, simmer the strained consommé again before serving. Never cover it completely while it is hot or it may spoil. If it is to be kept for some time in the refrigerator, reheat it to the boiling point every three days.

THE TOWN OF GRASSE *Provence*

Sautéed Chicken Provençal, Peasant Style
Poulet Sauté à la Paysanne Provençale
(Chicken, olive oil, onion, white wine, tomatoes, garlic, parsley, black olives)

Have a 4-pound chicken cut in serving pieces, wipe them dry, season them with salt and pepper, and dip them lightly in flour. In a broad sauté or frying pan brown them on all sides in 4 tablespoons of hot olive oil. Add 1 tablespoon of finely chopped onion and let it cook slowly until it is golden. Add ½ cup of dry white wine and cook until this is reduced by about half. Then add 4 medium-size tomatoes, peeled, seeded, and coarsely chopped, 1 small clove of garlic, chopped and mashed, and 1 teaspoon of finely minced parsley. Cover the pan and cook the chicken slowly for 15 to 20 minutes. Five minutes before it is done, add a dozen pitted black Italian olives. Serve with steamed potatoes. Serves four.

CHÂTEAU DE FUMICHON   *Normandy*

Escoffier's Chicken Sauté Normandy

Poulet Sauté à la Normande

(Chicken, mushrooms, onion, brandy, cream, meat glaze)

Have a 4-pound chicken cut into serving pieces, wipe them dry, and season them with salt and pepper. In a broad sauté or frying pan, heat together 2 tablespoons of butter and 1 tablespoon of oil. Sauté the chicken slowly in this, over moderate heat. After about 10 minutes, when the chicken is browned on all sides, add ½ pound of quartered mushrooms, first cooked in butter for about 5 minutes, and a generous tablespoon of chopped onion. Continue cooking the chicken slowly, without letting the onion burn, for about 15 minutes, or until the pieces of white meat are done. Remove these to a dish and cook the dark meat for another 5 minutes. Return the white meat to the pan, add 2 tablespoons of apple brandy (or good French brandy), and cook until it has almost completely evaporated. Then add ¾ cup of heavy cream and 3 tablespoons of hot stock (or hot water in which ½ teaspoon of meat glaze has been dissolved). Taste the sauce for seasoning and simmer all together for 2 minutes. If you like a thicker sauce, blend 1 teaspoon of potato starch into the cream before adding it. Serve the chicken in a deep hot dish with the mushrooms and sauce poured over it. Serves four.

CHÂTEAU DE ROCHERS *Brittany*

Cream-Puff Paste

Pâte à Chou

(Butter, water, salt, flour, eggs, flavoring)

The beauty of cream puffs is that, once baked (see *Narcisses* in the *Index*), they will freeze beautifully and can therefore be made far in advance.

In a heavy saucepan heat ¼ pound of unsalted butter, cut in pieces, together with 1 cup of water and a pinch of salt. When the mixture boils, take the pan off the fire, add 1 cup of sifted flour, and stir hard with a wooden spoon to blend well. Return the pan to a moderately high heat, and stir hard again until the paste forms a single mass and comes away from the sides of the pan; this will take about 1½ minutes. Then, off the fire, beat in 4 large eggs, one at a time, blending each one in well before adding the next. Add a few drops of orange flower water or vanilla extract. Use this paste, still warm, in a pastry bag, to make small or large cream puffs, éclairs and other pastries, and tiny hors-d'oeuvre puffs.

378

CITY HALL—LA CHARITÉ-SUR-LOIRE   *Nivernais*

Marinated Carrots

Carottes Marinées

(Carrots, white wine, herbs, seasonings, garlic, oil)

Scrape 6 to 8 young carrots (about 1 lb.) and cut them in quarters lengthwise. In a saucepan combine ¾ cup of dry white wine, 1 cup of water, and a *bouquet garni* composed of parsley, bay leaf, thyme, and a sprig or two of tarragon or chervil, all tied together. Add salt and pepper, 2 teaspoons of sugar, 1 crushed clove of garlic, and 5 tablespoons of olive oil. Bring the marinade to a boil and simmer it for 5 minutes. Add the carrots and boil them until almost done but still quite firm; cool them in the liquid. Arrange them prettily in a dish of suitable size and spoon some of the liquid over them. Chill them briefly in the refrigerator, and sprinkle them with finely chopped parsley before serving. Serve as one of a number of assorted hors-d'oeuvre.

379

VILLAGE SQUARE — SARE

Fresh Tomato Soup

Soupe à la Tomate

(Onion, carrot, butter, flour, tomatoes, parsley, sugar, rice)

Melt 2 tablespoons of butter in a large saucepan, add 1 onion and 1 small carrot, both sliced, and cook them together slowly without browning until the onion is soft. Stir in 2 tablespoons of flour and blend well. Add 3 large ripe tomatoes, coarsely cut, stir, and add 2½ cups of hot water, a sprig of parsley, salt, pepper, and 2 lumps of sugar. Bring the soup to a boil, cover, and simmer it for 45 minutes. Force it through a strainer fine enough to catch the tomato seeds. Return the soup to the stove, add a little chicken stock or water if it is too thick, and add ¼ cup of cooked rice and a lump of butter. Serves four.

THE TUILERIES   *Paris*

Mushroom Omelette Mornay

Omelette Richemonde

(Eggs, mushrooms, butter, chicken-stock base, sherry, cream, onion, cheese)

Sauté ¾ pound of sliced mushrooms in 2 tablespoons of hot butter for 5 minutes, or until the juice has almost evaporated. Season with salt and pepper, and blend in ¾ teaspoon of flour and ½ teaspoon of powdered chicken-stock base (or 2 teaspoons of brown juices from a roast chicken). Stir in gradually 1 tablespoon of sherry and ¼ cup of cream, simmer until the sauce thickens, and reserve.

Make a Mornay sauce: Over moderate heat blend 1½ teaspoons of flour into 1 tablespoon of melted butter, and add salt and pepper, a dash of nutmeg, and a slice of onion. Stir in gradually ½ cup of cream, or milk, simmer briefly, cover and reserve. Just before making the omelette, remove the onion from the sauce, add 2 tablespoons of grated American Cheddar cheese, and reheat, stirring, just long enough to melt the cheese. Make a 5- or 6-egg omelette, spoon the mushrooms into the center, and fold it out onto an oval heatproof dish. Spoon the Mornay sauce over the omelette, sprinkle with grated cheese and a little melted butter, and glaze briefly under a hot broiler. Serves three.

ANNECY   *Savoy*

Leek and Potato Soup Bonne Femme

Potage à la Bonne Femme

(Leeks, onion, butter, stock, potatoes, chervil, croutons)

Clean thoroughly 4 medium-size leeks and slice the white parts thinly; peel 1 onion and slice it thinly. Melt 3 tablespoons of butter in a soup kettle or a large saucepan, add the leeks and onion, and cook them slowly over a low fire until they are well softened but not brown. Add 1¾ quarts (7 cups) of hot chicken or beef stock, and salt and freshly ground pepper if needed, and bring the soup to a boil. Cover it, lower the heat, and allow it to simmer. Now peel and slice thinly 4 medium-size potatoes. Add these to the soup, cover again, and let the soup simmer until the potatoes are very tender. Taste for seasoning. Just before serving, remove the soup from the fire and stir in 2 tablespoons of butter divided into small pieces. Add 1 tablespoon of finely minced chervil, and sprinkle each serving with bread croutons fried in butter. Serves eight.

PASTORALE—PASSY   *Nivernais*

Farmer's Vegetable Soup

Potage Cultivateur

(Carrots, white turnips, leek, onion, stock, potatoes, bacon or salt pork)

Clean and cut in fairly large dice or slices 3 medium-size carrots, 2 small white turnips, the white part of 1 medium-size leek, and 1 small onion. Sauté the vegetables very slowly in 4 tablespoons of butter, adding salt and a good pinch of sugar. When the vegetables are a little softened and pale gold, add 6 to 7 cups of light stock (beef or chicken). Cover the soup and simmer it for 1¼ hours. Twenty-five minutes before it is done, add 2 medium-size potatoes, peeled and diced, and ½ cup of diced bacon or lean salt pork which has first been parboiled for 3 or 4 minutes in unsalted water. Serves six.

383

FORTRESS AT SOCOA

Pyrenees

Pineapple with Rum

Ananas au Rhum

Pour 6 tablespoons of rum over 6 large slices of fresh pineapple, sprinkle them with sugar, and let them marinate for several hours. In the top of a double boiler heat together ¼ pound of unsalted butter and 3 tablespoons of fine granulated sugar. When the butter is almost melted (do not let it cook), add 3 tablespoons of rum and stir in 3 beaten egg yolks. With a whisk beat the mixture over hot water just until it thickens. Place the pineapple slices on individual dessert plates, pour the hot custard over them, sprinkle with toasted slivered almonds, and serve at once. Serves six.

CHALONS-SUR-MARNE   *Champagne*

Cream of Spinach Soup

Potage Crème d'Epinards

(Spinach, butter, flour, milk, cream)

Wash 2 pounds of spinach and remove the stems. Drop the leaves into boiling water, boil them for 30 seconds, and drain them thoroughly. Then cook the spinach, covered, with 1 tablespoon of butter for 5 minutes, and purée it in an electric blender.

Make a cream-sauce soup base (béchamel): Blend 2½ tablespoons of flour into 2½ tablespoons of melted butter and add gradually 4 cups of hot milk; season with salt, pepper, and nutmeg. Simmer the béchamel for 5 or 6 minutes, stirring constantly with a whisk. Add the puréed spinach, reheat the soup, taste it for seasoning and, just before serving, add ⅓ cup of heavy cream. Serves six.

CHÂTEAU DE CHASSELAS, NEAR MACON   *Burgundy*

Veal Kidneys Dijon Style

Rognons de Veau en Casserole Dijonnaise

(Veal kidneys, herbs, spices, lemon juice, cream, mustard, mushrooms)

Clean 5 small veal kidneys, removing fat and skin and most of the hard core. Wash them well under running water and dry them on paper towels. Season them with salt, pepper, a pinch of thyme, and a dash of nutmeg. Melt 4 tablespoons of butter in an earthen or enamelled casserole and, when it is hot but not brown, cook the kidneys in it, over a brisk fire, for 3 minutes, turning them from time to time. Remove the kidneys, let them cool a little, and slice them. Return the slices to the casserole and sprinkle them with lemon juice, a little grated onion, and 2 teaspoons each of chopped chives and parsley. Into ¾ cup of cream blend 1 tablespoon of Dijon mustard, salt, pepper, and a dash of cayenne. Over the kidneys spread ¾ cup of small mushroom caps, or sliced mushrooms, first sautéed in butter for 3 or 4 minutes. Pour the seasoned cream over all, cover the casserole, and bake in a 350° oven for 15 minutes. Serves six.

CANNES *Riviera*

Baked Fish à la Niçoise

Poisson à la Niçoise

(Fish fillets, olive oil, tomatoes, garlic, parsley, orégano, butter)

This is a simple way to prepare any fish suitable for baking and it will add flavor to less interesting fish such as the humble haddock: Coat a baking dish with olive oil and place 2 pounds of fish fillets in it in a single layer. Season them with salt and pepper. Peel, seed, and chop coarsely 4 or 5 small tomatoes, mix them with 1 chopped and mashed clove of garlic, 1 tablespoon of minced parsley, ¼ teaspoon of dried orégano, and salt and pepper. Spread the mixture on the fish, sprinkle it with 4 tablespoons of olive oil, and dot it with 2 tablespoons of butter. Bake the fish in a 350° oven for 30 minutes, more or less, depending on the thickness of the fillets. Serves six.

MOULIN-À-VENT, IN THE BEAUJOLAIS   *Burgundy*

Poached Eggs with Onions

Oeufs Pochés Lyonnaise

(Eggs, onions, butter, flour, milk, stock, cheese)

Slice 4 onions thinly, drop them into boiling water, and boil them for 2 minutes. Drain them well, then cook them slowly in 2 tablespoons of hot butter until they are soft but not browned. Sprinkle them with 4 teaspoons of flour, blend well, and add gradually ½ cup each of milk and chicken stock. Cook the mixture, stirring, until it is rather thick, and season it with salt, pepper, and a dash of paprika. Butter a shallow baking dish small enough to hold 4 poached eggs close together, and spread some of the onion mixture in it. Poach the 4 eggs, place them carefully in the dish, season them lightly, and spoon the rest of the onion mixture over them. Sprinkle with grated cheese and a little melted butter, and glaze briefly under a hot broiler. Serves four.

LANDSCAPE NEAR ROQUEFORT   *Guyenne*

Roast Sirloin of Beef Bordelaise

Aloyau de Boeuf à la Bordelaise

(Sirloin of beef, olive oil, shallot, onion, herbs, stock, potato starch, vinegar)

Marinate a 3- to 4-pound boned sirloin of beef for 12 hours in ½ cup of olive oil, with 1 shallot and 1 small onion, both sliced, 2 bay leaves, a pinch of thyme, 2 sprigs of parsley, and salt and pepper; turn it once or twice. Remove it from the marinade, and roast it in a 325° oven for 16 to 18 minutes per pound for rare, or according to taste. Remove the roast to a serving platter and keep it warm.

Skim the fat from the roasting-pan juices, and deglaze the pan with ½ cup of stock (or a little meat glaze dissolved in hot water), stirring in all the brown bits. Add the strained marinade, 1 teaspoon of potato starch dissolved in a little water, and a few drops of vinegar. Reheat this sauce and serve in a sauceboat. Serves six to eight.

THE CHÂTEAU IN DAMPIERRE

Ile-de-France

Beef à la Mode Bordeaux Style

Le Boeuf à la Mode Bordelaise

(Rump of beef, salt pork, herbs, garlic, spices, vinegar, wine, onions, brandy)

Cut salt pork into strips ⅜ of an inch thick and several inches long. Dip them in brandy; roll them in a mixture of salt, pepper, and a little powdered cinnamon and clove; then roll them in finely minced parsley. With a larding needle, insert the pork here and there into a 4-pound piece of rump roast of beef. Place the meat in a bowl to marinate for 8 hours with pepper, a *bouquet garni,* 2 unpeeled cut cloves of garlic, a dash of nutmeg, 2 cloves, 1 tablespoon of wine vinegar, and 2 cups of red Bordeaux wine.

Drain the beef and pat it dry. Brown it on all sides in a heavy pot in 1½ table-of hot butter, together with 1 or 2 small onions. Add the marinade, ½ cup of diced parboiled salt pork, about 1 cup of stock or water, and 3 tablespoons of good brandy. Cover the casserole closely, bring it to a boil on top of the stove, then place it in a 300° oven. After 1½ hours, add ½. pound of small whole onions. Continue cooking the beef for another 1½ to 2 hours. Remove it to a deep hot platter, cut it into rather thick slices, and place the onions around it. If the sauce is too plentiful, reduce it quickly over a brisk fire; if you like a thicker sauce, blend in 1 teaspoon of potato starch per cup of sauce and simmer until it thickens. Pour it over the beef. Serves eight.

MOUNTAINS ABOVE TALLOIRES *Savoy*

Scalloped Eggs

Oeufs au Gratin

(Eggs, butter, flour, milk, cream, nutmeg, Parmesan, bread crumbs)

Make a cream sauce by blending 2 tablespoons of flour into 2 tablespoons of melted butter and adding gradually ½ cup each of milk and cream; season with salt, pepper, and nutmeg. Simmer the sauce for several minutes, stirring with a whisk to keep it smooth. Slice 6 hard-boiled eggs. Put a thin layer of cream sauce in the bottom of a shallow baking dish, add a layer of half the sliced eggs, and sprinkle with grated Parmesan cheese. Add half the remaining sauce, then the rest of the eggs and more cheese. Pour the rest of the sauce over the top, sprinkle with fine bread crumbs and melted butter, and brown the dish in a 450° oven for 10 minutes, or until the top is golden brown. Serves four.

THE CLOCK TOWER—CONCARNEAU   *Brittany*

Baked Clams Brittany

Palourdes à la Bretonne

(Clams, butter, shallot, parsley, white wine, lemon, bread crumbs)

Remove a dozen small hard-shell clams from their shells and poach them very briefly in their own liquor without letting it reach the boiling point. In a small saucepan melt 1 tablespoon of butter, add 1 chopped shallot, 1 teaspoon of minced parsley, 2 tablespoons of white wine, the juice of a small lemon, and a pinch each of salt and cayenne pepper. Simmer this slowly until the liquid is reduced to little more than a tablespoon. Brown 2 or 3 tablespoons of coarse bread crumbs lightly in plenty of butter and combine them with the reduced sauce. Replace each clam on a half shell, put some of the bread-crumb mixture on each one, and brown them briefly in a very hot oven. Serves two.

392

FARMHOUSE IN THE FINISTÈRE

Brittany

Poached Eggs Brittany

Oeufs Pochés Bretonne

(Onions, chicken stock, mushrooms, cream, egg yolk, eggs, French bread, butter)

Peel 8 small onions and simmer them in enough seasoned chicken stock to cover. When they are tender and the liquid is reduced to an almost syrupy consistency, add 4 quartered cooked mushroom caps and ½ cup of cream beaten with 1 egg yolk. Season the sauce with salt and pepper and heat it, stirring, until it is slightly thickened, but do not let it boil. Meanwhile, while the onions are simmering, poach 4 eggs and fry 4 slices of French bread on both sides in butter; have these ready before you start the sauce. Place one poached egg on each crouton, spoon onions, mushrooms, and sauce over each, and serve at once. Serves four.

RIVERFRONT AT DOLE *Franche-Comté*

Broiled Fish with Caper Sauce

Poisson Grillé, Sauce aux Câpres

(Broiled fish, butter, meat glaze, anchovies, vinegar, capers)

Any good broiled fish will be enhanced by this simple sauce: Melt ¼ pound of butter and add ½ teaspoon of meat glaze (or extract) and 2 chopped anchovy fillets. Stir until these are dissolved but do not let the butter boil. Add freshly ground pepper, a few drops of vinegar, and 2 teaspoons of drained capers. Be sure the sauce is very hot, and pass it in a sauceboat. Serves six.

MAISON D'ADAM — ANGERS   *Anjou*

Zucchini in Butter

Courgettes au Beurre

(Zucchini, butter, parsley)

Scrub but do not peel 8 small zucchini (Italian squash). Slice them into rather thin rounds, and put them in a saucepan with 3½ tablespoons of hot butter. Cook them very slowly, uncovered, shaking the pan occasionally, until they are lightly browned. Salt them lightly. Put them in a hot serving dish, add 1½ tablespoons of butter heated just until it foams, and sprinkle them with minced parsley. Serves four. Other young summer squash may be treated in the same way.

395

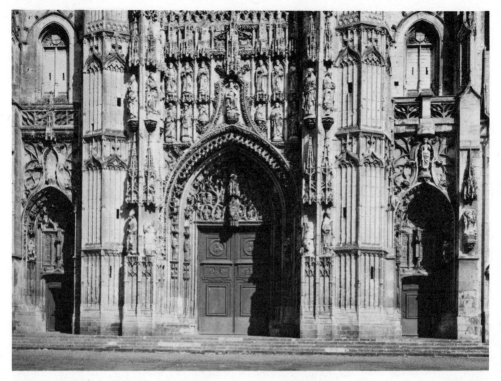

THE CHURCH AT ST. RIQUIER *Picardy*

Pears Condé

Poires Condé

(Rice, milk, sugar, butter, vanilla, egg yolks, pears, apricot sauce)

In a saucepan combine ½ cup of rice and 2 cups of water. Bring slowly to a boil, boil for 10 minutes, then drain. Meanwhile, in the top of a double boiler, heat together 2 cups of hot milk, ½ cup of sugar, and a pinch of salt. Add the rice, cover, and cook over boiling water for 30 to 40 minutes, or until the rice is tender. Remove it from the heat and stir in 1 tablespoon of soft butter, ½ teaspoon of vanilla, and 3 beaten egg yolks. Press the mixture gently into a mold and turn it out onto a serving dish.

Meanwhile, make a syrup by boiling together 2 cups of water and ¾ cup of sugar for 5 minutes. Add 1 teaspoon of vanilla. In the syrup poach 4 peeled, halved, and cored pears until they are just tender. Arrange the pear halves on the rice. Serve immediately, while still warm, with a hot apricot sauce poured over all. Make this with strained apricot jam, or stewed apricots, diluted with some of the pear syrup. Serves four.

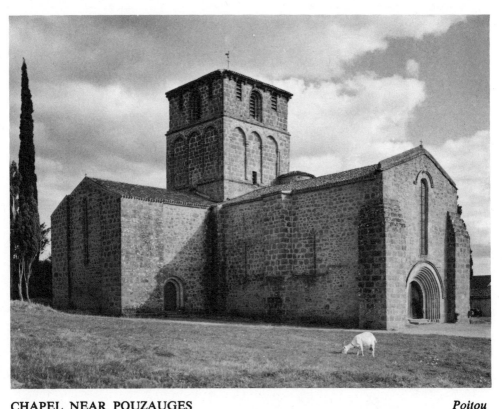

CHAPEL NEAR POUZAUGES   *Poitou*

Sorrel and Potato Soup

Potage Santé

(Leek, butter, potatoes, sorrel, egg yolks, cream, chervil, French bread)

Wash one leek thoroughly, slice the white part, and sauté it slowly in 1 table-spoon of butter until it is pale gold. Add 3 or 4 peeled and quartered potatoes. After about 4 minutes, add 5 cups of boiling water and salt and pepper. Simmer the soup for 20 to 30 minutes, or until the potatoes are tender. Pour the soup through a coarse strainer and press through the vegetables. Meanwhile wash and shred enough leaves of tender young sorrel to make 2 cups, loosely measured. Cook it down very slowly with a spoonful of water and 1½ tablespoons of butter until it is just soft. Add this to the soup and simmer it 10 minutes. Beat 3 egg yolks with ½ cup of cream and, off the fire, add this gradually to the soup. Stir in 1 tablespoon of sweet butter divided into bits, and add a little chopped chervil or parsley. Reheat the soup without boiling, and ladle it into plates containing thin slices of toasted French bread. Serves six.

FORTRESS AT AUQRESSELLES, NEAR BOULOGNE   *Picardy*

Purée of Celery Soup

Potage Purée de Céleri

(Celery root, celery, onion, butter, milk, parsley, croutons)

Peel about ¾ pound of celery root (celeriac), and slice it into thin julienne strips or grate it coarsely. Scrape 5 or 6 outer stalks of celery (remove the leaves), and slice it thinly. Chop 1 large onion. Melt 2 tablespoons of butter in a heavy saucepan, add the three vegetables, cover, and simmer them very slowly without browning for 15 minutes. Add 3 cups of hot water and salt and pepper, and simmer the soup for 35 to 40 minutes. Drain the vegetables in a sieve, reserving the liquid, then mash them through the sieve into a saucepan (or purée them in an electric blender). Stir the liquid into the purée, and add 1¼ cups of hot milk. Reheat the soup and, off the fire, stir in a lump of butter. Add 1 teaspoon of chopped chervil or parsley, and serve with small fried bread croutons. Serves four.

398

CHÂTEAU DE CHAMBORD   *Orléanais*

Cream Puffs

Narcisses

(Cream-puff paste, egg, almonds, pastry cream)

These are similar to the well-known *choux à la crème* and are called *Narcisses* by some French chefs: On ungreased baking sheets form mounds of cream-puff paste (see *Index*) with a pastry bag, using a ¾-inch tube; make them about 2 inches in diameter, place them 2 inches apart, and lift the tube with a slight twist to make a peak in the center of each one. Brush the tops with egg beaten with a little water (be sure not to let this run down to the base or they will not rise), and sprinkle with a few slivered almonds. Bake the puffs in a 425° oven for 15 minutes, or until about twice their original size. Then lower the heat to 375°, and bake them for a few more minutes; they should be golden brown, firm, and crisp. With a sharp knife slit them around the sides to release the steam, and take out any soft center dough which might make them soggy. Cool. Fill the lower halves with pastry cream (see *Index*), and replace the tops. The recipes referred to will make enough for 10 to 12 *Narcisses*.

ENTRANCE TO THE PLACE DAUPHINE *Paris*

Artichoke Soufflé Bénouville

Soufflé aux Artichauts Bénouville

(Artichokes, flour, milk, lemon juice, eggs, Sauce Mousseline)

Boil 6 artichokes for 40 minutes or until they are tender. Scrape the tender part from the base of each leaf and add the bases of the artichokes, with the "chokes" removed. Mash together well, sprinkle with lemon juice to keep the pulp from darkening, and force it through a strainer. Put this purée in a saucepan, stir in 1½ tablespoons of flour, and add gradually ½ cup of hot milk. Cook the mixture for 2 or 3 minutes, stirring, remove it from the fire, and add salt and pepper and 1 tablespoon of lemon juice.

Beat the yolks of 4 eggs lightly and add these to the cooled artichoke mixture, stirring well. Beat the whites of 6 eggs until stiff (save the 2 extra yolks for the sauce, below), and fold them into the yolk mixture. Pour the batter into a buttered 2-quart soufflé mold or deep baking dish, and bake the soufflé in a 475° oven for 10 minutes, or until it rises; then lower the heat to 275° and cook it for about another 15 minutes. Turn the soufflé out gently onto a warm serving dish, and serve with Easy Sauce Mousseline (see *Index*). Serves six.

400

CAMARET-SUR-MER   *Brittany*

Stuffed Fillets of Sole Prosper Montagné

Délices de Sole Prosper Montagné

(Sole, butter, mushrooms, shallot, shrimp, white wine, cream, egg yolks)

Use 9 small fillets of sole. Put one of them through the finest blade of a meat grinder and mash it smooth with a pestle. Sauté 8 mushroom caps and 1 shallot, all finely minced, for 2 or 3 minutes in 1 tablespoon of hot butter. Combine this with the chopped fish and season well with salt and pepper. Stuff the remaining fillets by rolling each one around a spoonful of this mixture; fasten them with toothpicks. Stand the rolls upright and close together in a buttered baking dish.

Cook 12 shrimp for 10 minutes in water to cover, with a slice of onion, a *bouquet garni*, and salt and pepper; drain, reserving the liquid, and peel the shrimp. Pour over the fillets ½ cup each of dry white wine and the shrimp stock, and add a little salt and pepper. Cover the dish with buttered paper, and cook the sole for 25 to 30 minutes in a 325° oven, basting occasionally. Meanwhile, sauté 8 whole mushroom caps in butter. When the fish is done, remove all the liquid to a small saucepan with a basting syringe and reduce it over a hot fire to ¾ cup. Stir in, off the fire, 2 tablespoons of sweet butter broken into bits. Beat together ¼ cup of cream and 2 egg yolks, add this to the sauce, and reheat it, stirring, just until it thickens. Arrange 4 shrimp down the center of the dish, spoon the sauce over all, place a sautéed mushroom cap and a shrimp on each fish roll, and serve at once. Serves four.

KERITY   *Brittany*

Mussels Ravigote

Moules Ravigote

(Mussels, herbs, onion, white wine, vinegar, oil, capers)

Scrape and wash 3 pints of mussels. Put them in a kettle with a *bouquet garni,* a few peppercorns, 1 sliced onion, and ½ cup of white wine. Steam them until they open and remove them from their shells. Strain the juice through several layers of cheesecloth, simmer it until it is reduced to about ½ cup, and let it cool. Make a cold sauce with 1½ tablespoons of wine vinegar, 4 tablespoons of oil, and salt, pepper, 1½ teaspoons of capers, and 1 teaspoon each of chopped parsley, chives, and tarragon. Mix the juices from the mussels and the sauce together, add the mussels, and chill before serving. This makes an interesting addition to the hors-d'oeuvre tray.

402

PETIT ANDELY ON THE SEINE *Normandy*

Normandy Salad

Salade Normande

(Lettuce, heavy cream, lemon juice, salt, pepper, fresh herbs)

Dress tender green garden lettuce with the following *sauce normande:* Mix together 5 parts of heavy sweet cream, 1 part lemon juice, salt and pepper to taste, and a generous sprinkling of chopped fresh parsley, tarragon, and chervil, or other fresh green herbs depending on what is available. Make the dressing and toss the salad in it both at the last minute.

LA LLAGONNE   *Pyrenees*

Cherries in Bordeaux Wine

Cerises au Vin de Bordeaux

(Cherries, sugar, cinnamon, orange, currant jelly, red wine)

Pit 1 pound of ripe cherries. Put them in an enamel saucepan with 1 cup plus 2 tablespoons of fine granulated sugar, a very small bit of cinnamon stick, the grated zest of half an orange, and 6 tablespoons of currant jelly. Pour in 1½ bottles of good red Bordeaux wine. Cover the pan and heat the mixture, stirring now and then, until it boils. Remove the pan from the fire, and let the cherries poach, still covered, in the liquid for 12 minutes. Then uncover, cool, and chill in the refrigerator.

Serve a few cherries to each person in a champagne glass and fill the glasses with the cold and delicious red-wine juices. A spoon accompanies each glass and small cakes, lady fingers, or macaroons are passed at the same time. This is best for a summer afternoon party, though it may be used as a dessert. Serves eight to ten.

EGUISHEIM   *Alsace*

Alsatian Cabbage Salad

Salade à l'Alsacienne

(Cabbage, seasonings, vinegar, bacon)

Shred a small young cabbage finely, removing the heavy center stalk and the larger ribs of the leaves. Pour boiling water over the cabbage and let it stand for 10 minutes. Drain it thoroughly and sponge it dry. Put it in a bowl, add salt, freshly ground pepper, and 2 tablespoons of wine vinegar. Dice 4 or 5 strips of bacon, and heat them slowly in a frying pan until they have given out most of their fat and are just beginning to brown. Add the bacon and the hot fat to the cabbage, toss it lightly with two forks, and serve warm. Serves four.

CANAL NEAR PONT DE PANY *Burgundy*

Cheese Fondue with Truffles

Fondue de Fromage aux Truffes

(Swiss cheese, milk, cream, flour, egg yolks, butter, toast, truffles)

Grate ½ pound of imported Swiss cheese and melt it slowly in the top of a double boiler with 2 tablespoons of milk, stirring constantly. Measure out 1 cup of heavy cream, blend 1 tablespoon of flour smoothly with a little of the cream, and gradually stir in the rest of the cup. Add salt and pepper and 6 egg yolks, and beat this mixture well with a whisk. Add it gradually to the melted cheese, stirring constantly. Never let the *fondue* boil. When the cheese, cream, and egg mixture has thickened, stir in a lump of butter and pour it onto 4 slices of toast. Sprinkle thinly sliced truffles on top and serve immediately. Serves four.

ST. CÔME *Guyenne*

Sautéed Chicken with Parsley

Poulet Persillé

(Chicken, white wine, veal stock or meat glaze, parsley, lemon, sweet butter)

Have a 4-pound chicken cut into serving pieces, wipe them dry, and season them with salt and pepper. In a broad sauté or frying pan, heat together 2 tablespoons of butter and 1 tablespoon of oil and brown the chicken on all sides in this, over moderate heat, for about 10 minutes. Then cover the pan and continue cooking the chicken for 20 minutes, or until the white meat is tender. Remove it to a dish and cook the dark meat 5 minutes longer. Then return the white meat to the pan, add ½ cup of dry white wine, and simmer it until it is reduced by about half. Add ¼ cup of rich veal stock (or ¼ teaspoon of meat glaze dissolved in ¼ cup of hot water), and simmer briefly. Arrange the pieces of chicken on a hot platter and sprinkle them with 1 tablespoon of finely minced parsley. Add the juice of half a small lemon to the sauce left in the pan, and reheat it, stirring well. Off the fire, melt 2 teaspoons of the best sweet butter, divided into bits, into the sauce, and pour it over the chicken. Serve at once, with steamed potatoes or rice. Serves four.

VINEYARDS NEAR ST. HIPPOLYTE *Alsace*

Chicken in White Wine

Coq au Vin Blanc

(Chicken, butter, onions, stock, bacon, brandy, white wine, herbs, mushrooms)

Over low heat, lightly brown 12 small white onions on all sides in 1 tablespoon each of hot butter and oil, turning them often. After 10 minutes, add ½ cup of hot chicken stock, cover, cook slowly for 30 minutes, or until the onions are almost tender, and reserve them. Meanwhile, parboil 3 ounces of lean diced bacon for 3 minutes. Drain and dry it, and in a large skillet sauté it in 2 tablespoons of butter until it is golden; remove the bacon and reserve it also.

Have a 3-pound chicken cut into serving pieces. Dry them well, and in the fat remaining in the skillet brown them lightly on all sides, over moderate heat, for about 10 minutes. Pour on 3 tablespoons of warm brandy and flame it. Then add the reserved bacon, 1¾ cups of dry white wine, 1 cup of chicken stock, a *bouquet garni,* and salt and pepper. Cover, and simmer for 30 to 40 minutes.

Meanwhile wash, dry, and quarter ½ pound of mushrooms. Sauté them for 5 minutes in 2 tablespoons of butter and 1 tablespoon of oil. Ten minutes before the chicken is done, add the reserved onions and the mushrooms. Then remove all but the sauce to a hot serving casserole. Reduce the sauce if there is more than about 2 cups, skim off the fat, and thicken the sauce with 1½ tablespoons of butter creamed with 2 tablespoons of flour; simmer, stirring, until it coats the spoon, and pour it over the chicken. Serves four.

LES MONTS DE CHAMPAGNE *Champagne*

Creamed Cucumbers

Concombres à la Crème

(Cucumbers, butter, flour, milk, nutmeg, parsley, cream)

Peel 1½ pounds of cucumbers (3 or 4 of average size), cut them into 1½-inch lengths, and cut these into quarters; remove the seeds and drop the pieces into a bowl of cold water as they are done. Then drain, drop them into a saucepan of boiling salted water, boil them for 20 to 25 minutes, and drain again very thoroughly. Blend 3 tablespoons of flour into 1½ tablespoons of melted butter and add gradually 1½ cups of hot milk. Add salt, pepper, a dash of nutmeg, and a sprig of parsley. Stir to keep the sauce smooth, and simmer it until it is reduced to 1 cup (after 10 minutes remove the parsley). Then add ½ cup of cream and the cucumbers, and reheat. Serves six.

CHÂTEAU DE LA BRETSCHE *Brittany*

Hot Salmon Mousse

Mousse de Saumon

(Salmon, seasonings, egg whites, cream)

Chop 1 pound of uncooked salmon, free of bones and skin, by putting it through the finest blade of a meat grinder. In a bowl work it smooth with a pestle or a wooden spoon, adding plenty of salt and freshly ground white pepper. Work in gradually the whites of 2 small eggs. Chill the mixture for 1 hour in the refrigerator, then work in 1 cup of heavy cream, and finally fold in the stiffly beaten whites of 2 more eggs. Put the mixture in a buttered mold, stand it in a pan of hot water, cover the mold with a buttered paper, and bake the mousse in a 350° oven for 20 to 25 minutes or until it is firm and elastic to the touch. Let the mousse stand 6 or 8 minutes before turning it out on a hot platter. Serve with Easy Sauce Mousseline (see *Index*). Serves six.

PLACE DU MARTROI—BEAUGENCY   *Orléanais*

Roast Tenderloin of Beef Charentais

Filet de Boeuf Rôti à la Mode des Laitiers Charentais

(Beef tenderloin, oil, vinegar, herbs, spices, salt pork, wine, shallot, cream)

Marinate a 2-pound piece of tenderloin of beef overnight in ½ cup of olive oil and 2 tablespoons of wine vinegar, with a *bouquet garni,* 3 cloves, and a dash of nutmeg. Remove the meat from the marinade, tie a thin sheet of salt pork over the top, and roast it for 45 minutes in a 350° oven, or until cooked but still rare. Baste it occasionally with the marinade. Remove it to a hot platter and keep it warm.

Remove most of the fat from the pan juices, deglaze the pan with ½ cup of dry white wine, and strain this sauce into a small saucepan. Add 1 teaspoon of wine vinegar, 1 finely minced shallot, and salt and pepper if needed, and simmer the sauce for 10 minutes. Add 1 teaspoon of chopped tarragon leaves and one fourth as much heavy cream as you have sauce. Reheat and, off the fire, melt in 1 teaspoon of soft sweet butter. Slice the tenderloin, pour the sauce over it, and serve with French-fried potatoes and sautéed mushrooms. Serves six.

411

THE BEACH AT YPORT *Normandy*

Hot Leek Pie

Flamiche aux Poireaux

(Pie crust, leeks, bacon, butter, flour, milk, nutmeg)

Make a pie-crust dough from a good standard recipe, roll it out about ⅛ inch thick, and line a 10-inch pie plate with it; prick the bottom here and there with a sharp pointed knife. Bake the shell in a 400° oven for 10 to 12 minutes.

Clean and wash several leeks thoroughly and slice the white parts only into very thin rings; use about ½ pound, or enough to make 1¾ cups. Cut 2½ ounces of lean bacon into ¼-inch dice, put them in a saucepan of cold water, and bring slowly to the boiling point; boil for 1 minute, drain, and dry thoroughly. Then sauté the bacon briefly in 2 tablespoons of butter, add the leeks, and cook together over a low fire for 15 minutes, without browning. Blend in 3½ tablespoons of flour and cook the mixture briefly, stirring, again without browning. Add gradually 1¾ cups of milk, season with salt, pepper, and nutmeg, and simmer over very low heat for about 25 minutes, stirring often. Pour this mixture into the pie shell, dot it with 2 tablespoons of butter divided into small bits, and put the pie immediately into the lower part of a preheated 375° oven. Bake for 15 minutes, or until the crust is golden brown. Serves six or eight.

LAC DE NANTUA   *Bresse*

Tenderloin of Beef with Artichokes and Peas

Tournedos de Boeuf à la Clamart

(Beef tenderloin, butter, Madeira, stock, artichoke bottoms, peas, cream)

Have 4 slices of beef tenderloin cut 1 inch thick, and tie them around the edges with string to keep each little steak round. Brown them quickly in 2 tablespoons of hot butter and cook them for 3 to 4 minutes on each side, keeping them rare in the center. Place them on a hot platter, remove the string, and season with salt and pepper. Pour the surplus fat from the pan, and add ¼ cup of Madeira and ⅓ cup of stock. Reduce this over a brisk flame to about ¼ cup, stirring in all the brown juices left in the pan, and spoon a little of the sauce over each steak. Garnish with small artichoke bottoms (canned ones are fine) sautéed in hot butter just long enough to heat them through; fill these with tiny canned peas first drained and heated with a little butter and heavy cream. Serves four.

413

ROADSIDE NEAR LES EYZIES-DE-TAYAC   *Périgord*

Boiled Beef with Herbs

Boeuf Bouilli à la Mode de Mon Jardinier

(Cold boiled beef, assorted fresh herbs, tomato, egg, garlic, seasonings)

When you have some cold beef left from a *pot-au-feu* or other boiled-beef dish, slice it thinly and serve it as an hors-d'oeuvre or first course covered with the following green dressing: Take a handful each of chervil and parsley, the leaves from a branch of tarragon, some chives, 2 leaves of fresh sage, 2 leaves of mint, a sprig of basil, and a clove of garlic; chop these all rather finely. Peel and seed 1 small tomato and chop it coarsely. Mix these all together with 1 finely chopped hard-boiled egg, 3 tablespoons or more of red-wine vinegar, and salt and pepper. Obviously, this is a recipe for someone with an herb garden but, even if you cannot obtain all the ingredients, you can make your own combinations provided you use fresh, not dried, herbs.

CHAPEL OF NOTRE DAME — CAMARET-SUR-MER *Brittany*

Baked Halibut in White Wine

Poisson Bonne Hôtesse

(Halibut, butter, onion, mushrooms, white wine, lemon, herbs, spices, brandy)

A 2-pound slice of halibut or any fine white fish may be used for this dish: Put the fish in a buttered baking dish with a few slices of onion, 8 or 10 sliced mushroom stems, enough white wine almost to cover the fish, 1 teaspoon of lemon juice, a sprig of parsley, salt and pepper, and a tiny pinch each of nutmeg and clove. Bake the fish in a 350° oven for about 30 minutes.

Remove it to a hot platter and pour the juices into a small saucepan. Over a hot fire reduce them to 1¼ cups. Strain the sauce into another pan, add 1 tablespoon of warm brandy, and flame it. Stir in 1 tablespoon of butter first thoroughly blended with 1 tablespoon of flour. Add a pinch of cayenne, reheat the sauce, stirring, until it is slightly thickened, pour it over the fish, and serve at once. Serves six.

415

THE BEACH AT ETRETAT

Normandy

Mackerel with Tarragon Butter

Maquereaux au Beurre d'Estragon

(Mackerel, olive oil, butter, tarragon, tarragon wine vinegar)

Have 4 small tinker mackerel cleaned and split without completely separating the halves. Spread them, skin sides down, in an oiled baking dish, season them well with salt and pepper, and pour a little olive oil over them; let them marinate for an hour before cooking. Place the fish in a 400° oven, or under the broiler, and cook them for about 20 minutes or until the meat separates easily from the backbones which you may now carefully remove. Meanwhile, mash 1 generous tablespoon of chopped fresh tarragon in a mortar, and mix in gradually 4 tablespoons of soft butter, salt and pepper, and about 2 teaspoons of tarragon wine vinegar. Spread the butter on the still broiling-hot fish and serve at once. Serves four.

TOWN GATES OF RICHELIEU   *Touraine*

Green Beans Peasant Style

Haricots Verts Paysanne

(Green beans, bacon, butter, onions, tomatoes, potatoes)

Wash and string 1½ pounds of young green beans and cut them in pieces. Dice enough bacon to make ½ cup, parboil it for 3 minutes, and drain it well. In a heavy saucepan brown the bacon lightly in 2 tablespoons of hot butter, then remove and reserve it. In the remaining fat cook slowly 2 finely chopped onions until they are soft and lightly browned. Add 4 peeled, seeded, and coarsely chopped tomatoes, salt and pepper, the beans, the bacon, and ½ cup of hot water. Cover the pan and simmer slowly for about half an hour, or until the beans are tender. The water should have almost entirely evaporated but do not let the dish become too dry. Meanwhile peel 2 potatoes and cut them into ½-inch dice. Cook these slowly in butter until tender and golden brown. Add them to the beans at the last minute. Serves six.

DOORWAY OF THE CHURCH OF ST. LAZARE — AVALLON *Burgundy*

Braised Salmon Trout

Truite Saumonée Braisée Castel de Nérac

(Trout, vegetables, herbs, wine, Madeira, shrimp, brandy, lemon, mushrooms, tomato)

Put a fine 2-pound salmon trout in an oval baking dish on a bed of 1 small carrot and 1 onion, both sliced, a little chopped celery, a pinch of thyme, 1 bay leaf, and a sprig of parsley. Season with salt, pepper, and paprika, and add 1 cup or more of dry white wine and 1 tablespoon of Madeira. Bake the fish in a 350° oven, basting occasionally, for 30 to 40 minutes, or until firm.

Meanwhile, peel and devein 6 or 8 shrimp, sauté them in 1 tablespoon of butter for 2 or 3 minutes, and flame them with 1 tablespoon of warmed brandy; sprinkle with a little lemon juice. When the fish is three quarters cooked, add the shrimp and their juice, 4 or 5 quartered mushroom caps, and 1 peeled, seeded, and coarsely chopped tomato. Cook the fish another 10 minutes, or about 40 minutes in all, then remove it to a hot serving dish. Place the shrimp and mushrooms around it, and discard the parsley and bay leaf. Pour the remaining pan juices into a saucepan and reduce them quickly. Off the fire, stir a lump of butter into the sauce, and pour it over the fish. Serves four.

418

MANOR COURTYARD

Brittany

Cheese Omelette

Omelette au Fromage

(Eggs, Parmesan cheese, Swiss cheese, butter)

With a fork beat together 4 eggs and 2 teaspoons of water for about 30 seconds. Add pepper, a small pinch of salt, 1 tablespoon of grated Parmesan, and 1 tablespoon of grated Swiss cheese or American Cheddar; beat until the cheese is well mixed with the eggs. Heat 1 tablespoon of butter in an omelette pan until it stops foaming. Pour in the eggs, stir them once or twice as they begin to harden on the bottom, and cook the omelette until it is creamy but not dry; shake the pan back and forth to keep it from sticking. Fold the omelette out onto a platter, sprinkle a little more cheese on the top, and serve immediately. Serves two.

CHÂTEAU D'O, NEAR MORTRÉE *Normandy*

Eggs Aurore

Oeufs à l'Aurore

(Eggs, cream sauce, seasonings, croutons, Parmesan, butter)

Cut 6 hard-boiled eggs in half lengthwise and remove the yolks. Cut the whites into fine strips. Make 1¼ cups of cream sauce by blending 2 tablespoons of flour into 2 tablespoons of melted butter and stirring in gradually 1¼ cups of rich milk (or half milk, half cream). Add salt, a pinch of cayenne, and a dash of nutmeg. Fry triangles of bread in butter until they are crisp, and arrange them upright around the edge of a shallow baking dish. Combine the egg whites and the cream sauce, and pour half of this into the center of the dish; sprinkle with grated Parmesan. Rub half the egg yolks through a coarse sieve over the cheese. Add the remaining egg whites and cream sauce, sprinkle again with grated Parmesan and with the rest of the sieved yolks. Sprinkle with melted butter, reheat the dish briefly in a 400° oven, and serve at once. Serves four.

420

CATHÉDRALE ST. FRONT-PÉRIGUEUX   *Périgord*

Fried Eggs Bordelais

Oeufs Frits Bordelais

(Tomatoes, olive oil, garlic, parsley, bread crumbs, mushrooms, shallots, eggs)

Halve 2 large tomatoes, shake out the seeds, and prepare them *à la Provençale:* Season them with salt and pepper and cook them lightly on both sides in 3 tablespoons of hot olive oil; then add 1 minced clove of garlic and cook them another 2 or 3 minutes. Remove the tomatoes to a hot platter and sprinkle them with minced parsley. Add 1 or 2 tablespoons of coarse bread crumbs to the frying pan, brown these lightly, and sprinkle them over the tomatoes.

Meanwhile, in one pan sauté together in hot butter 4 large mushrooms, sliced, and 1 shallot, minced. When the liquid has evaporated, spread these on the tomatoes. At the same time, in another pan, fry 4 eggs slowly in combined butter and oil. Trim the edges of the eggs to make neat rounds and place one on each half tomato. Serves four.

421

CHAPEL AT SÉRANON, NEAR CASTELLANE — *Provence*

Leeks Peasant Style

Poireaux à la Paysanne

(Leeks, bacon, butter)

Clean a bunch of leeks, remove most of the green parts, wash the leeks thoroughly under cold running water, and cut them crosswise into 1-inch lengths. Cut ¼ pound of lean bacon, or Canadian bacon, into small dice and brown these slowly in 3 tablespoons of melted butter. Add the leeks, and cook them slowly, stirring often, for about half an hour. Salt them lightly to taste, and serve at once. Serves two.

ST. RIQUIER *Picardy*

Pastry Cream

Crème Pâtissière

(Eggs, sugar, flour, milk, vanilla, flavoring)

Beat together 5 large egg yolks and 1 cup of sugar until very thick and pale in color. Add ½ cup of sifted flour and beat until well blended. Add gradually 2 cups of hot milk in which a vanilla bean has been steeped. Cook this custard, stirring with a whisk, just to the boiling point; then continue cooking for 2 minutes over moderate heat, still stirring to keep it smooth. Flavor with a few drops of almond extract, a liqueur, or any flavoring you may wish. Cool. Use to fill cream puffs (*Narcisses*; see *Index*).

THE RIVER INDRE—LOCHES *Touraine*

Braised Sorrel

Oseille Braisée

(Sorrel, butter, flour, salt, sugar, stock, eggs, cream)

Wash thoroughly 2 pounds of tender young sorrel. Heat it in a large saucepan with 1 cup of water, adding about one-half of the sorrel at a time and turning it over until it shrinks and is well softened. Turn it out into a sieve and let it drain for at least 20 minutes. Purée the sorrel in an electric blender, or force it through the sieve. In a small casserole, melt 1½ tablespoons of butter and blend in 2 tablespoons of flour. Add the sorrel purée to this *roux*, and add also ½ teaspoon of salt, 1 tablespoon of powdered sugar, and 1¼ cups of light stock. Let this come to a boil, cover the casserole, and cook the purée in a 325° oven for about 1½ hours. Then beat 2 eggs well with ¼ cup of heavy cream, combine this gradually with the sorrel, and simmer, stirring, for 2 or 3 minutes. At the end and off the fire, add 2 tablespoons of butter broken into bits. Serve with broiled shad or roast meats. Serves four to six.

VALLEY NEAR MÉGÈVE   *Savoy*

Cream of Onion Soup

Potage Crème d'Oignons

(Onions, butter, milk, nutmeg, egg yolks, croutons)

Peel, slice, and chop finely 5 or 6 large mild onions. Melt ¼ pound of butter in a soup kettle or earthen casserole, add the onions, and cook them over a low fire, stirring often, until they are soft and transparent. Add 1¾ quarts (7 cups) of hot rich milk and simmer the soup for about half an hour. Season it with salt and white pepper to taste, and add a good dash of nutmeg. Strain the soup through a fine sieve, mashing through as much of the onion as will go easily. Beat 4 egg yolks in a bowl, stir in gradually a little of the hot soup, and pour this back into the kettle, off the fire, to thicken the soup slightly. Serve it at once, and pass bread croutons fried in butter to sprinkle on top. Serves eight.

CHURCH AT CUNAULT *Anjou*

Stuffed Shoulder of Lamb
Epaule d'Agneau Farcie
(Boned shoulder of lamb, bread crumbs, parsley, scallions, herbs, eggs, stock)

On a board spread out a boned shoulder of lamb, skin side down; it should weigh about 3¼ pounds after boning. Season it with salt and pepper, and spread on it the following stuffing: Combine 1 cup of soft bread crumbs first soaked in a little milk then squeezed almost dry, salt and pepper, ½ cup of finely chopped parsley, 2 scallions with a little of their green stems (or 1 small onion), finely chopped, ⅛ teaspoon each of powdered rosemary and powdered thyme, and 1 chopped hard-boiled egg. Mix the ingredients lightly but thoroughly with a fork, and bind with 1 beaten raw egg. Roll the meat into a cylinder shape, and tie it with kitchen string at rather close intervals to hold it in shape. Roast it to your taste (or about 18 minutes per pound in a 350° oven for medium rare), and remove the string before serving. Skim the fat from the pan juices, add ½ cup of stock to the pan, and stir in all the brown scraps. Reheat this sauce, strain it, and serve it with the meat. Serves six to eight.

426

SEMUR-EN-AUXOIS

Burgundy

Chicken Breasts Hunter Style

Suprêmes de Volailles Chasseur

(Chicken breasts, croutons, mushrooms, shallots, brandy, wine, tomato paste, stock)

Have the bones and skin removed from the breasts of 3 chickens; flatten the six fillets by pounding them lightly between sheets of waxed paper. Season them lightly with salt and pepper and dust them with flour. In a broad frying pan heat ¼ pound of butter and cook the chicken breasts slowly in it for 4 to 5 minutes on each side; do not let the butter brown too much. Meanwhile, in another pan, brown 6 slices of bread in butter on both sides. Place a cooked chicken breast on each crouton, remove them to a hot serving dish, and keep them warm.

Add ½ pound of sliced mushrooms and 2 finely chopped shallots to the butter left in the first frying pan, and cook them for 2 or 3 minutes. Add 3 table-spoons of good brandy and ½ cup of dry white wine, then reduce the liquid by half. Add 2 tablespoons of tomato paste, 1 cup of strong hot chicken stock (in which you may dissolve ½ teaspoon of meat glaze), and 1 teaspoon of minced parsley. Simmer the sauce to reduce it to about 1 cup, and spoon it over the chicken breasts. Serves six.

LA ROCHE-POT

Burgundy

Bananas Parisian

Bananes à la Parisienne

(Bananas, sugar, vanilla, kirsch, whipped cream, strawberries)

Boil together 2 cups each of sugar and water for 5 minutes. Add a few drops of vanilla extract. In this syrup poach 6 bananas, keeping the liquid just below the boiling point, until they are softened. Lift the bananas out carefully and cool them. To serve, cut 6 ovals of sponge cake each long enough to hold one banana, dip the cake in a little of the syrup, and sprinkle with kirsch. Arrange the cake around the edge of a round platter, place a banana on each piece, and fill the center of the dish with whipped cream mixed with a few mashed fresh strawberries. Decorate with halved strawberries. Serves six.

PONT ROYAL

Paris

Steak Lapérouse

Entrecôte Lapérouse

(Steak, wine vinegar, shallot, tarragon, white wine, meat glaze, butter)

Broil a thick, juicy steak large enough to serve four, and serve it with the following sauce: In a small saucepan combine 2 tablespoons of red-wine vinegar, 1 minced shallot, 1 tablespoon of fresh tarragon leaves (or 1 teaspoon of dried tarragon), and ½ cup of dry white wine. Simmer the mixture until it is reduced to half its original quantity. Then add a little pepper and ½ teaspoon of meat glaze dissolved in ½ cup of hot water. Simmer the sauce again until it is reduced to about ⅜ of a cup. Taste for seasoning and, off the fire, stir in 1 teaspoon of butter. Put the steak on a hot platter, strain the sauce over it, and carve it at the table. Serve with creamed potatoes.

429

LOW TIDE AT ST. SERVAN *Brittany*

Fillets of Bass Fermière

Filets de Bar Fermière

(Bass fillets, butter, mushrooms, shallots, parsley, red wine)

In a shallow buttered baking dish arrange 6 bass fillets weighing about 2 pounds in all. Season them with salt and pepper, and cover them with a mixture of 6 or 7 large chopped mushrooms, 2 chopped shallots, and 1 tablespoon of minced parsley. Pour over them ⅓ cup of red wine and ⅔ cup of fish stock (obtained by simmering the heads and bones of the fish in water to cover, together with a slice of onion, a *bouquet garni,* and salt and pepper). Poach the fish slowly in a moderate oven or on top of the stove just until it can be flaked with a fork. Remove the fillets carefully to a hot serving dish. Pour the juices into a small saucepan and reduce them over a hot fire to about ¾ of a cup. Blend 3 tablespoons of butter with 2 teaspoons of minced parsley and, off the fire, add this to the sauce bit by bit; move the pan with a rotary motion to melt in the butter. Spoon the sauce over the fish and serve at once. Serves six.

430

ST. HIPPOLYTE   *Alsace*

Pork Loin Strasbourg Style

Porc Mariné Strasbourgeoise

(Pork loin, red wine, onion, carrot, garlic, herbs, spices, lemon, currant jelly)

Make a marinade by simmering together for 20 minutes 2½ cups of red wine, 1 sliced onion, a few slices of carrot, 1 chopped clove of garlic, 1 tablespoon of tarragon vinegar, 4 or 5 crushed peppercorns, salt, 2 cloves, and a *bouquet garni.* Place a piece of boned loin of pork (weighing 2½ pounds after boning), with fat removed, in an earthenware bowl. Pour the cooled marinade over it, cover, and let it stand in the refrigerator for two days, turning it once or twice.

Remove the pork from the marinade, wipe it dry, and brown it on all sides in a casserole in 1 tablespoon of hot lard. Add the strained marinade, cover the casserole, and cook the pork in a 350° oven for 1½ to 2 hours, more or less, depending on the thickness of the meat. Place the pork on a deep hot platter. You should have about 1 cup of juices in the casserole. Reheat them in a small saucepan with the grated rind of half a lemon and 2 tablespoons of red currant jelly. Carve the pork, pour a little of the sauce over it, and pass the rest separately. Serves six.

431

CHÂTEAU AT BOURDEILLES   *Guyenne*

Roquefort Cream Salad

Salad Aveyronnaise

(Lettuce, Roquefort cheese, cream, lemon juice, herbs)

Mash 4 tablespoons of crumbled Roquefort cheese in a bowl; the best cheese will be creamy or waxy in appearance, light in color, and not too strong in flavor. Blend it smoothly with ⅔ cup of heavy cream, 4 tablespoons of lemon juice, and a good dash of freshly ground pepper, but no salt as the cheese should supply enough. Add 1 teaspoon each of chopped fresh chervil (or parsley) and tarragon. Mix this dressing with lettuce enough for six, which has been cut across the head to shred it coarsely. Serves six.

Menus

❦

HORS-D'OEUVRE VARIÉS

These are the classic luncheon hors-d'oeuvre. Though elaborate variations are possible, the ones listed below are some of the most usual and they are so rudimentary that actual recipes are given for only seven of them. A balanced selection of three or four items from the total list is quite sufficient for one meal. It is a good cook's pride every now and then, however, to set forth a splendid tray of a dozen or so in matching raviers, *oblong china dishes that are traditional at home as well as in restaurants. It is legitimate, and in fact expected, that the family cook should use her imagination in putting together* hors-d'oeuvre variés *and that she should often use up leftovers in the process. Quantities should be small and French bread and unsalted butter are necessary accompaniments.*

Radishes, eaten with salt, sweet butter, and French bread

Black olives, Greek or Italian type

Vegetable salads, each vegetable in its own dish, with French dressing, minced parsley and/or minced chives or onion. Some possibilities: sliced tomatoes or cucumbers; cooked green beans, white beans, cauliflower, beets or leeks.

Celery root with rémoulade sauce, 372

Cucumbers à la grecque, 265

Onions à la grecque, 294

Mushroom salad, 274

Grilled peppers, 264

Mixed-vegetable salad, cooked, diced, and dressed with mayonnaise

Potato salad

Hard-boiled eggs, halved, with mayonnaise, sometimes garnished with a piece of anchovy

Salami, or any hard sausage of the same type, thinly sliced

Marinated beef, 313

Liver pâté, 238 (or any meat pâté of your choice)

Sardines, with lemon

Canned tuna fish, with lemon, or with mayonnaise and capers

Herring, pickled in oil or white wine

Shrimp, the smaller the better, cooked in a well-seasoned *court-bouillon* (see page 350), chilled, and served with lemon or mayonnaise

433

LUNCHEONS

Radishes, butter   Tomato salad
Sardines
Omelette with herbs, 277
Cheese
Fruit

Red *or* white wine

❧

Hors-d'oeuvre variés, 217
Calves' brains with black butter, 90
Steamed potatoes
Spinach purée
Strawberry tart, 7

Red *or* white wine

❧

Cheese tart, 133
Niçoise salad, 55
Fruit

Rosé wine

❧

Eggs poached in cream, 113
Braised endive, 126
Swiss cheese
Apples
French butter cookies, 88

White wine

❧

Poached eggs with onions, 388
Chicory salad, French dressing
Swiss cheese
Stewed apricots

White wine

❧

Fried eggs Gascony, 278
Romaine salad, French dressing
Roquefort or blue cheese
Fresh pears

Red wine

Black olives   White bean salad
Salami
Basque omelette, 250
Cheese
Fruit

Red *or* rose wine

❧

(Burgundian snails, 147)
Jellied ham with parsley, 122
Salad (chicory)   Cheese
Strawberries with whipped cream, 50

Chablis *or* Meursault Charmes
or California Pinot Blanc

❧

Riviera pizza, 73
Lobster Alexander, 56
Fruit

White Burgundy
or California Riesling *or* Pinot Blanc

❧

Hot cheese and ham sandwiches, 30
Green salad with fines herbes
Flambéed bananas, 72

Meursault
or California Pinot Chardonnay

❧

Stuffed onions, 231
Potato salad with water cress
Port Salut or Oka cheese
MacIntosh Apples

Red wine

❧

Basque salad, 325
Italian bread, sweet butter
Baked eggs Héloïse, 304
Sliced navel oranges

White wine

PARTY LUNCHEONS

Asparagus and shrimp salad, 230
Ripe Brie, hot French bread
Stuffed pineapple with strawberries, 319
White Bordeaux *or* Finger Lakes Elvira
Demitasse

❧

Cucumber sticks, coarse salt   Toasted almonds
Chicken-liver foie gras, 264   Homemade Melba toast
Dry sherry
Fresh spinach purée, garnished with stuffed mushrooms, 334
Macaroon cream omelette, 298
Pouilly-Fuissé *or* California Pinot Chardonnay
Demitasse

SUPPERS

Purée of celery soup, 398
Boiled beef with herbs, 414
Cream cheese   Currant jelly
Toasted French bread
Red wine

❧

(Onion soup, 17)
Mirasol pork and veal pâté, 128
Green salad (escarole)
Caramel baked pears, 155
Red wine

❧

Alsatian ham and beef broth, 186
Ardennes stuffed baked potatoes, 82
Liver pâté, 22   Endive salad
Caramel custard, 51
Beer *or* Alsatian white wine
or California Riesling

❧

Marseilles fish soup, 222
Cold sliced ham or prosciutto
Spinach Italian style, 259
Fresh figs and shell almonds
White Chianti
or California Pinot Blanc

Sorrel and potato soup, 397
Cold roast beef, pickled gherkins
Sliced cucumbers, French dressing
Camembert, Muscat grapes
Red wine

❧

Pumpkin soup, 102
Stuffed baked tomatoes, 177
Mashed potatoes
Chocolate mousse, 107
White wine

❧

Split-pea soup, 108
Burgundian snails, 147
Green salad (lettuce, chicory)
Creamed Camembert, 43
Red Burgundy
or California Cabernet

❧

Fresh tomato soup, 380
Burgundian cheese pastry, 246
Green salad, French dressing
Chocolate cream, 235
Red Burgundy
or California Cabernet

PARTY SUPPERS

Baked oysters with almonds, 24
Foie gras   Normandy potato salad, 211   Green salad with fines herbes
Flambéed fresh figs, 162
Champagne   *Demitasse   Liqueurs*

❧

Steamed artichokes, lemon butter
Sliced prosciutto
Potato and mussel salad Dumas, 273
Ripe Brie or Camembert   Hot French bread
Fruit compote, 269
White Burgundy (*such as* Meursault *or* Batard Montrachet)
Demitasse   Liqueurs

❧

Russian caviar
with lemon, black bread, and sweet butter
Creamed crabmeat omelette, 351
Marinated carrots, 379   Water cress
Fresh blueberries and raspberries, with sugar and Kirsch
Champagne
Demitasse   Liqueurs

DINNERS

Consommé
Pheasant with endive, 185
Francine's chocolate cream, 66
Bordeaux (*such as* Léoville-Poyferré)
or California Pinot Noir

❧

Broiled steak
Turnips Bordelaise, 292
Green salad, French dressing
Bananas in cream, 249
Red Bordeaux
or California Pinot Noir

Creamed water cress soup, 5
Squab with new peas, 158
Flambéed apricot omelette, 131
Red Bordeaux
or California Pinot Noir

❧

Chicken Casserole Bonne Femme, 368
Buttered spinach
Assorted cheeses, French bread
Cherries in Bordeaux wine, 404
Bordeaux Médoc
or California Cabernet

436

Burgundian beef stew, with rice, 94
Salad (*garden lettuce, water cress*)
Cheese (*Camembert, Gorgonzola*)
Poached peaches, raspberry sauce, 182
Red Burgundy
or California Pinot Noir

❦

(*Epicures' canapés, 75*)
Fish sauté Romagnole, 193
Steamed potatoes
Baked zucchini,* 110
Fruit
Rosé wine

❦

(*Burgundian snails, 147*)
Chicken in red wine, 21
Steamed potatoes
Salad (*garden lettuce*)
Cheese (*Roquefort*)
Hot apple mousse, 179
Red Burgundy
or California Pinot Noir

❦

(*Leek and potato soup, 54*)
Roast leg of veal with mustard, 136
Buttered noodles
Germaine's creamed spinach,* 63
Hot apple mousse, 179
Red Bordeaux, Arbois, *or* Bourgeuil
or California Cabernet

❦

Broiled chicken Languedoc, 359
Sautéed mushrooms
Broiled eggplant   Tomato sauce, 278
Roquefort or blue cheese
Fresh fruit
Beaujolais (red, *such as* Moulin
à Vent *or* Fleurie)

(*Shrimp Nantua, 148*)
Duck with glazed onions, 161
Asparagus, egg and butter sauce,* 199
Fruit
Red Burgundy (*such as* Grands-
Echézeaux) *or* California Cabernet

❦

(*Baked eggs with mushrooms, 44*)
Stuffed shad, 23
New potatoes
Spinach purée
Strawberries and cream, 187
Vouvray *or* Pouilly-Fuissé
or New York State Elvira

❦

(*Stuffed crab Armoricaine, 115*)
Breton roast lamb with white beans, 15
Salad (*romaine*)
Cheese (*Pont l'Evêque, Brie*)
Pears amandine, 18
Pouilly-sur-Loire
or California Pinot Blanc

❦

(*Mushrooms on toast, 208*)
Poached salmon, green mayonnaise,
109
Cucumber-stuffed tomatoes, 109
Cheese (*Camembert, Bel Paese*)
Grand Marnier soufflé, 166
Meursault *or* Traminer, *or* California
Folle Blanche *or* Pinot Chardonnay

❦

Beef consommé, 375
Broiled double loin lamb chops
Water cress garnish
Kidney-bean purée Ali-Bab, 270
Apricot cream, 26
Côtes du Rhône (red, *such as* Château
Grillet *or* Hermitage)

* separate course

437

SUNDAY & MIDDAY DINNERS

Marinated mackerel, 229
Tomato and pepper salad, 254
Italian bread
Boeuf en daube Provençale, 287
Buttered macaroni
Lemon mousse, 305
Côtes du Rhône
or California Zinfandel

Sliced tomato salad, French dressing
Chicken-liver pâté, 232
Hot French bread
Poached chicken Mère Brazier, 301
Steamed new potatoes
Cheese and fruit
Meursault
or California Pinot Chardonnay

❦

Onions à la grecque, 78
Herring fillets pickled in oil
Cucumber salad   Black olives
Pork tenderloin Lorraine, 27
Brussels sprouts and chestnuts, 28
Green salad (endive, water cress)
Crème brulée, 198
Traminer, Sylvaner, or Riesling
or California Riesling

Tomato salad   Liver pâté, 22
Celery root with rémoulade sauce, 156
Radishes, butter   Black olives
Fowl with rice, 47
Braised carrots, 10
Cheese (Port-du-Salut, Camembert)
Francine's apple fritters, 124
Sancerre or Pouilly-Fuissé
or California Pinot Chardonnay

❦

Black olives
Radishes and sweet butter
Sardines with lemon
Hot French bread
Beef and chicken stockpot, 365
Assorted cheeses
Fresh strawberries and cream
Côtes du Rhône (red, such as
Châteauneuf-du-Pape)

Radishes and sweet butter
Sliced salami
Leek salad, 335
Hot French bread
Lamb à la poulette, 299   Rice
Pont l'Evêque
Fresh fruit salad, 338
Imported Chablis or California
Folle Blanche

❦

Chicken-liver pâté, 232
Toasted French bread
Roast pork with potatoes and apples,
315
Endive and water cress salad
Cottage-cheese fritters, 236
Alsatian Riesling
or California Pinot Blanc

Tomato and pepper salad, 254
Baked fish steaks, 356
Parsley potatoes
Creamed cucumbers, 409
Sliced peaches
Muscadet
or California Riesling

438

Radishes, butter   Salami
Leeks with French dressing
Veal chops en cocotte, 103
Green salad (romaine)
Roquefort   Pears

Beaujolais *or* Côtes du Rhône
or California Pinot Noir

Hors-d'oeuvre variés, 217
White wine rabbit stew, 167
Eggplant purée, 146
Cheese (Port-du-Salut, Brie)
Fruit

Arbois *or* Beaujolais
or California Sauvignon Blanc

❧

❧

(Eggs in aspic with Madeira, 129)
Black-pepper steak, 130
Green beans with onions, 92
Chestnut pudding, 65

Red Burgundy *or* Côtes du Rhône
or California Cabernet

(Hot Lorraine tart, 2)
Roast of veal bourgeoise, 117
Cold asparagus salad, French dressing
Puréed apricots and cream, 189

Red Bordeaux
or California Pinot Noir

DINNER PARTIES

Consommé, 375
Steak Lapérouse, 429
Creamed potatoes
Tomatoes stuffed with mushrooms, 255
Cold lemon soufflé, 366

Red Burgundy (*such as* Chambertin
or Clos de Vougeot)

Demitasse   Liqueurs

Cherrystone clams on the half shell
Tenderloin of beef
with artichokes and peas, 413
Green salad, French dressing
Pineapple with rum, 384

Red Burgundy (*such as* Richebourg
or Pommard)

Demitasse   Liqueurs

❧

❧

Roast sirloin of beef Bordelaise, 389
Potatoes Anna, 268
Glazed carrots and onions, 218
Green salad, French dressing
Cherries in Bordeaux wine, 404

Red Bordeaux (*such as* Château
Gruaud-Larose)
or California Pinot Noir

Demitasse   Liqueurs

Mussels ravigote on lettuce leaves, 402
Toasted buttered French bread
Chicken Limousin, 309
Spinach purée
Chilled melon bowl, 283

Red Bordeaux (*such as* Château
Margaux) *or* California Cabernet

Demitasse   Liqueurs

439

Oysters on the half shell

Pouilly-Fuissé
Roast duck Rouennaise, 284
Sautéed new potatoes
Escarole salad, French dressing
Assorted cheeses
Red Burgundy (*such as* Volnay
or Corton)

Flambéed pears, 271
Demitasse   Liqueurs

❦

THANKSGIVING
(*or Christmas Day*)

Oysters on the half shell
Chablis *or* California Pinot Blanc
Roast turkey, chestnut stuffing, 125
Mashed potatoes   French peas, 37
Chambertin *or* California Cabernet
Endive salad
Assorted cheeses
Upside-down apple tart, 93
Demitasse   Liqueurs

❦

FORMAL DINNER

Chicken consommé velouté, 192
Scallops Saint-Jacques, 39
Puligny-Montrachet
Avignon flambéed filets mignons, 52
Pommard-Epenots

Foie gras
Garden lettuce salad with fines herbes
Assorted cheeses
Poached peaches, raspberry sauce, 182
Château La Tour Blanche
Demitasse   Liqueurs

* Separate course

Stuffed mushrooms, 334
Sautéed chicken with parsley, 407
Steamed new potatoes
Imported *or* California Chablis

Cold fresh asparagus, French dressing*
French crêpes with currant jelly, 317
California Muscat de Frontignan
or Sweet Sémillon
Demitasse   Liqueurs

❦

CHRISTMAS EVE

Oysters on the half shell
Chablis *or* California
Pinot Chardonnay
Christmas Eve smothered beef, 215
with steamed potatoes
Red Bordeaux *or*
California Pinot Noir

Water cress salad   Camembert, 43
Crêpes Grandgousier, 216
Champagne
Demitasse   Liqueurs

❦

BANQUET

Cold Madrilène consommé, 140
Trout with almonds and cream, 57
Alsatian Gewürztraminer
Roast tenderloin of beef jardinière, 86
Musigny (*also with next course*)

Guinea hen chasseur, 173
Water cress and lettuce salad
Assorted cheeses
Coupe Jacques, 169
Champagne
Demitasse   Petits fours   Liqueurs

440

Menu Planner

The bilingual recipe index which follows is designed to serve as a menu planner as well as to locate recipes by name. The English entries, therefore, include the following categories:

Classics of the Family Kitchen

HORS-D'OEUVRE

Céleri rémoulade, 156
Pâté de foie, 22
Salade de boeuf, 97

SOUPS

Potage aux légumes, 45
Potage parisien, 54
Purée de lentilles, 204
Purée Saint-Germain, 108
Soupe à l'oignon, 17
Soupe au potiron, 102

CHEESE DISHES

Croque Monsieur, 30
Quiche Lorraine, 2
Soufflé au fromage, 123

EGGS

Oeufs cocotte à la crème, 113
Oeufs en gelée au madère, 129
Omelette chasseur, 213
Omelette fines herbes, 61

SHELLFISH

Coquilles Saint-Jacques, 39
Moules marinière, 207

FISH

Filets de sole au vin blanc, 64
Raie au beurre noir, 176
Saumon poché, sauce verte, 109
Sole meunière, 190

POULTRY

Canard à l'orange, 114
Coq au vin, 21
Pigeons aux petits pois, 158
Poule au pot Henri IV, 178
Poule au riz, 47
Poulet en cocotte, 194
Poulet Marengo, 121

BEEF

Boeuf à la mode, 33
Boeuf bourguignon, 94
Miroton de boeuf, 168
Pot-au-feu, 165
Steak au poivre, 130
Tournedos béarnaise, 9

LAMB

Epaule de mouton à la boulangère, 214
Gigot à la bretonne, 15
Navarin de mouton, 74
Rognons de mouton en brochette, 143

VEAL

Blanquette de veau, 40
Cervelles au beurre noir, 90
Côtes de veau en cocotte, 103
Foie de veau à la française, 14
Paupiettes de veau, 149
Rôti de veau bourgeoise, 117

HAM & PORK

Choucroute garnie alsacienne, 87
Côtes de porc aux navets, 80
Jambon, sauce madère, 145
Rôti de porc campagnarde, 191
Saucisses au vin blanc, 81

RABBIT

Lapin en gibelotte, 167

VEGETABLES

Carottes Vichy, 10
Céleri ménagère, 171
Chou farci Aristide, 174
Endives braisées, 126
Garniture bourgeoise, 117
Gratin dauphinois, 35
Haricots verts à la lyonnaise, 92
Petits pois à la française, 37
Pommes gratinées à la normande, 180
Ratatouille, 89
Salade niçoise, 55
Tomates farcies, 177
Tomates provençale, 101

DESSERTS

Bananes flambées, 72
Beignets de pommes, 124
Crème renversée, 51
Mont-Blanc, 65
Mousse au chocolat, 107
Tarte aux fraises, 7

BREAD

Pain de ménage, 120

Regional Specialties

Recipe Index

455

460

List of Illustrations